Protecting President Lincoln

Protecting President Lincoln

The Security Effort, the Thwarted Plots and the Disaster at Ford's Theater

FREDERICK HATCH

McFarland & Company, Inc., Publishers
Jefferson, North Carolina, and London

LIBRARY OF CONGRESS CATALOGUING-IN-PUBLICATION DATA

Hatch, Frederick, 1945–
Protecting President Lincoln : the security effort, the thwarted plots and the disaster at Ford's Theatre / Frederick Hatch.
p.   cm.

Includes bibliographical references and index.

ISBN 978-0-7864-6362-6
softcover : 50# alkaline paper ∞

1. Lincoln, Abraham, 1809–1865 — Assassination.   2. Presidents — Protection — United States — History —19th century.   3. Assassination — United States — History —19th century.   4. United States. Secret Service — History —19th century.   5. Secret service — United States — History —19th century.   I. Title.
E457.5.H325 2011   973.7092 — dc23   2011036507

British Library cataloguing data are available

© 2011 Frederick Hatch. All rights reserved

No part of this book may be reproduced or transmitted in any form or by any means, electronic or mechanical, including photocopying or recording, or by any information storage and retrieval system, without permission in writing from the publisher.

Front cover: Eyes of Private Detective Allan Pinkerton; background and blood © 2011 Shutterstock

Manufactured in the United States of America

McFarland & Company, Inc., Publishers
Box 611, Jefferson, North Carolina 28640
www.mcfarlandpub.com

James O. Hall (1912–2007)
Mentor, example, friend.

Table of Contents

Preface   1

Introduction   3

1. National Crisis   5
2. President Elect   10
3. Inauguration —1861   19
4. Protecting President Lincoln   25
5. Presidential Health   42
6. Reelection   51
7. Confederate Secret Service   58
8. John Wilkes Booth   69
9. Conspiracy   77
10. A Night of Horrors   91
11. Cause of Death   102
12. The Missing Guard   109
13. The Hand of the Avenger   118
14. The Long Good-bye   132
15. Rest in Peace   144
16. Aftermath   149

Appendix 1: Weapons of the Assassination Conspirators   167
Appendix 2: Presidential Succession   170
Notes   175
Bibliography   187
Index   195

Preface

Unfortunately, we are all too familiar with the dangers encountered by our political and social leaders. Since Lincoln's time, we have seen numerous attacks upon our leaders, as well as problems sometimes severe enough to disable, if not end, a political career. The safety of our leaders cannot be left to chance, nor can considerations of health, both physical and mental. All of these problems can be seen in the administration of Abraham Lincoln. If such problems were not so familiar to his contemporaries, they are very much so to us. Perhaps there are even lessons to be learned from the study of Lincoln's protection that can be of use today, especially the fatalism Lincoln seemed to have had about himself, a fatalism that we have encountered in later leaders, and which has posed similar problems for those who must try to protect them.

There are more books about Abraham Lincoln than almost any other person. Even if we confine ourselves to the assassination alone, there remain hundreds of book-length works expressing a wide variety of information and opinions. It is interesting and surprising, not only to discover how much diversity of opinion exists among the legions of Lincoln enthusiasts, but also to note the strength of passion for their subject and the certainty of their beliefs. Lincoln is not only rated as our greatest president, but he can also be seen as the embodiment of the American archetype. His rise from the humblest beginnings to achieve the pinnacle of leadership makes him, perhaps more than any other, the kind of person we think of as best representing the title "American." Because so much has been written about Lincoln, an author of our time is faced with a challenge. A simple repetition of the Lincoln story is not needed. It is necessary to inquire into the details of his life to seek out that which is less familiar. This also serves to limit our story. Obviously, the essential facts of Lincoln's assassination must form the largest part of any study of his protection. But some readers may object to the inclusion, or exclusion, of this or that person, place, or event. This book is not intended to stand as the most comprehensive or definitive version of the story of the assassination, with all of its hundreds of characters, its many twists and turns of fate, or resemblance to other events. Our focus is, and must be, on the role played by those who posed the greatest threat to the president and those who sought to deter them.

It is likewise necessary, in studying the massive amount of potential research sources, to pick and choose. The sources listed here are not presented as the only ones available, and it is certainly possible that in some cases better sources could be found. We must recognize that opinion and individual judgment will always play an important part in evaluation of sources, as in the judgment of the work as a whole. The sources used here come from a wide variety of places, both old and new, and in between. Readers seeking additional information are urged to examine the many items listed in the bibliography, as well as in bibliographies found in those books.

An effort has been made to follow the historical record, and not to wander astray after theories and conjecture. But, of course, all authors are human, and to be human is to care about your subject, and to care means that it is impossible to avoid an occasional excursion down the road of speculation. When that happens, the reader will probably recognize it, even if he encounters no signpost.

Some of the material in this book has previously appeared in the *Journal of the Lincoln Assassination*, but has been revised and sometimes extensively rewritten to conform to the story told here.

A word of acknowledgment is in order. The higher we would reach, the higher must be the pyramid of those upon whose shoulders we stand. It would be impossible to list all of those who contributed both information and encouragement, but it would be unjust not to make mention of those whose contributions, both in quantity and quality, truly stand out. At the top of the list must be Dr. James O. Hall. No one else has spent more time on and uncovered more details about Lincoln's assassination than he, and his willingness to share his information and his well-informed wisdom is well known to his friends and disciples. He has been an inspiration and a model to us all. Others who have been most helpful, listed alphabetically, are David R. Barbee, John C. Brennan, Joan L. Chaconas, Dr. William Hanchett, Michael W. Kauffman, Dr. John K. Lattimer, Steven G. Miller, Dr. Richard D. Mudd, Richard E. Sloan, Edward Steers, Jr., Laurie Verge, and Frank J. Williams. Special mention must also be made of the staff, past and present, of those institutions wherein the records of our history reside. For this book, that would include the Surratt Society, Georgetown University, University of California at Los Angeles, University of Southern California, University of Arizona, University of Texas, the Lincoln Museum at Ford's Theatre, the National Park Service, the Library of Congress, and the National Archives. My wife Virginia has helped in many ways, large and small. Of course, there are many more, and to them, as well as to those listed above, the author extends his heartfelt thanks and best wishes.

Introduction

In a time of crisis unequaled in American history before or since, Abraham Lincoln emerged on the national scene. Little was expected of him at first, and it took time for him to gain the experience and knowledge necessary to achieve his goals. Lincoln's moment in history was brief. Little known on the national scene before his debates with Stephen Douglas in 1858, he was often vilified and taken for granted during his four-year presidency. It also took time for the American people to get to know him and to begin to appreciate his uniqueness. The process of discovery was not completed on April 15, 1865. With Lincoln's death at the end of the most costly war in American history, Americans began to realize what an extraordinary man they had had and lost. He was suddenly gone, and Americans have been awakening to his importance and greatness ever since.

Lincoln had his share of personal tragedies, and a huge and bloody civil war must be the ultimate tragedy for a nation to have to endure. It can be argued that his death by assassination was the capstone of his career and guaranteed his place in history.

Because Lincoln was assassinated, it is often assumed that either he was not protected at all or that his protection was flawed and inadequate. As we shall see, neither of these assumptions is entirely true, or entirely false. Lincoln was a target for would-be assassins from the moment of his victory in the election of 1860. There were at least four overt attempts on his life, the fourth being successful. In addition, there were plans to kidnap him. All of these plots were known to the authorities, and unprecedented measures were taken to protect the life and health of President Lincoln.

It is extraordinarily difficult to protect a public figure such as the president of the United States from harm. Nearly every president in American history has been the subject of serious threats, or has suffered injury or disease. Four American presidents have died from assassination, Lincoln being the first. The possibility of assassination had been imagined and talked about, with varying degrees of seriousness, almost since the beginning of the presidential institution. An assassination attempt had been made upon President Andrew Jackson in 1835. With feelings running high and the American Union splitting asunder, the possibility of an attack upon the president was no longer mere conjecture.

That Lincoln was assassinated is very well known, but the nature of the difficulties faced by his protectors is not so widely recognized. Nor is it appreciated so much today that Lincoln was a controversial figure, and that, both before his election to the presidency and especially after his taking office, he was the subject of much vilification and even outright hatred. Whatever is said of our political leaders today pales in comparison with the bitter criticism that was directed at Abraham Lincoln. The iconic, god-like figure of the Lincoln

Memorial, and of countless statues, portraits, motion pictures, radio and television broadcasts, and even advertisements, cannot clarify our understanding of how Lincoln was regarded by his contemporaries. The adulation, the near-deification of Lincoln, came almost entirely after his death. The manner and timing of that death helped to ensure that all of the bitter controversy and hatred would fade and be largely forgotten in time, leaving the benign, all-wise, far-seeing Lincoln that we see portrayed today.

If our understanding of the real Abraham Lincoln is inadequate and faulty, if we discover that he was a human being with weaknesses and problems comparable to people we know today, if he had very human traits, desires, moods, even prejudices, just as we encounter today, we should not judge him any more harshly than we would our contemporary leaders. Does it not add to, not detract from, our appreciation of Lincoln, to discover that he was a human being who had to contend with his own self-criticisms and self-doubts, along with the resistance he encountered from others? In evaluating Lincoln, as with any other historical figure, we should judge him by the standards of *his* time more than our own. We should seek to understand the problems he faced and the possibilities for, and restrictions upon, his efforts to achieve his goals.

Ultimately, Lincoln is a larger than life figure, one who will stand the test of time regardless of how he is viewed through the ages. In that sense, the marble statue in the Grecian temple is both appropriate and honest.

We should not be surprised that Lincoln died by assassination, but rather that his life was spared for as long as it was, largely through the actions of dedicated men and women. This book is the story both of those who sought Lincoln's life and of those who attempted to preserve that life. That they managed to prevent the disaster, with the assistance of fate, for as long as they did is a testament to their loyalty, perseverance, and courage.

1. National Crisis

> Much is being said about peace; and no man desires peace more ardently than I. Still I am yet unprepared to give up the Union for a peace which, so achieved, could not be of much duration.
>
> Abraham Lincoln

Abraham Lincoln, the sixteenth president of the United States, serving from March 4, 1861, to April 15, 1865, presided over nearly the entire course of the Civil War. Although he was controversial throughout his presidency, it was his death, coming at the very end of the hard-fought and bitter conflict, that both shocked the nation and helped to pull it back together. After his death, opposition to Lincoln was largely forgotten and he was regarded as a martyr to the cause of liberty and union. His life represents the image of the self-made man, the story of the rise from humble poverty to national leadership, and the traits of compassion, wit, humility, iron resolve and individual responsibility that Americans celebrate. In many ways, in both truth and legend, Abraham Lincoln has come to represent the American ideal.

Born in a rough log cabin on Sinking Springs farm, near Hodgenville, in Hardin (now Larue) County, Kentucky, on February 12, 1809, Lincoln was largely self-made. His father was Thomas Lincoln (1778–1851), and his mother was Nancy Hanks Lincoln (1784–1818). They had been married June 12, 1806, in Beechland, Kentucky. Their first child, Nancy (1807–1828), was commonly called Sarah. Abraham was the second child, and Thomas, Jr. (1811–1813), the third and last. Searching for a better life, the family moved to southern Indiana in 1816, then an undeveloped wilderness. Lincoln's mother died October 5, 1818, and his father returned to Kentucky, leaving the children with relatives. He returned with a new wife, Sarah Bush Johnston Lincoln (1788–1869), and her three children. His stepmother raised Abraham as her own, and he became close to her.[1]

Young Abraham's schooling was only occasional and probably of poor quality. Although books were scarce in the rude frontier, Lincoln had an early love of reading and would borrow books whenever possible. As with many in that time and place, he was mostly self-educated. His early occupations derived from his humble origin: farm laborer, boatman, store clerk, surveyor. His sister Sarah married Aaron Grigsby (1801–1831), but died in childbirth. In 1828, Lincoln made his first trip away from home when he and a friend sailed a flatboat downriver to New Orleans, returning by steamer. River navigation became a subject of great interest to him. After moving to Illinois in 1830, Lincoln made another flatboat trip to New Orleans in 1831. Upon his return he moved to the town of New Salem, Illinois, setting out on his own.[2]

Continuing to read and study, Lincoln first ran for the Illinois General Assembly in 1832, but was not elected. Volunteering for the militia in the Black Hawk Indian War, he was chosen captain of his company. During this period he earned a living as a store clerk, becoming a partner with William F. Berry (1811–1835), and had to work hard as a laborer to pay their debts when the store failed. He established a reputation for honesty and integrity, which he retained throughout his life. Coming to the attention of influential people, Lincoln became postmaster of New Salem from 1833 to 1836, and deputy surveyor of Sangamon County. Having demonstrated ability as a speaker, Lincoln was elected to the Illinois House of Representatives in 1834. He became friends with John Todd Stuart (1807–1885), a lawyer, who helped him study the law. As a member of the Whig Party, Lincoln supported his party's issues, especially canal and river navigation, and the chartering of a state bank.[3]

It was at this time that Ann Rutledge (1813–1835) died. The true nature of their relationship remains unknown. Popular legend has it that Lincoln loved Ann, and was devastated by her death. Debate has raged over this story ever since Lincoln's death. Lincoln did suffer from depression and was often moody and lost in his own thoughts, but he is better known for his sense of humor and enjoyed telling stories and reading from joke books. He had a natural-born politician's knack for communicating with people, especially the humble and unsophisticated.[4]

Reelected to the legislature in 1836, Lincoln was among those instrumental in moving the state capital to Springfield. By 1837, Lincoln had become a lawyer, and began practicing as a partner of his friend John T. Stuart. He gained experience in a wide variety of cases, both civil and criminal. Elected to a third term in the legislature in 1838, Lincoln became the Whig leader in the house. He was reelected again in 1840, and was also a Whig elector in the presidential contest that year.[5]

Lincoln first met Mary Ann Todd (1818–1882) in 1839. She had been born in Lexington, Kentucky, on December 13, 1818. Mary's father, Robert Smith Todd (1791–1849), was a highly successful merchant and financier, and was very prominent in public affairs, having served as city councilman, a magistrate and sheriff, and in the Kentucky state assembly and state senate. Mary's mother was Eliza Ann Parker Todd (1794–1825), whose early death, combined with Robert's business affairs and prolonged absences, resulted in Mary's attending boarding school. By 1837, when Mary went to Springfield, Illinois, to live with her sister Elizabeth Edwards (1813–1888), she had learned the ways of society and could speak fluent French. Mary was courted by several of Springfield's prominent men, including Stephen Arnold Douglas (1813–1861), who would become a U.S. senator and Lincoln's nemesis in their famous debates. But it was the tall, homely, awkward Abraham Lincoln who finally won Mary's hand. Their courtship was far from trouble free, the engagement being broken altogether for a time, but on the evening of November 4, 1842, Mary Todd and Abraham Lincoln were married. Engraved on her ring was the sentiment "Love Is Eternal."[6]

The image of Mary Lincoln as a shrewish burden to her husband is mainly the work of Lincoln's friend and law partner, William Henry Herndon (1818–1891). One of the early Lincoln biographers, he considered her a would-be aristocrat, with her social airs and wealthy family, and she disliked Herndon's low standing in society, and especially his drinking. A neighbor of the Lincolns in Springfield described Mrs. Lincoln as a "cheerful woman" who was "fond of home." The only letters between Lincoln and his wife that survive show closeness and mutual affection.[7]

The Lincolns' first child was born August 1, 1843, and Mary named him for her father,

Robert Todd Lincoln (1843–1926). Their second child, born March 10, 1846, she named Edward Baker Lincoln (1846–1850), after Edward Dickinson Baker (1811–1861), a family friend. Little Eddie died on February 1, 1850, the first of several tragedies that the Lincolns were to endure. The third child, another son, born December 21, 1850, was named William Wallace Lincoln (1850–1862), after Mary's brother-in-law, William S. Wallace (1802–1867), a doctor who had married one of Mary's older sisters. The fourth and final child, also a boy, born April 4, 1853, was named Thomas Lincoln (1853–1871), after Lincoln's father. The baby's large head prompted his father to call him "Tadpole," which was further modified to become "Tad." Mary's sister described the relationship of Abraham and Mary as "not ... an unhappy life at all. She was devoted to him and their children and he was certainly all to her a husband could have been."[8] The Lincoln family moved into the house at Eighth and Jackson streets, Springfield, in 1844, and lived there until the family went to Washington in 1861.[9]

Lincoln's second law partner was Stephen Trigg Logan (1800–1880), also a member of the legislature, with whom he shared a law practice from 1841 to 1844. His next law partner was William Henry Herndon, whose Lincoln biography remains influential today. In 1846, Lincoln won his party's nomination for Congress, and won election handily. Moving to

Lincoln was the second choice of the majority of the delegates and was nominated on the third ballot, defeating the original front runner William H. Seward. Republican victory in 1860 was made possible by the division of the Democratic Party (Library of Congress).

Lincoln the candidate. Photograph taken in Springfield, Illinois, August 13, 1860 (Library of Congress).

Jefferson Davis. Born in Kentucky, only a few months and less than a hundred miles apart from Lincoln, Davis served as president of the Confederacy (Library of Congress).

Washington the following year, Lincoln was soon involved in the Whig opposition to the Mexican War. President James Knox Polk (1795–1849) had stated that Mexican soldiers fired on American troops on American soil. Knowing that the battle had been fought in a disputed area, Lincoln introduced his "spot resolutions," challenging the president to name the spot on American soil. Although he disputed the need for the war, Lincoln did vote for appropriations for the armed forces, and he supported General Zachary Taylor (1784–1850) when the war hero became the Whig candidate for president in 1848. Not being offered an appointment he wanted in the Taylor administration, and having previously agreed not to run for reelection to Congress, Lincoln returned to practicing law in Springfield in 1849.[10]

Probably believing that his political career had run its course, Lincoln concentrated on his legal practice for the next several years, being very successful in many different kinds of cases. The growing unrest over the slavery question reawakened Lincoln's interest in politics. Lincoln was a candidate for United States senator in 1855, and was very disappointed when he failed to win the nomination. In 1856 he joined the new Republican Party, campaigning enthusiastically for the party's nominee for president, John Charles Frémont (1813–1890).

In 1858 Lincoln was named the Republican candidate for U.S. senator, opposing the incumbent Democrat Stephen A. Douglas. The two candidates met in a series of debates in different towns around Illinois, drawing crowds of thousands. The issue of slavery dominated the debates, with Lincoln opposed to its spread into the territories and Douglas wanting the question to be settled locally. The legislature, then the deciding electors for the Senate, voted 54 to 46 for Douglas, reflecting the party strength in Illinois at that time.[11]

The national publicity achieved by the debates gained Lincoln a following, and he began making appearances outside of Illinois. On February 27, 1860, he spoke to an audience of 1,500 people at Cooper Union in New York City. His friends now began their efforts to win the Republican nomination for president for Lincoln. Prominent in that effort were David Davis (1815–1886) and Norman Buel Judd (1815–1878). At the national convention in Chicago, Senator William Henry Seward (1801–1872) of New York, Simon Cameron (1799–1889) of Pennsylvania, and Salmon Portland Chase (1808–1873) of Ohio, were Lincoln's principal rivals for the nomination. Seward led on the first ballot, while his opponents rallied behind Lincoln as an acceptable alternative to those, such as Seward or Chase, whose position on slavery was considered by many to be too extreme. On the third ballot, Lincoln won the nomination. His vice presidential running mate was Senator Hannibal Hamlin (1809–1891) of Maine.

In the election of 1860, the Democratic Party, like the country, split over the slavery question. Democrats in much of the South supported Vice President John Cabel Breckinridge (1821–1875), while northern Democrats favored Senator Steven A. Douglas. Another split saw border state support for former Senator John Bell (1797–1869). With such divisions among their opponents, the Republicans won, but with a minority of the popular vote, only 39.82 percent. With Lincoln's victory came secession, South Carolina leading the way, followed soon after by Mississippi, Florida, Alabama, Georgia, Louisiana, and Texas.[12]

Aware that he faced a crisis unique in American history, as he had acknowledged in his farewell speech to the people of Springfield, Lincoln did not have any grand strategy in mind. The one thought that fixed itself in his mind throughout the entire course of the long and terrible war was of the Union. Lincoln belonged to that line of American leaders who saw the future of his country as one of pulling together the separate strands with which it had been made into a single fabric, solid and inseparable. Not only that, but he believed that such a nation as he envisaged, made strong by its unity, could become a beacon among the nations, a great light shining for all the world. He called it "the last, best hope of earth." Not only would the permanent dissolution of the Union be the end of the nation the Founding Fathers had created and passed along to Lincoln's generation, but America would be broken and vulnerable, perhaps for all time. Lincoln did not know exactly how to save the Union, but he never wavered in his determination to do so.[13]

2. President Elect

> What if I rush, And with a blow strike life from out his heart?
> Richard Taylor Shiel, *The Apostate*

The times were charged with high emotion, and there is no reason to doubt that Lincoln was in constant and sometimes extreme danger. No sooner had he been named president elect than the threats and warnings began. A letter to the *Cincinnati Commercial*, in December 1860, predicted that Lincoln would be shot on inauguration day. Senator William H. Seward, soon to be Lincoln's secretary of state, warned Lincoln by letter of a plot by secessionists to take over Washington and prevent the inauguration. Lincoln replied that he was worried that Congress might not meet, or, if it did, might not have a quorum to certify the election. Capital police arrested a man named Columbus Edelin, who had supposedly offered to shoot Lincoln. Private military organizations were drilling in the District of Columbia and outgoing Secretary of War Joseph Holt (1807–1894) expressed his personal belief that these, or other groups, planned to seize the capital.[1]

One of these schemers was Senator Louis T. Wigfall (1816–1874) of Texas. Born in South Carolina, Wigfall had served in the Seminole War in Florida in 1837. After studying law and being admitted to the bar, he moved to Texas in 1848. He served in the Texas House of Representatives from 1849 to 1850, and in the state senate from 1857 to 1859. Elected United States senator to fill a vacancy, Wigfall served from December 5, 1859, to March 23, 1861.[2] A rabid secessionist, Wigfall approached Secretary of War John B. Floyd (1807–1863) about cooperating in his plan to kidnap President James Buchanan (1791–1868), in order to make vice president John C. Breckinridge president. What the plotters of this scheme seemed not to know was that the Vice President did not succeed to the presidency unless the president had either died or resigned. President Buchanan, even in the hands of kidnappers, would still have been president. This would have posed serious problems for the government, but Breckinridge would have had no legal authority to act as president. Floyd, though he would later serve the Confederacy, would have no part of Wigfall's plot.[3]

Washington was ill prepared to counter such schemes. Outgoing President Buchanan, hoping to avoid hostilities before he left office, was unwilling to antagonize the secessionists by calling for more troops. It was the task of General Winfield Scott (1786–1866), commanding officer of the army, and pro–Union officers such as Colonel Charles Pomeroy Stone (1824–1887), who was named inspector general for the District of Columbia militia at the beginning of January 1861, to rally the pro–Union men of Washington and organize them into military units capable of maintaining order and deterring schemes such as Wigfall's.[4] General Scott, hero of the War of 1812 and of the Mexican War, was old and infirm, but his loyalty to the Union was unshakable and obvious to all who spoke with him. "While I command the army there will be no revolution in the City of Washington!" he told his visitors.[5]

"A large number of communications were received.... All concurred in the declaration that a plot existed to assassinate President Lincoln and General Scott. They agreed singularly in the details, and sometimes in fixing the same dates for the attempt." General Scott's residence was moved from the 6th Street location to Mrs. Duvall's house, no. 159, south side of Pennsylvania Avenue, between 17th and 18th Streets. "For several nights, until arrangements were made for an aide to lodge in the house, I [E.D. Townsend] rested on a sofa in the outer room, next the General's chamber. With sword and revolver at hand, fully expecting that some attempt would be made upon us."[6] The *Cincinnati Commercial* reported on February 27, 1861, that "General Scott has received 130 letters, from fifteen different states, threatening his own life. Some are anonymous, but the bulk of them are evidently genuine."[7]

> Col. Keyes [Erasmus Darwin Keyes (1810–1895) of Massachusetts, military secretary to Gen. Scott from January 1, 1860, to April 19, 1861] ... says the evidence in his possession of a widespread and powerful conspiracy to seize the Capital are overwhelming, and he has no doubt whatever on the subject. Now the only thing to prevent the attempt will be the presence here of a sufficient force to hold this city against all comers, which he does not expect will be had. He says that in addition to the 600 or 700 regulars now here, there should be at least 10,000 volunteers. He has the gravest apprehensions that this Capital will be taken. All of the departments are filled with traitorous clerks, who would do all in their power to surrender up the buildings to a hostile force.... I am satisfied that we must soon begin to prepare for the worst.[8]

Lincoln's secretary, John G. Nicolay (1832–1901), received a letter from Colonel Edwin Vose Sumner (1797–1863), already a distinguished soldier of nearly forty-two years' service, who would gain additional distinction in the coming Civil War:

> The political excitement is becoming so intense, that a feeling of personal hostility, and bitterness, is increasing every day. I have heard of threats against Mr. Lincoln, and of bets being offered that he would never be inaugurated. I know very well that he is not the man to live in fear of assassination; but when the safety of the whole country depends upon his life, I would respectfully suggest to him, whether it would not be well to give this matter some attention. It has occurred to me that if any such attempt should be made, it would most likely be made at Springfield. Mr. Lincoln's habit of walking about alone at night, gives an opportunity to make the attempt, with a good chance of escaping detection. I would respectfully urge him to carry such arms about him, when walking alone at night, as will make him secure against any crazy fanatics.[9]

There is no evidence that Lincoln ever carried any sort of weapon except a small pocket knife and a cane.

Congressman John Addison Gurley (1813–1863), R-OH, wrote Lincoln a strong letter that must have provided him some cheer. "I hope you will lose no sleep from the rumors of plots to assassinate, etc., etc. We will see to that. God help the men who engage in them, in the next world, for if our people get hold of them in this, their time will be short. All we want is a President in the White House with the courage and determination of a lion, and the cry of disunion would at once cease."[10]

Senator William H. Seward made a practical suggestion: "Habit has accustomed the public to anticipate the arrival of the President elect in this city [Washington] about the middle of February and evil minded persons would expect to organize their demonstrations for that time. I beg leave to suggest whether it would not be well for you keeping your own counsel, to be prepared to drop into the city a week or ten days earlier. The effect would probably be reassuring and soothing."[11]

J. Medhill combined the sentiments of Gurley with the advice of Seward. "It is the plan of the disunionists to have an army in this city within five weeks, to drive out the Republican members and to prevent your inauguration by force. It is expected that in 30 days Maryland will pronounce for the disunionists. Who can say that she will not? ... [W]ould it not be a coup d'etat were you to quietly, with only a carpet sack, get on the cars [train] and drop down in this city some day next week or very soon. Would it not knock over and disarrange all the plans of the traitors, and show them they had a second Jackson to deal with.... It is all important that you should take the oath of office here on the 4th of March on the steps of the Capitol. The moral effect will be worth an army of 10,000 men."[12]

Lincoln received a letter from James Henry Lane (1814–1866), Republican senator elect for the new state of Kansas, offering to raise a thousand men from Kansas to escort Lincoln to his inauguration. In considering such an offer, Lincoln was mindful of his delicate position. He had been elected president, but had no authority to act until his inauguration on March 4, 1861. Until then, he had to be careful not to appear to be assuming power that was not yet legally his.[13]

Lincoln sent a close friend, Leonard Swett (1825–1889), to Washington to meet with Colonel Stone and others concerned about the tense situation in the capital. Swett, a friend since Lincoln's circuit-riding days, had been one of those who had worked hard to secure the Republican presidential nomination for Lincoln. For several days Swett conferred with General Scott, Colonel Stone, and others, gathering information to take back to Springfield for the president elect.[14]

In a letter from Horace White (1834–1916), secretary of the Illinois Republican State Central committee, dated December 11, 1860, Lincoln was warned to be mindful of his safety. "$40,000 had been subscribed in the St. Charles Hotel, New Orleans, to procure the assassination of yourself and Hamlin.... The state of feeling in Louisiana and Mississippi [is] that of pure frenzy.... People are getting mad very fast in this latitude."[15]

Only a few days later, Horace Greeley (1811–1872), the New York newspaper editor, wrote Lincoln a similar warning. "...Your life is not safe, and it is your simple duty to be very careful in exposing it. I doubt whether you ought to go to Washington via Wheeling and the B & O Railroad unless you go with a very strong force. And it is not yet certain that the Federal District will not be in the hands of a pro-slavery rebel array before the 4th of March."[16]

George Washington had started the tradition of the new president making a long journey to his inauguration, showing himself to the public at many points along the way. Curiosity about Lincoln was heightened not only by the secession crisis, but also by the fact that he was still unfamiliar to most of his countrymen. The War Department sent four officers to protect Lincoln on the journey, and one of these, Captain George W. Hazzard (?–1862), advised using disguises and avoiding Baltimore. Captain Hazzard carried a knife, eye shields (goggles) and brass knuckles on the journey to Washington.[17] Another officer traveling with the Lincoln family, Elmer Ellsworth (1837–1861), was asked by the railroad to take charge of security. In addition, Lincoln's friends encouraged Ward Hill Lamon (1828–1893), who was also traveling with the president elect, to take extra precautions. Lamon hardly needed to be asked. Lincoln would chide him many times about Lamon's concern for his friend's safety. The concern was justifiable, for not far along the line, at State Line, Indiana, an engineer discovered an obstruction on the tracks in the path of Lincoln's train that would have derailed it. After leaving Cincinnati, a hand grenade was found on the train. Near Pittsburgh a freight train ahead of Lincoln's train was derailed, delaying the presidential train for two hours.

Lincoln was traveling in a special train, whose composition changed along the way as it passed from the domain of one railroad into that of another. Typically, it consisted of an especially plush car for the president elect and his close advisors, including those who were watching out for his security, with a baggage car and other passenger cars making up the rest of the train. Locomotives were changed as the train passed from one rail line to another. As the train traveled, the number of politicians and well-wishers aboard grew. Many rode only part of the way.

Ward Hill Lamon. Lincoln's friend accompanied him from Springfield to Washington for the first inauguration. Lamon often warned Lincoln of danger (Library of Congress).

Having to speak at every stop was fatiguing, and Lincoln's voice grew hoarse. Local leaders relished the opportunity to introduce him to the crowds of admirers gathered at train depots. At Girard, Pennsylvania, the Lincoln party was startled by the unexpected arrival of Horace Greeley. Although equipped with a valise and blankets, Greeley rode only the twenty miles to Erie. Lincoln greeted him cordially. Greeley was a prominent and easily recognizable person, but the ease with which he boarded the train unexpected and unannounced indicates that the president elect's security was not as tight as it might have been.[18]

Coincidences occurred on this journey that would later be remarked upon. One of the military guards, Major David Hunter (1802–1886), would later preside over the military commission that tried the assassination conspirators. His shoulder was dislocated by the jostling of the crowd in Buffalo, though this was only an accident; Lincoln was unhurt. The crowd was estimated to number ten thousand, and although a company of soldiers was on hand to assist the local police, the pressure of the eager crowd posed a serious, though unintended, threat to the Lincoln party's safety. Lincoln's train arrived in Albany, New York, on February 18, the same day the young actor John Wilkes Booth (1838–1865) opened at the Gayety

Theatre on Green Street, and Booth may well have been in the crowd that greeted the president elect, though there is no evidence to link him with any conspiracy at this time. In New York City Lincoln went to a performance of Verdi's opera *Un Ballo in Maschera*, which deals with the murder of a ruler.

After Lincoln had arrived safely in Washington, it was reported

> by gentlemen connected with the party of Mr. Lincoln since he left home for Washington that there were several attempts to take his life during the journey through Indiana and Ohio. The one which threatened the more serious consequences took place on the Presidential train leaving Cincinnati, when a grenade of the most destructive character was discovered in the car occupied by Mr. Lincoln, his family and personal friends. It was found in a small carpet bag, which had been deposited in a seat of the car by some unknown person. Attention was drawn to it from the fact that no baggage was allowed in the cars. On examination, the grenade concealed in the carpetbag was discovered to be ignited, and so arranged that within fifteen minutes it would have exploded with a force sufficient to have demolished the car and destroyed the lives of all persons in it. Of course, the "infernal machine" was speedily removed and properly disposed of.
>
> Great precautions were taken at the various points on the route to guard against any injury to the person of the President from malicious designs of enemies. Before entering the cars the conductors of the line were accustomed to thoroughly examine the seats and the cushions to see that there was no dangerous machine or person secreted in the carriage. This precaution shows that not only was there danger, but that danger was at least partially known to Mr. Lincoln and his friends. It is well understood that Gen. Scott advised Mr. Lincoln, before leaving home, to have his family at all times around him on his journey to the Federal Capital.

Precautions to be taken for the journey across New York State were announced in advance in the press. "A pilot engine will be sent in advance of the train, after which all switches will be spiked and guarded until the special train passes. Every possibility of accident will be guarded against, so that Mr. Lincoln's journey may be an indubitably safe one. Col. Bowen, the Superintendent of the Illinois Great Western Road, has taken every step to insure increased safety, speed and comfort. Special orders have been sent to telegraph operators to be on duty when the train passes, and to report its time immediately to Indianapolis. Every employee of the line is particularly instructed to be on the track and know that all is right before the train is allowed to pass."[19]

Horace Greeley, New York newspaper editor. Though pro–Union, Greeley often disagreed with Lincoln over the course of the war (Library of Congress).

Lincoln began growing a beard even before he left for Washington. This was never intended as a disguise, for his election as president started an avalanche of engravings and photographs through which his countrymen could familiarize themselves with the new leader of the government. As soon as it became known that Lincoln had grown a beard, new images of the bearded president elect were produced. Lincoln received a letter from supporters describing themselves as "true Republicans," advising growing a beard and wearing high collars to improve his appearance. It was a similar letter, however, received only a few days later, that became one of the most famous pieces of correspondence he received. A young girl, Grace Bedell (1848–1936), of Westfield, New York, not only was widely credited with prompting Lincoln to grow his whiskers, but she was also personally greeted by the president elect when the train made a stop at her hometown.[20]

Between his election on November 6, 1860, and his inauguration on March 4, 1861, Lincoln made very few public speeches. The secession crisis boiled over, and everyone, North and South alike, waited eagerly to see what he would do. While not revealing his plans, he was busy organizing the new administration, tying up business in Springfield, and preparing for the journey to Washington. In late January he traveled to Farmington, Illinois, to visit his step-mother, Sarah Bush Johnston Lincoln. The old woman was full of foreboding. "I did not want Abe to run for President, did not want him elected — was afraid somehow or other ... that something would happen [to] him ... and that I should see him no more."[21]

As Abraham Lincoln was preparing for his journey from Springfield to Washington in February 1861, Samuel Morse Felton (1809–1889), president of the Philadelphia and Baltimore Railroad, received a visit from Dorothea Dix (1802–1887), the philanthropist. She had been touring the South, visiting hospitals, and had had many conversations with prominent Southerners. She described to Felton the details of a plan to prevent Lincoln's inauguration, capture Washington and usurp the government. Felton had previously heard rumors, but now he had details of a plot that was, in his own words, "a coup d'etat." As the plan involved cutting off Washington from communication with the North, Felton's railroad was in jeopardy, as bridges were to be burned. Felton learned that it was planned to murder President Elect Lincoln to assure that he would never take office.[22] Alarmed, Felton sent a man to Washington to advise General Winfield Scott of this information. A few days later Felton received a report from another source that Lincoln's train was to be stopped outside Baltimore by setting fire to a bridge. Men were to rush aboard the train and "Mr. Lincoln [was] to be put out of the way."[23] Felton contacted a private detective, Allan Pinkerton (1819–1884), founder of the agency that still bears his name. Pinkerton, born in Scotland, had been a detective on the Chicago police force, and had founded his detective agency in 1850. He had built a reputation both for competence and honesty in the decade since.

Pinkerton sent two of his best operatives, Kate Warne (1833–1868) and Timothy Webster (1821–1862), to Maryland to infiltrate the pro-secessionist organizations. Warne used the alias "Mrs. Cherry," among other names, and was described as "quite captivating" and able "to make a favorable impression at once." Webster, whom Pinkerton considered his best detective, joined the secessionists at Perrymansville, Maryland. Pinkerton went with them to Baltimore, where he posed as a stockbroker named John H. Hutchinson. His method was to profess friendship and sympathy with the secessionists to gain their confidence and obtain information.[24]

The Baltimore police would not be helpful, for the chief of police, George Proctor Kane (1817–1878), was, as Pinkerton said, "a rabid rebel." Kane was born in Baltimore on August 21, 1817, of Irish immigrant parents. Becoming a grain merchant in Baltimore, he was involved in the relief effort for the Irish potato famine of 1845–1849. The always popular Kane held several offices, including collector of the Port of Baltimore, from 1849 to 1853. By 1861 Maryland had a large pro–Confederate population, and Kane was involved in efforts to bring the state into the Confederacy, or at least to impede the federal government's efforts to prevent Maryland secession. Pinkerton's opinion of Kane was confirmed by the police chief's refusal to provide Lincoln with a police escort.

Felton, the railroad president, had meanwhile "organized and armed a force of about two hundred men, whom I distributed along the line between the Susquehanna and Baltimore, principally at the bridges. These men were drilled secretly and regularly by drill-masters, and were apparently employed in whitewashing the bridges," the whitewash doing double duty as a fire retardant. A train was kept standing by to pick up the guards and rush them to the scene of trouble anywhere along the line. These precautions, and a change in Lincoln's schedule, forced the conspirators to abandon action on Felton's line.[25]

The railroad tracks did not run through Baltimore, making it necessary to transfer to another train at another station. Lincoln was to arrive at the Calvert Street Station, take a carriage to the Eutaw House hotel, then on to the Camden Street Station to board the train for Washington. The conspirators had changed their plans. They would surround Lincoln's carriage in the streets. Eight men would be designated to attack Lincoln, assuring that no failure of nerve would prevent action.

Kate Warne, Pinkerton's detective, met in New York with Norman Judd, and told him about the plot. Judd agreed to tell Lincoln, but decided to wait until they arrived in Philadelphia. By this time Pinkerton and his operatives had learned the details of the plot. When the train arrived at Baltimore's Calvert Street Station on February 23, the assassins would create a diversion to distract the police, then move in on their victim. Lots had been drawn to choose the one who would thrust a dagger into the president elect. The assassins would then be spirited away and smuggled to the South. Pinkerton had two men among the conspirators and both were greatly relieved not to have drawn the deadly lot.

It was necessary to convince Lincoln himself of the reality of the plot and the danger to himself if he did not agree to change his plans. Pinkerton was aided in this by the arrival of Frederick William Seward (1830–1915), son of the senator who would become Lincoln's secretary of state. He brought a message from his father and from General Scott describing what they had independently learned about the plot and urging caution.[26]

The plot was described to Lincoln by Pinkerton, who urged him to change his plans and proceed immediately to Washington. With Frederick Seward's arrival the same evening, Lincoln took this as corroboration of the story he heard from Pinkerton, but, on the detective's advice, didn't reveal that he had agreed to modify his travel plans. Refusing to cancel public events in Philadelphia and Harrisburg, Lincoln did agree to change the time of his passage through Baltimore, and to make the final phase of his trip incognito. Just before his train's arrival in Harrisburg, it was decided by the railroad officials to transfer the Lincoln party to another car. This was probably a security measure, for "a great crowd was awaiting him near his own car."[27]

New York Superintendent of Police John Alexander Kennedy (1803–1873) had also heard of the plot. Born in Baltimore, Maryland, on August 9, 1803, Kennedy was the son of a teacher from the north of Ireland. After being educated in Baltimore, Kennedy moved to New York City and went into business with his brother. He was appointed a commissioner of immigration in 1849, and was elected to the common council in 1854. After serving as superintendent of Castle Garden, he became superintendent of the metropolitan police in 1860.

Rumors of a rebel takeover of Washington, and of a plot to kill Lincoln as he passed through Baltimore, reached New York and were reported to the police there. Superintendent

Kennedy already knew about the rumors, having begun investigating possible rebel plots in Washington as early as December 1860. Upon receiving a request from Congressman Schuyler Colfax (1821–1885), R-IN, that he send detectives to Washington, Kennedy, along with one of his men, personally visited the Capital. Meeting with Colfax and other congressmen, Kennedy found a divergence of opinion regarding rebel intentions. Meeting with Colonel Stone (1824–1887), Kennedy promised to have his detectives in Washington report to Col. Stone whatever they learned. Stone later wrote Kennedy that he had received "dozens of letters and reports from other sources, addressed sometimes to the General-in-Chief [Scott] and sometimes to myself, which served to convince both of us that there was imminent danger that Mr. Lincoln's life would be sacrificed should he attempt to pass through Baltimore at the time and in the manner published in the newspapers as the programme of his journey.... I recommended that Mr. Lincoln should be officially warned ... it appeared to me that Mr. Lincoln's personal dignity was of small account in comparison with the destruction, or, at least, dangerous disorganization of the United States government, which would be the inevitable result of his death by violence in Baltimore." Col. Stone was the one who had informed Senator Seward of the danger, prompting him to send his son to Harrisburg to urge Lincoln to change his plans.

Slipping away from official functions in Harrisburg, Lincoln joined Pinkerton for their secret departure. Lincoln's friend and unofficial bodyguard, Ward Hill Lamon, accompanied them, armed with several revolvers and knives. Lamon offered Lincoln a weapon, but the president elect declined. Boarding at the rear of the train, they settled into their sleeping compartment screened from view. Pinkerton described Lincoln as calm, but he noted that none of the three men slept that night. Lincoln did not wear a disguise, but exchanged his familiar stovepipe hat for a soft cap, and stooped over, as if he were much older, when walking to the train. Arriving in Baltimore in the middle of the night, Pinkerton was especially alert as they traveled between stations. Although suspicious men had been seen watching their train in Philadelphia, no incidents occurred in Baltimore.[28]

Just before Lincoln's train departed from Harrisburg, Superintendent Kennedy personally boarded the train and traveled through Baltimore as additional security, unknown to Lincoln and his party.[29]

Arriving in Washington, a man called to Lincoln and grabbed at his arm. Pinkerton bumped the man aside, and was preparing to punch the persistent man when Lincoln recognized him as a friend, Congressman Elihu B. Washburne (1816–1887), and restrained the detective. Washburne joined them as they hurried out of the station and got into a carriage for the trip to Willard's Hotel. Washburne had found out about Lincoln's unscheduled arrival from Seward. Pinkerton apologized to the congressman, and Washburne admitted he should have been more discreet.[30]

Although Marshal of Police Kane always denied that there ever was any real danger to Lincoln, he did admit that there were individuals who might present an "annoyance" to the president elect. Because of this, Kane asked John S. Gittings, president of the Northern Central Railroad, to entertain the official party at his home and "relieve them from the crowd and excitement." This was done when Mrs. Lincoln and the Lincolns' three sons came through Baltimore at the time originally scheduled, after Lincoln's secret nighttime passage.

There is no doubt that "the Baltimore Plot," as it came to be known, was a real threat to Lincoln and to the preservation of the Union. When Baltimore crowds heard that Lincoln had already passed through their city, they denounced him as a coward. But it seemed to be common knowledge that had Lincoln come through as planned, to quote one Baltimorean, "he would have been torn to pieces." Newspapers caricatured Lincoln, cringing in fear, dressed in a Scottish outfit and looking ridiculous as he sneaked through Baltimore. Such criticism was embarrassing to Lincoln and it took him some time to live it down.[31]

Lincoln's safe arrival in Washington took everyone by surprise. "At first the news was not believed, but an inspection of the register at Willard's Hotel, where 'A. Lincoln, Illinois,' was palpably written down, satisfied the most skeptical.... He was domiciled at parlor No. 6, Willard's Hotel, tired, and declining to see company."[32]

3. Inauguration —1861

> Men looked searchingly into the eyes of every stranger, to discover whether he were a traitor or a friend.
>
> Isaac N. Arnold

As the new year of 1861 began, persons of pro–Union sentiments were especially concerned for the situation in Washington, DC. Secession was already a fact, and while Virginia was still officially part of the Union, few expected the state to remain, opposing its neighbors to the south. There was the further concern that Maryland might join the rebellion. If both these states broke from the Union, Washington, the capital city, would be surrounded by hostile territory. If that happened before inauguration day, March 4, it would be impossible for the government of the new Lincoln administration to convene in the capital city. Even if Maryland, at least, could be held for the Union, and Lincoln could be inaugurated in Washington, could a functional government be established and commence operations against a rebellion growing in size and hostility?

In December 1860, President James Buchanan summoned the commanding officer of the United States Army, Lieutenant General Winfield Scott to meet with him in Washington and discuss the growing crisis. Scott was a legendary soldier. Though born in Virginia, he was thoroughly pro–Union. An army officer since the days of Thomas Jefferson, Scott had become a national hero in the War of 1812, and again in the Mexican War of 1846–

Gen. Winfield Scott. Hero of previous wars, Scott was too old to command the vast armies required for the Civil War, but he was a key figure in arranging security for the first inauguration (Library of Congress).

1848. Running for president in 1852, Scott's anti-slavery position cost him much support, especially in the South, and he lost to Franklin Pierce (1804–1869). Continuing as army commander, he was promoted by brevet to the rank of lieutenant general in 1855, the first American officer to hold that rank since George Washington.

While in the capital, Scott also met with Charles Pomeroy Stone. A native of Massachusetts, Stone graduated from West Point in 1845. He served under General Scott in the Mexican War, and was influential in planning defenses on the west coast in the postwar years. Leaving the army in 1856, Stone did surveying for the Mexican government until the outbreak of the Civil War. Scott appointed Stone inspector general of the District of Columbia militia, with the rank of colonel, on January 1, 1861. In addition to raising volunteers to defend the capital city, Stone assumed the responsibility for security for the inauguration of Lincoln.

Colonel Stone found the defenses of the city of Washington to be meager. At the marine barracks were stationed between three and four hundred marines. The Washington Arsenal had only about one hundred regular army troops. Supplementing these forces were one company of militiamen in Georgetown, the Potomac Light Infantry, one company of volunteers in Washington, the National Rifles, and a few under strength militia units, for a total of fewer than five hundred men. To make matters worse, not all of these soldiers could be said to be totally loyal to the Union. The previous secretary of war, John B. Floyd, a Virginian, had sent most of the regular army soldiers to distant posts on the far frontiers, and had ordered that one of the volunteer companies, the National Rifles, commanded by a pro-secession lieutenant, should have all the rifles, ammunition, and supplies they needed from government stores. With the cooperation of the new secretary of war, Joseph Holt (1807–1894), Stone ensured that he would have authority over all such orders. Moving rapidly, Stone was able to raise thirty-three companies of infantry and two troops of cavalry, and saw them equipped and under regular drill, all in only six weeks. He employed detectives to watch those whose loyalty to the Union was questionable. Stone claimed that his quick actions had thwarted a plan to seize the capital for the rebels.

Of his newly raised soldiers, Colonel Stone said, "These were

Col. Charles P. Stone and daughter. Stone was invaluable in arranging security for the first inauguration, and raising troops to defend Washington, DC (Library of Congress).

the troops which insured the regular inauguration on the steps of the Capitol of the Constitutionally elected President. I firmly believe that without them Mr. Lincoln would never have been inaugurated. I believe that tumults would have been created, during which he would have been killed, and that we should have found ourselves engaged in a struggle, without preparation, and without a recognized head at the Capital."[1]

Lincoln's arrival in the capital city by no means spelled a lessening of danger to his person. In his hotel room he found an abusive, threatening note, and the papers were depicting him as cowardly and frightened, sneaking his way into the capital in a disguise.[2]

The local police added little to the security of the city. As with all other segments of society at that time, the policemen exhibited divided loyalties, and the organization of the police — some paid by the city, others by the federal government — worked against efficiency and effectiveness. Eventually, the military police had to assume normal police duties in Washington, and the police force was entirely reorganized.[3]

Colonel Stone took personal charge of military security for the inauguration on the steps of the Capitol. Riflemen were posted in the windows of the Capitol. The plans for the inaugural procession were carefully made by General Scott and his staff, including Colonel Stone. President Buchanan would be driven from the White House the short distance to Willard's Hotel, at Pennsylvania Avenue and 14th Street, where President Elect Abraham Lincoln would join Buchanan for the ride up the avenue to the Capitol. Stone assigned double files of cavalry to ride on both sides of the carriage carrying the outgoing and incoming presidents. A company of troops would march in front of the carriage and another company behind. Riflemen were on the roofs of buildings along the procession route, watching both the crowds below and the adjacent rooftops and windows. Additional cavalrymen would block the side streets as the procession passed by, riding ahead and taking up positions at the next intersection after the carriage's passage.

On the night before the ceremony, Stone received word that an attempt would be made to blow up the inaugural platform. Stone ordered additional troops to surround the platform and block entrances to prevent anyone who did not belong from getting in. Plainclothes policemen mingled with the crowd, under orders to observe closely any suspicious actions.

Stone personally escorted the carriage containing the two presidents on inauguration day, handling his horse in such a way as to slightly disrupt the cavalrymen's order. Thus he sought to ensure that the random movements would

James Buchanan. Lincoln's predecessor in the presidency was greatly relieved to be able to turn over the government to Lincoln just before the war broke out (Library of Congress).

Lincoln and Cabinet. Left to right: Secretary of War Edwin M. Stanton, Secretary of the Treasury Salmon P. Chase, Secretary of the Navy Gideon Welles, President Abraham Lincoln, General Ulysses S. Grant, Secretary of State William H. Seward, Attorney General James Speed, Secretary of the Interior John P. Usher, and Postmaster General Montgomery Blair (Library of Congress).

spoil the aim of marksmen.[4] Many in the crowd were, or could be presumed to be, pro–Southern. "Men looked searchingly into the eyes of every stranger, to discover whether he were a traitor or a friend.... Lincoln's calmness arose from an entire absence of self-consciousness; he was too fully absorbed in the gravity of the occasion and in the importance of the events around and before him, to think of himself." When Lincoln had finished delivering his inaugural address, one of the first to congratulate him was Senator Stephen A. Douglas, who had been a political opponent of Lincoln's for years, but who now assured the new president that he would have Douglas's full support.

Among those present at the inauguration was newspaper editor Horace Greeley, who afterward described his unease as Lincoln spoke of his hopes for a peaceful resolution of the secession crisis. "I sat just behind him as he read [the inaugural address] on a bright, warm, still March day, expecting to hear its delivery arrested by the crack of a rifle aimed at his heart; but it pleased God to postpone the deed, though there was forty times the reason for shooting him in 1860 that there was in '65, and at least forty times as many intent on killing him or having him killed. No shot was fired then, however; for his hour had not yet come."[5]

After the ceremony, the procession was repeated in reverse, as the carriage of Lincoln and Buchanan was escorted back down the avenue to the White House. Former President

Lincoln with Nicolay (left) and Hay. John Nicolay was Lincoln's official private secretary, but John M. Hay was also needed as Nicolay's assistant. As Lincoln's administration progressed, other secretaries were added (Library of Congress).

Buchanan received a military escort for his departure from the White House.⁶ The White House had been made ready by the outgoing administration. "A competent chef, with efficient butler and waiters, under the direction of the accomplished Miss Harriet Lane [the bachelor president's niece], had an elegant dinner prepared, and it is needless to say, after the excitement and fatigue of the day, it was most thoroughly appreciated. But physical fatigue was of minor account — we went out not knowing what the day might bring forth. Bristling guns, mounted artillery, and belching cannon were too fearfully suggestive of what might be apprehended, and it was a moment of intense relief when 'Old Edward,' who had served through many administrations, opened the doors of the Executive Mansion, admitted us, and our President was safely housed."⁷

Thanks to the work of Pinkerton, Stone, and many others, Lincoln had been conducted safely to Washington and inaugurated president, something many secessionists had sworn would never happen. But this was only a bare beginning. An Alabama newspaper stated, "Mr. Lincoln's life would not be worth a week's purchase after a single gun had been fired against Fort Sumter." There were still very few regular troops in the capital, only volunteer outfits such as those organized by James Henry Lane (1814–1866) of Kansas and Cassius Marcellus Clay (1810–1903) of Kentucky. They guarded the White House and drilled in the streets and open ground around the White House and Treasury building.⁸

In those first few days of his presidency, Lincoln received news of a Confederate plan to slip a group of men headed by Benjamin Franklin Ficklin (1827–1871) into Washington, and kidnap or kill the president. The rebels were said to be planting a mortar battery in the Virginia hills overlooking the capital city. When Lincoln and his family suddenly became ill it was rumored they had been poisoned, until it was discovered they had eaten bad fish. Lincoln expressed no concern for his personal safety, but his anxiety for the Union cause bore down upon him. Looking out the window for any sign of the ships that would bring his volunteers, he was overheard to mutter, "Why don't they come? Why don't they come?"[9]

4. Protecting President Lincoln

> It would never do for a president to have guards with drawn sabers at his door, as if he fancied he were, or were trying to be, or were assuming to be, an emperor.
> Abraham Lincoln

Lincoln, with his disdain for security and his fatalistic attitude, showed little concern for his safety. Many others, however, were constantly worried. Foremost among these was Ward Hill Lamon. Lincoln appointed his old friend Lamon to the post of United States marshal for the District of Columbia. Lamon assumed as one of his official duties the protection of the president. He often cautioned Lincoln, as in this letter.

> Continental Hotel
> Aug. 17, 1861
> Philadelphia
>
> Hon. A. Lincoln — Dear Sir:
>
> I very much fear that there are Eaves Droppers and traitors lurking about the White House. I would suggest that no one be allowed upstairs except such as you permit — after their sending up their cards.... I am sure there are dangerous persons who get access or at least information.... I am so fully convinced that there are dangerous persons lurking about the White House that I think it necessary to employ a secret detective — Pinkerton if we can get him, or some other shrewd person. I wish you would look after it at once, and by all means keep everybody downstairs only those on business.[1]

Or the following note to Lincoln's personal secretary.

> New York, Dec. 15, 1864
>
> I may be unnecessarily frightened about Mr. Lincoln's personal safety — but I do assure you I think I have good reasons for my uneasiness about him.
> See that he don't go out alone either in the day or night time.
> Ward Hill Lamon

Lamon was not the only one expressing such concerns. At a private dinner in Washington in 1861, it was said that Senator James Asheton Bayard, Jr. (1799–1880), D-DE, declared he would give $10,000 if Lincoln were assassinated. Bayard denounced the story as false before a Senate committee in 1869. At that time, it was revealed that the source of the story was a "citizen of African descent" named James Yellowplush, who said he had stood behind the senator and had overheard his remark.[2] Whether the story was true or not, such things were being said throughout the Lincoln administration.[3]

Even before his inauguration, Lincoln received abusive, threatening letters. Typical of these is this one, dated February 20, 1861:

> May the hand of the devil strike you
> down before long — You are destroying
> the country.
> Damn you — every breath you take —
> (signed) Hand of God against you

One correspondent passed on threats while simultaneously applying for a job: "I have heard several persons in this place [Lynchburg, VA] say that if you ever did take the President chair that they would go to Washington City expressly to kill you ... have you had any application for this post [presumably bodyguard] if not I wish you would let me have it." Lincoln might have been amused at one letter, which, after using much vile language to describe the president elect, the writer apologized: "excuse me for using such hard words with you, but you need it you are nothing but a goddam Black nigger."

Even as Pinkerton, Seward, and others were informing Lincoln of the danger they perceived in Baltimore, Lincoln received this letter, dated February 22, 1861: "I was advised last night by a gentleman that there existed in Baltimore a league of ten persons, who had sworn that you should never pass through that city alive." The writer signed this letter, "God defend and bless you — The prayers of many go with you. A Lady."

Lafayette C. Baker. The feared head of the War Department detective force, Baker and his men never worried about the fine points of the law, only about furthering the Union government's interests (Baker, *History of the U.S. Secret Service*).

At least one letter was short and to the point:

> You will be shot on the 4th of March 1861 by a Louisiana Creole
> We are decided and our aim is sure.

Escaping the dangers of the Baltimore Plot and of his inauguration, Lincoln continued to receive letters threatening him, or relating rumors of such threats: "The same who warned you of a conspiracy Novr. 18th 1862 is now compelled to inform you, that, 'Your days are numbered.' You shall be a dead man in six months from date Dec. 31st 1863." A letter dated November 1864 received more attention than most: "Abe must die, and now. You can choose your weapons. The cup, the knife, the bullet. The cup failed us once, and might again." This is one of the letters said to have been left in a streetcar in New York City. When shown the letters, Lincoln "seemed to attach very little importance to them." The remark about "the cup," suggesting poison having been tried before, reawakened memories of the bad fish incident (see chapter 3) and later seemed to foreshadow one of the Booth conspirators, David Herold, who had worked in a drugstore.

Lincoln was certainly aware of these and many other threatening or warning letters. One letter, signed "Horace Greeley," the widely known newspaper editor and Lincoln critic, requesting a meeting with the president to discuss a conspiracy, has "Forgery" written on the back in Lincoln's hand. Some of these letters Lincoln told his secretaries to burn. Others were filed in a large envelope upon which Lincoln wrote "Assassination."[4]

To his secretary John M. Hay (1838–1905), Lincoln expressed doubts that the many threatening letters received at the White House represented any real danger. General Benjamin F. Butler (1818–1893), arriving at the White House in the middle of the night in 1861, could find no guards at all. Lincoln had objected to the formal guards originally posted at the White House, making him seem like an emperor, he said, so the guards were withdrawn. In those times a large part of the president's working day consisted of receiving callers, not only officials but also ordinary citizens, and Lincoln always felt that it was especially important that he be accessible to the people. Of course, there were people to see before one could gain access to the president himself. The White House had a doorkeeper, there was an usher on the second floor, and the president's secretaries, originally only two, later increased as the volume of business increased. None of these people were intended to

Lincoln with Allan Pinkerton (left) and Gen. John A. McLernand. Pinkerton, whose detective agency still bears his name, accompanied Lincoln on the inaugural journey and provided security (Library of Congress).

be guards, but John Hay took it upon himself to add security to his other duties, checking the White House rooms while the Lincolns slept. Colonel Charles Halpine (1829–1868), of General Halleck's staff, wrote of how he had entered the White House "many times" and progressed all the way up to the offices without being challenged. It seemed to him that the attendants who were supposed to be on duty had assumed that no one would be coming up after hours. To all of this, Lincoln gave his standard reply, that if anyone wanted to get to him they would, guard or no guard.

Similar recollections appeared in a newspaper following Lincoln's assassination. "It has been charged that Mr. Lincoln was ... 'culpably negligent.'" When visiting Lincoln, "no guards intercepted our movements, no examination of our persons was required, no evidence of necessity for caution was manifested. We went into the presence of Mr. Lincoln, who was alone. Had we been assassins, there were more than a dozen avenues of escape presented to us." Another report contradicts this: "Gen. James Lane also leads a gallant band, largely composed of his old Kansas confers. Last night they occupied the East Room of the White

House, so that between their vigilance and that of the 'President's Mounted Guard,' Mr. Lincoln's safety was assured. The last named corps is the crack light-horse volunteer company of the District, and is proud to be responsible for the President's nightly security." These conflicting reports can be reconciled by understanding that they refer to different times during Lincoln's presidency. Presidential security, even during such perilous times, was not uniform or consistent.[5]

Once Lincoln had arrived in Washington and assumed the office of president, General Winfield Scott, commanding general of the army, took it upon himself to see to it that Lincoln received security. Beginning in March 1861, Scott assigned cavalrymen to the White House, standing guard both outside and in the mansion. The original group of guards, nicknamed "Scott's 900,"* were replaced by Company K of the 150th Pennsylvania Regiment, known as the "Bucktails" for the feathers they wore in their hats. These soldiers not only guarded the president's house and grounds, but also escorted him when he went out. The president disliked being guarded, and made his dissatisfaction known, though he treated his soldier guards with courtesy and respect.

In his characteristic way, Lincoln told his soldier guards a joke that he said summed up his feelings about the need for their presence. "You boys remind me of a farmer friend of mine in Illinois, who said he could never understand why the Lord put the curl in a pig's tail. It never seemed to him to be either useful or ornamental, but he reckoned the Allmighty knew what he was doing when he put it there."[6]

The capital of the United States that Abraham Lincoln knew was very different from the city of today. It had very much the air of a small city of the Old South. Census figures from 1860 show the District of Columbia had about 75,000 people, 35,000 male and 40,000 female. 61,000 were white and 14,000 black. By age, 10,000 were under five, 17,000 from 5 to 14 years old, 22,000 were 15 to 24, another 22,000 were 25 to 44, and 3,000 were age 45 or older. Of the 75,000, about 63,000 lived in the city of Washington, which did not extend beyond Boundary Street, today's Florida Avenue. Most of the streets were unpaved, the Potomac River flowed nearly as close in as the Washington Monument, and sometimes overflowed its banks as far as Pennsylvania Avenue. Bad sanitation and lack of air conditioning made the city very unpleasant in summer; foreign diplomats considered it to be an undesirable post, unsafe for their families because of cholera, typhoid, malaria, and other diseases.[7]

The city had an unfinished look, a look that was reflected in the Capitol building. Expansion of the Capitol had been authorized in 1850, with the addition of two new wings, containing larger chambers for the Senate and House of Representatives, still under construction as Lincoln took the oath of office on March 4, 1861. The Capitol expansion also included replacing the old dome with a much larger, grander one, only about half finished at the beginning of Lincoln's administration. While some expected this expensive work to be halted once the Civil War broke out, Lincoln ordered that it continue, "as a sign that we intend the Union shall go on." The Capitol was completed on December 2, 1863, with the installation atop the dome of the nineteen-foot high Statue of Freedom.[8]

The White House in Lincoln's time was not as large and complex as it is today. The wings with the executive offices were not added until early in the twentieth century. Lincoln's

---

Named for Assistant Secretary of War Thomas A. Scott, a friend of Colonel James B. Swain, who had organized the regiment.

office was in the White House proper, on the east end of the second floor. Today this room is the Lincoln bedroom. Journalist George Alfred Townsend (1841–1914) has left us a description of Lincoln's office. "The room is long and high, and so thickly hung with maps that the color of the wall cannot be discerned. The President's table ... adjoins a window at the farthest corner; ... there is a large table before an empty grate, around which there are many chairs, where the Cabinet used to assemble. The carpet is trodden thin, and the brilliance of its dyes is lost. The furniture is of the formal cabinet class, stately and semi-comfortable; there are bookcases sprinkled with the sparse library of a country lawyer.... [T]he maps ... are from the coast survey and engineer departments, and exhibit all the contested grounds of the war; there are pencil lines upon them where someone has traced the route of armies and planned the strategic circumference of campaigns."[9]

In addition to the troops guarding the White House, there were servants whose functions were not primarily that of security, but who could provide a degree of protection at times. There was the doorkeeper, who would receive visitors and send word of their arrival. Records from the administration of Andrew Johnson listed two doorkeepers, probably indicating they worked two shifts. Also listed are two night watchmen, suggesting that someone was on duty at any hour of the day or night. Another position on the list is that of fireman, although he may have had more to do with heating the house than protecting it. One or two "messengers" were on hand to deliver and receive messages, and to run errands such as arranging for presidential visits to the theatre. Charles Forbes, who went with the Lincolns to Ford's Theatre the night of the assassination, was often described as the president's "messenger." The names of these servants, in addition to Forbes, were

Edward McManus, doorkeeper, retired during Lincoln administration.
O'Leary, "
Edward Burke, "
J. R. Vernon, night watchman.
James Kelly, "
Alphonso Donn, assistant doorkeeper.
Thomas H. Cross, fireman.
Thomas F. Pendel, messenger.

There were other household servants, but their duties would not have involved any sort of security for the house or for the president.

Late in Lincoln's administration, full-time guards were provided from the ranks of the Washington Metropolitan Police. These are discussed in chapter 12.

When the Lincoln family took up summer residence at the Soldiers Home, they were guarded by the army.

Washington, Sept. 5, 1862

Your Excellency

I have ordered a portion of the Provost Guard of the Army of the Potomac to take post at the Soldiers Home for the purpose of guarding your Excellency's residence.

The officer in command is instructed to deliver this note and receive your orders.

Very respectfully, your obt. Svt.
George B. McClellan, Maj. Gen.[10]

The war brought about major changes in Washington, from a quiet, small, Southern-oriented city to a bustling capital, headquarters of the war effort, a war far larger and costlier than any previous conflict in American history. Troops drilled on streets and in open areas and stood guard at public buildings. By war's end the number of troops in and around the city exceeded 200,000. Soldiers were quartered in the Capitol, and other public buildings. Hotels and even churches were converted to hospitals and camps containing thousands of tents were set up in and around the city. Homeless persons also sought shelter in the Capitol building. A ring of forts were built, usually out of piled-up earth and tree trunks, with cannon as large as 15."[11]

It is not commonly understood today that Abraham Lincoln was very controversial, that he was hated and even feared by many in his time. Expressions of anti–Lincoln sentiment, some even advocating violence toward him, were to be seen and heard everywhere.

Alphonso Taft to Senator Benjamin F. Wade, September 8, 1864: "Providence must have some punishment in store for Lincoln.... How it is to come about, is yet to be seen."[12]

Senator John Sherman on the habeas corpus question: "I never met with anyone who claimed that the President would, by a proclamation, increase the regular army. The legal power to suspend the writ of habeas corpus has been recently claimed for the President, but I am convinced that by the plain meaning of the Constitution, Congress alone must determine cases in which the public safety requires its suspension.... I could not say [such suspensions] were strictly legal or within his designated powers."[13]

Editorial from the *London Times*:

> [The Lincoln administration] has destroyed a vast mass of property and happiness, and scattered to the winds the best hopes of the American people.... The Republican majority in Congress ... deserve a foremost place among those representatives of the people who from time to time have made themselves notorious in the history of the world by surrendering the liberties of their country into the hands of a dictator or tyrant.... The office of President, plain and republican as it came from the hands of the founders ... is hardly recognizable beneath the mass of powers with which it is overlaid. The first citizen of the republic, the servant of the people, the head of an executive, exercising certain few and clearly defined powers, has become, by the treason of a legislature ... the most absolute autocrat on earth.[14]

Letter of Col. Wm. Marshall Anderson to Sam Medary: "My hope, my prayer is, that when monarchical power is concentrated and centralized in Washington; that one thousand daggers may pierce the heart of the first crowned villain!"[15]

A mass meeting of conservative Democrats in Syracuse, New York, on October 26, 1864, displayed transparencies bearing the following slogans: "A despot has his parasites, and liberty hath her avengers." "American soil scourged by an unconditional despot in Abraham Lincoln." "If Seward touches his bell again, the people will stretch his neck." (A reference to William H. Seward's claim that he need only ring a small bell on his desk to order the arrest of anyone.) "Lincoln has murdered three white men to free one negro." "Free ballots or free bullets. Crush the tyrant Lincoln before he crushes you." "Resistance to a tyrant is obedience to God."[16]

Elder statesman and presidential advisor Francis P. Blair, Sr.: "Under no possible emergency, not even an insurrection, or amid the terrors of Civil War, can this government justify interference with the freedom of speech or of the press, any more than it can with the freedom of the ballot. The licentiousness of the tongue and of the pen is a minor evil compared with the licentiousness of arbitrary power."[17]

And from the *London Herald*: "It would not be at all surprising if some of Mr. Lincoln's victims, despairing of legal redress for their sufferings, have resolved to attempt the employment of violence to rid the country of their oppressor and its disgrace."[18]

Of course, we now know that Lincoln enjoyed the approval and confidence of the majority of his countrymen, and a posthumous near-deification, but in his time, as in ours, the voices of discontent can be loud and frequent, and can give the impression of carrying more weight than they actually do. But we also know that discontent, whether sincere or not, need not command legions to accomplish its wicked ends.

Official, full-time protection for the presidents did not begin until 1902, after three presidents, Lincoln, Garfield, and McKinley, all inadequately protected, had been assassinated in a thirty-six-year period.[19]

"The simple habits of Mr. Lincoln were so well known that it is a subject for surprise that watchful and malignant treason did not sooner take that precious life which he seemed to hold so lightly. He had an almost morbid dislike for an escort, or guard, and daily exposed himself to the deadly aim of an assassin."

Lincoln's dislike of security measures was personal, but in his statements on the subject he used logical arguments as well. "Our friends on the other side [the Confederates] would make nothing by exchanging me for Hamlin," he noted, referring to his vice president's more radical views. When friends pressed him on the subject of his safety, he replied, "I cannot be shut up in an iron cage and guarded ... if to kill me is within the purposes of this rebellion, no precaution can prevent it. You may guard me at a single point, but I will necessarily be exposed at others.... The truth is, if any man has made up his mind that he will give his life for mine, he can take mine." Logical this statement may be, but there is more than a trace of fatalism in it, too. There are many references in Lincoln's conversations and speeches to the idea that he might not survive the war, or that he might come to a bad end. When first elected president, Lincoln had seen in a mirror the double image of his face — one sharp and distinct, the other shadowy and ghost-like. He concluded that this meant he would serve one term but not live through a second. To Congressman Owen Lovejoy (1811–1864) he remarked, "This war is eating my life out; I have a strong impression that I shall not live to see the end."

There was every reason to justify Lincoln's fatalism and the fears of his supporters. Not only did people speak openly of assassination, they even published such ideas, in the North as often as the South. The New York Copperhead of July 11, 1863: "Behave yourself in future, boss, or we shall be obliged to make an island of your head and stick it on the end of a pole." The La Crosse, Wisconsin, *Democrat,* August 29, 1864: "The man who votes for Lincoln now is a traitor.... He who calls and allures men to certain butchery, is a murderer, and Lincoln has done all this.... If he is elected to misgovern for another four years, we trust some bold hand will pierce his heart with dagger point for the public good." The Illinois State Register of August 7, 1864: "The doom of Lincoln and black republicanism is sealed. Corruption and the bayonet are impotent to save them. The sovereign people have willed it, and the would be despots at Washington must succumb to their fate." The Richmond Dispatch of November 9, 1864: "A vulgar tyrant, who has never seen a shot fired in anger, who has no more idea of statesmanship than as a means of making money; whose career has been one of unlimited and unmitigated disaster; whose personal qualities are those of a low buffoon, and whose most noteworthy conversation is a medley of profane jests and obscene anecdotes — a creature who has squandered the lives of millions without remorse and without even the decency of pretending to feel for their misfortunes."

General Thomas Ewing (1829–1896), who would later serve as a defense counsel at the trial of the conspirators, sent the following letter to Secretary Stanton early in 1865. "The president could be seized any reception evening, in the midst of the masses assembled round him, and carried off by fifty determined men armed with bowie knives and revolvers — and once out could be put into a market wagon guarded by a dozen horsemen, and bourne off at will — the conspirators having first set a dozen or twenty hacks in motion to distract attention. Look out for some such dash soon."

In spite of threats and the obvious danger to his safety in the midst of a bitter civil war, President Abraham Lincoln frequently went out unprotected, sometimes entirely alone. No permanent guards were assigned to him until relatively late in his administration, the guards at the White House being sporadic, sometimes more effective than at other times. Noah Brooks (1830–1903), Lincoln's journalist friend, sometimes accompanied him on walks around town, describing how Lincoln believed the lack of advance publicity about his movements provided his best security. The president's seeming confidence in his safety was not shared by Brooks. In the summer of 1863, the reporter walked back with Lincoln from the War Department to the White House, a short distance that could not have taken many minutes. "I fancied that I saw in the misty moonlight a man dodging behind one of the trees. My heart for a moment stood still, but, as we passed in safety, I came to the conclusion that the dodging figure was a creature of the imagination." Expressing his concern for Lincoln's safety, Brooks was shown a walking stick, and heard some of Lincoln's fatalistic philosophy. "He laughed and showed me this slight weapon, and said, but with some seriousness, 'I long ago made up my mind that if anybody wants to kill me, he will do it. If I wore a shirt of mail, and kept myself surrounded by a bodyguard, it would be all the same. There are a thousand ways of getting at a man if it is desired that he should be killed.'"

Brooks was not the only one to be concerned for the president's safety. The following letter was sent to the editors of the Chicago Tribune in April 1865. "Last fall, while a member of the Sons of Liberty [an extremist group], in this city, I heard and instantly reported to General Sweet, which reports were forwarded to the War Department at Washington, a distinct proposition made to raise $50,000 to send a man to Washington to assassinate President Lincoln, and I have not a particle of doubt the plan originated with and was executed by the 'Sons of Liberty.'"

Congressman James S. Rollins (1812–1888), Conservative-MO, received a visit from "Colonel Lane," a constituent, who told him of a Southern plot to kill Lincoln by sending a box filled with explosives to the White House, rigged to explode when opened. When Lincoln was told about this, he said, "I don't pay much attention to such things. I have received quite a number of threatening letters since I have been President, and nobody has killed me yet, and the truth is, I give very little consideration to such things."

John M. Hay, assistant to Lincoln's private secretary, recorded in his diary another warning of danger on Friday, May 13, 1864. "Jim Lane [James Henry Lane (1814–1866), congressman from Indiana, 1853–1855, senator from Kansas, 1861–1866] came into my room this morning and said the President must now chiefly guard against assassination. I pooh-poohed him and said that while every prominent man was more or less exposed to the attacks of maniacs, no foresight could guard against them. He replied by saying that he had by his caution and vigilance prevented his own assassination when a reward of one hundred thousand dollars had been offered for his head." Hay obviously did not hold Lane in very high esteem, though he had been known to express concern for Lincoln's safety on other occasions.[20]

In perhaps the only exception to his dismissive attitude about his security, Lincoln once remarked, apparently seriously, "so far as my personal safety is concerned, Gurowski is the only man who has given me a serious thought of a personal nature. From the known disposition of the man, he is dangerous wherever he may be. I have sometimes thought that he might try to take my life. It would be just like him to do such a thing."

Adam Gurowski was born September 10, 1805, in Russian-occupied Poland. An early injury resulted in poor eyesight for most of his life. Even as a schoolboy he was in trouble with the authorities for his Polish patriotism. Studying philosophy in Berlin, Germany, with Georg Friedrich Hegel (1770–1831) from 1820 to 1825, and in Heidelberg, Jena and Leipzig, he returned to Poland and was involved in plots against the Russians in 1829–1830, which resulted in exile and the confiscation of his estates. Making a sudden turnaround, he renounced the cause of Poland and upheld Russia as the champion of the Slavic peoples. This enabled him to return home and even to obtain a position in the Russian Ministry of Public Information, but by 1844 he was exiled again, wandering between Heidelberg, Munich, Berne, Naples, and Paris, always scheming and seeking political favor. The failure of the 1848 revolutions throughout Europe caused Gurowski to abandon the old world for the new.

He arrived in New York in 1849 with letters of introduction from European friends and was soon making the acquaintance of such notable Americans as historian William Hickling Prescott (1796–1859); poets Henry Wadsworth Longfellow (1807–1882), James Russell Lowell (1819–1891), and Walt Whitman (1819–1892); and statesmen Charles Sumner (1811–1874) and Edward Everett (1794–1865). His new friends rescued him from manual labor and got him work writing articles on history and European affairs. He involved himself in the debate on slavery, arguing against it with a passion and enthusiasm that knew no bounds.

In 1861 Gurowski got a job with the State Department reading and translating foreign newspapers. It was not long before he knew most of the influential people in the capital, who were impressed with his intelligence and beguiled by his charm. However, his intrusive ways and lack of respect for the privacy of his hosts got him into trouble. So, too, did his outspoken opinions. His criticism of President Lincoln and Secretary of State William H. Seward, blaming them for all America's misfortunes in the early months of the war, resulted in Gurowski's being fired from the State Department.

To make a living, Gurowski published his diary, beginning in 1862. The diary was as uninhibited as its author's conversation. A libel suit against Gurowski only helped sales. His condemnation of the country's leaders was thorough. "Traitors as Seward, imbeciles as Lincoln who ought to be shortened by the head, they carry the day.... Every day that Mr. Seward remains in the Cabinet the country's ruin is accelerated with lightning like velocity."

Was Gurowski a serious threat to Lincoln? He had been known to make threats and sometimes to carry a pistol, but if he had any serious thoughts to do harm to the president, he passed up many opportunities. He was a revolutionary, to be sure, but did not, as far as is known, belong to any anti-administration organizations. His anti-slavery and pro–Union sentiments were known by all and were apparently sincere.

The slow but steady success of the Union cause and the triumph of the Radical Republicans in the 1864 elections softened Gurowski's attitude. By the time of the assassination, he was in a forgiving mood. "This oozing blood almost sanctifies Lincoln.... Whatever sacrifices his vacillations may have cost the people, those vacillations will now be forgiven."

Gurowski died of typhoid on May 4, 1866. His funeral was attended by many prominent people, both friends and enemies. He was buried in Washington's Congressional Cemetery.[21]

After the assassination, Attorney General James Speed (1812–1887) wrote, "The principal police of the city was by Federal soldiers, the public offices and property in the city were all guarded by soldiers, and the President's house and person were, or should have been, under the guard of soldiers."[22]

From the middle of 1862 on, a company of soldiers was assigned to the White House grounds. According to John W. Nichols, a member of Co. K of the 150th Pennsylvania volunteers, which formed part of the guard, the soldiers' quarters were "immediately in front of the South porch of the Executive Mansion. Just to the east of our quarters was our guard tent, where a portion of the bodyguard remained when on duty." Security was often tightened, Nichols says, with the soldiers being ordered to be extra vigilant. Sometimes the guard was doubled.

On his excursions out of town, Lincoln had a cavalry escort, whose clanking swords and spurs made so much noise that Lincoln and his carriage mates were disturbed. Sometimes Lincoln would encourage his coachman to try to outrun the soldiers, who would be forced to chase after him. In the hot summers especially, Lincoln and his family would retreat to the Soldiers Home in the woods outside of Washington.[23] In the summer of 1864, as Lincoln was riding back alone to the Soldiers Home after a day's work at the White House, a shot was fired, the bullet passing through his hat. Lincoln came riding hard up to the grounds of the Home, where John W. Nichols was on duty. Examining the hat later, Nichols reported that the "person who fired the shot had secreted himself close to the roadside." Lincoln said, rather unconvincingly, that he thought it must have been an accident, but Nichols remarked that "after that the President never rode alone."[24]

Only once during the Civil War was Washington, DC, directly threatened by a Confederate army. In late June 1864, General Robert E. Lee (1807–1870) conceived a bold plan to invade Maryland, liberate the thousands of Confederate prisoners being held at Point Lookout, the southernmost spot in Maryland, and capture the federal city. A Union army commanded by Major General David Hunter (1802–1886), later to preside over the military commission at the trial of the assassination conspirators, had been run out of the Shenandoah Valley, leaving the way open for a Confederate army under Lieutenant General Jubal Anderson Early (1816–1894) to advance northward. Early's Army of the Valley, counting nearly 18,000 men, began their march on June 28.

From Staunton, Virginia, the Confederates moved along the valley pike, arriving at Winchester on July 2. They crossed the Potomac River at Shepherdstown on July 5 and 6. The division commanded by the youthful Major General Stephen Ramseur (1837–1864) arrived at Frederick, Maryland, on July 9. Union Major General Lew Wallace (1827–1905), who would also serve on the military commission at the conspiracy trial, and was at this time commanding the Middle Department at Baltimore, upon hearing of the invasion, immediately ordered all the troops available to converge on the town of Monocacy Junction, southeast of Frederick. With only about 6,000 men, Wallace knew he couldn't stop Early's army, which some reports overestimated to be 30,000 to 40,000, but by giving battle at Monocacy, Wallace hoped to slow down the Confederate advance. This is what happened, with Wallace's hopes aided by Early taking time to loot $200,000 from the city of Frederick, and also having to recall some of his troops who had chased the retreating Union forces. By midday on July 11, leading elements of Early's army entered the District of Columbia and came within sight of the Capitol dome.

Washington was ringed by a series of forts spaced closely enough to support each other, with guns of varying sizes. General Ulysses Grant (1822–1885) had sent the greater part of the forces defending Washington south to increase the pressure on Lee's army between Richmond and Petersburg, Virginia. As a result, the total number of defenders in place at the beginning of Early's invasion of Maryland was only about 9,000. Pro-rebel spies in Washington had already reported to Lee on the weakness of the city's defenses.

The advance of a strong Confederate army into Maryland, and the rebel victory at the Monocacy, spread uneasiness and even panic among the people of Maryland and Washington. Union army chief of staff, Major General Henry Wager Halleck (1815–1872), telegraphed General Grant on July 6, advising him that the enemy force was much larger than that of a cavalry raid and urging him to send reinforcements to Washington. Grant, still believing the invasion to be only a diversion, allowed elements of the XIX Corps, which had been sent up from New Orleans to support the siege of Petersburg, to proceed to the capital city. After the battle of Monocacy, even senior government officials felt alarm. Secretary of War Edwin McMasters Stanton (1814–1869) gave his clerk over $5,000, with instructions to hide the money from the rebels. The secretary also made efforts to safeguard War Department records. President Lincoln remained calm, telling visitors from Baltimore, "Let us be vigilant but keep cool. I hope neither Baltimore nor Washington will be taken."

Fort Stevens, near the Seventh Street Road in the north-central part of the District of Columbia, had been named for Brigadier General Isaac Ingalls Stevens (1818–1862), killed at Chantilly, Virginia, on September 1, 1862. The 25th New York Cavalry arrived at Fort Stevens at midnight, July 10. Around noon of the following day, Confederate troops arrived before the fort. As the rebels probed the defenses, the soldiers at Fort Stevens were aided by the guns of the two other nearby forts, Fort Slocum to the east and Fort DeRussy to the west.

A legend grew around the incidents of Lincoln's visits to Fort Stevens on July 11 and 12. As reported by the president's assistant secretary, John Hay, here is the account of the action on July 11: "He was in the fort when it was first attacked, standing upon a parapet. A soldier roughly ordered him to get down or he would have his head knocked off." In Hay's account for the following day, July 12, he said, "The President again made the tour of the fortifications; was again under fire at Ft. Stevens; a man was shot at his side."

In 1938, Alexander Woollcott (1887–1943) published a volume entitled Long, Long Ago, in which appeared an account corresponding to the July 11 events in the Hay diary. Woollcott stated that the soldier who had spoken roughly to the president was none other than Oliver Wendell Holmes, Jr. (1841–1935), son of a famous poet, and who later became a distinguished jurist, serving as an associate justice of the United States Supreme Court from 1902 to 1932. Woollcott heard the same story from Professor Harold Laski (1893–1950), the British political scientist and educator, and from Supreme Court Justice Felix Frankfurter (1882–1965). Laski's version said, "The President, rising his tall, gaunt figure to see better, became at once a target for snipers. 'I lost my nerve,' Holmes used to say, 'and yelled at the President, get down you fool! The President turned to me quietly, and said with a twinkle in his eye, "Colonel Holmes, I am glad you know how to talk to a civilian.""'

As with many stories about Lincoln, there has been much skepticism about this one. That Justice Holmes told the story to these two men, and others as well, is reliably supported, though Holmes left no written account of the incident. Margaret Leech (1893–1974) reported the "Get down, you fool!" story in her Reveille in Washington, but both Carl Sandburg (1878–1967) and Bruce Catton (1899–1978) left out the Holmes connection from their histories.

How much truth, if any, is there in the Holmes story? We have already seen that Hay reported that someone "roughly ordered" Lincoln to get down. Could it have been Holmes? Hay does not mention Holmes on either July 11 or 12, but Hay did not accompany the president to Fort Stevens on either of those days; at least, he makes no mention of having done so. In his entry for July 13, however, we have this account: "I rode out to the front this morning, R.T.L. [Robert Todd Lincoln, the president's son], and I. We visited Wright's headquarters first.... At Crystal Spring we met young Captain O.W. Holmes, Wright's A.D.C. [aide de camp]. He joined us and we proceeded through the encampment ... we went to Ft. Stevens and had a good view from the parapet of the battlefield of yesterday." This is the only mention of Holmes in the Hay diary, establishing that Holmes was there, but had he been the soldier who "roughly ordered" the president of the United States to "Get down, you fool!" would he have led his distinguished young visitors to the very parapet where it had happened and yet said nothing to them about it? If Holmes had told the story to Hay, would Hay have left such a colorful incident out of his diary?

The Holmes story aside, the fact of Lincoln's presence at the fort is undisputed. As we learned from Hay, who heard it from Lincoln himself, the president was under enemy fire on both days of the battle, dangerously close to the action, and showing an almost reckless disregard for his own safety. He is the only American president to come under enemy fire on a battlefield while serving as president.

As he was accustomed to doing in the hot summer nights, Lincoln rode out to the Soldiers Home, where he and his family enjoyed the breeze. He made the journey, as usual, on the evening of July 10, as Early's forces approached. Stanton, alarmed to have the president spending the night only a little over two miles from a rebel army, strongly urged Lincoln to return to the White House, sending a carriage to bring back the First Family. The Lincolns heeded the secretary of war's insistence, returning to the White House around midnight. Assistant Secretary of the Navy Gustavus Vasa Fox (1821–1883) arranged for a ship to be available at the Sixth Street wharf, should it be necessary to evacuate the president from the capital city. Hearing of this precaution, Lincoln felt embarrassed.

Lincoln arose early and aimed a telescope from the south windows of the White House. He was looking for signs of the ships carrying elements of the Sixth Corps, which Grant had dispatched from his army in Virginia. At Fort Stevens, Major General Christopher C. Augur (1821–1898) arrived to see for himself the condition of the defenses of the city for which he was responsible. At dawn on July 11, Augur found only 209 soldiers at Fort Stevens. General Augur immediately ordered every available man to Fort Stevens, including "orderlies, messengers, military riff raff, invalids ... indeed, every man in government employ who could put on a uniform, or carry a musket."

The Confederates were finding the going rough. General Early noted that the mid–July day was "an exceedingly hot one and no air stirring. When marching, the men were enveloped in a suffocating cloud of dust and many of them fell by the way.... I pushed on as rapidly as possible ... [but] it became necessary to slacken our pace." It was not until noon that real fighting broke out, with the Union pickets retreating behind the fortifications. The Union defenders, inferior both in quantity and quality, were fearful, but Early's men were barely able to mount an attack. As the battle was beginning, six hundred Union cavalrymen arrived to reinforce the fort. When the guns of Forts Stevens, Slocum, and DeRussy opened up on them, the Confederates had to retire to await the arrival of their comrades.

The exact time Lincoln arrived at Fort Stevens on July 11 is disputed. John Hay's diary says Lincoln "was in the fort when it was first attacked," which would have been around noon, and that he returned to the White House "at three o'clock." Other accounts have him at Fort Stevens in the late afternoon. All agree that the president was at the Sixth Street wharf to greet the arrival of Major General Horatio Governor Wright's (1820–1899) Sixth Corps, or at least two divisions of it, about 10,000 men, at around two o'clock. Wright, who had graduated second in his class at West Point in 1841, had spend most of his army service in the Corps of Engineers, but had seen plenty of combat in the battles of First Bull Run, Secessionville, Gettysburg, the Wilderness, Cold Harbor, and Petersburg. Wright's men began arriving at Fort Stevens by three o'clock.

On July 12, as a major battle began shaping up on Washington's doorstep, many civilians, including prominent citizens and officials of the government, rode out to see the action. Among these were writer-naturalist John Burroughs (1837–1921); Registrar of the Treasury Lucius Eugene Chittenden (1824–1900); Navy Secretary Gideon Welles (1802–1878); Senator Benjamin Franklin Wade (1800–1878); army provost Major William Emile Doster (1837–1919), who would be one of the defense lawyers at the conspiracy trial; Secretary of War Stanton; and President and Mrs. Abraham Lincoln.

General Wright described the scene:

> The President evinced a remarkable coolness and disregard of danger. Meeting him as I came out of my quarters, I thoughtlessly invited him to see the fight in which we were about to engage without for a moment supposing he would accept.... He took his position at my side on the parapet, and all my entreaties failed to move him, although in addition to the stray shots that were passing over, the spot was a favorite mark for sharpshooters.
>
> When the surgeon was shot and after I had cleared the parapet of everyone else, he still maintained his ground till I told him I should have to remove him forcibly. The absurdity of the idea of sending off the President under guard seemed to amuse him, but in consideration of my earnestness in the matter, he agreed to compromise by sitting behind the parapet instead of standing upon it.... After he left the parapet he would persist in standing up from time to time, thus exposing nearly one-half of his tall form.

The surgeon referred to was C. V. A. Crawford, of the 102nd Pennsylvania Regiment. A ricochet bullet struck Crawford in the thigh as he stood only a few feet from the president.

Others beside O. W. Holmes claimed to have urged Lincoln to take cover. Private John A. Bedient of the 150th Ohio National Guard was one. Private Peter W. Kaiser and Private Robert W. McBride, both of Ohio, left accounts supporting General Wright's.

An attack was mounted to clear out the rebel sharpshooters who were endangering the distinguished visitors. Though a Union force of six regiments went forward, supported by the guns of the forts, the Confederates sprayed them with deadly fire, killing or wounding between 280 and 375 men. But by the evening of July 12 it was all over. Early withdrew his men the following morning, and Washington was finally "free from alarm or anxiety," as Chittenden reported.[25]

Late in 1863, Ohio Governor David Tod (1805–1868), concerned for Lincoln's safety, suggested organizing a unit of cavalrymen to be sent to Washington to protect the president. Stanton agreed, and by the end of the year the 7th Independent Troop of Ohio Cavalry, known as the "Union Light Guard," went to Washington. They were an elite group, gathered from all over the state. Barracks were built for them near the Treasury building. They were also detailed to reinforce the capital city's defenses and to patrol the city as needed. Their horses were stabled on the north side of E Street, near 15th Street.

When the Lincolns took up residence at the Soldiers Home, located about three miles north of the White House, the Ohio Volunteers would escort Lincoln on his way between the home and the White House. Lincoln's usual route was up Vermont Avenue to Rhode Island Avenue, then along the 7th Street Road to Rock Creek Church Road. On occasion, Lincoln would fail to notify the soldiers of his departure, and would make the trip unescorted, sometimes entirely alone.

Walt Whitman observed the president, and left a description which includes information about his guards.

> I see the President almost every day, as I happen to live where he passes to or from his lodgings out of town. He never sleeps at the White House during the hot season, but has quarters at a nearby location some three miles north of the city, the Soldiers' home, a United States military establishment. I saw him this morning about 8½ coming in to business, riding on Vermont avenue, near L street. He always has a company of twenty-five or thirty cavalry, with sabers drawn and held upright over their shoulders. They say this guard was against his personal wish, but he let his counselors have their way. The party makes no great show in uniform or horses. Mr. Lincoln on the saddle generally rides a good-sized, easy-going gray horse, is dress'd in plain black, somewhat rusty and dusty, wears a black stiff hat, and looks about as ordinary in attire, etc., as the commonest man. A lieutenant, with yellow straps, rides at his left, and following behind, two by two, come the cavalry men, in their yellow-striped jackets. They are generally going at a slow trot, as that is the pace set them by the one they wait upon. The sabers and accountrments clank, and the entirely unormantal cortege as it trots toward Lafayette square arouses no sensation, only some curious stranger stops and gazes.... Sometimes the President goes and comes in an open barouche. The cavalry always accompany him, with drawn sabers. Often I notice as he goes out evenings — and sometimes in the morning, when he returns early — he turns off and halts at the large and handsome residence of the Secretary of War, on K street, and holds conference there. If in his barouche, I can see from my window he does not alight, but sits in his vehicle, and Mr. Stanton comes out to attend him. Sometimes one of his sons, a boy of ten or twelve, accompanies him, riding at his right on a pony. Earlier in the summer I occasionally saw the President and his wife, toward the latter part of the afternoon, out in a barouche, on a pleasure ride through the city.... The equipage is of the plainest kind, only two horses, and they nothing extra.

Obviously, if Whitman could so easily observe Lincoln, passing on a regular schedule along the same streets, others could have, too, perhaps kidnappers or assassins.

The cavalrymen had volunteered hoping to see action, and many were disappointed when they found out their duty was to serve as a presidential bodyguard. Likewise, Lincoln resisted having a formal guard assigned to protect him. However, the president and his guards came to like and respect each other, and developed a mutual affection. One of the guards, Robert Wesley McBride (1842–1926), underscored the importance of their duty. "It is probable that the only man in Washington who, if he thought upon the subject at all, did not think that Mr. Lincoln was in constant and imminent danger, was Mr. Lincoln himself." The White House grounds had not been organized with security in mind. A stone wall between three and four feet in height was all that bounded the property on the south. On the north side of the White House was an iron fence with two gates for the driveway, similar to today's arrangements, but not as sophisticated. The two gates each had two mounted guards, supervised by a corporal of the guard, who was usually dismounted. Lincoln made daily trips to the nearby War Department building in order to review the messages from the war fronts. He often spent long hours there, especially when anxiously awaiting news of a great battle. The path from the White House to the War Department passed beneath several large trees, and the soldier guards, posted at the mansion doors or gates, would watch with concern as the president walked through the shadows, often alone.

On February 10, 1864, at about 8:30 in the evening, the White House stables caught fire. Robert McBride described seeing "a tall and hatless man come running from the direction of the White House. When he reached the boxwood hedge that served as an enclosure to the stables he sprang over it like a deer. As he approached the stable he inquired if the horses had been taken out. On learning that they had not, he asked impatiently why they had not, and with his own hands burst open the stable door. A glance within showed that the whole interior of the stable was in flames, and that the rescue of the horses was impossible. Notwithstanding this, he would apparently have rushed in had not those standing around caught and restrained him." Fearful that the fire might have been set in order to draw the president out of the mansion, making him a target for assassins, the soldiers hurried Lincoln back indoors. Later, McBride found Lincoln in the White House East Room, weeping. The president's young son Tad told McBride that one of the horses had belonged to his brother Willie whose death two years before had caused his parents devastating grief. The next day, Patterson McGee, who had been fired from his job as the president's coachman, was arrested and charged with setting the stables afire, but was not prosecuted, there being insufficient evidence.

The cavalrymen would also provide security inside the White House. Receptions were held on several occasions, requiring the president to personally greet the public. Lincoln would have to stand for hours, shaking hundreds of hands. He knew many of the guests, but as these were public receptions, there would always be, mixed among the congressmen, generals, and other officials, many anonymous citizens. Sometimes the soldiers had their hands full managing the crowds.[26]

When the strife of the 1864 election campaign was added to the bitterness of the war, those around Lincoln became especially concerned for his safety. Mary Lincoln requested that some of her husband's cavalry escort be stationed inside the White House. Eight or ten soldiers attended official receptions, checking the guests' cloaks for weapons. The soldiers disliked this duty, as it made them feel they were low-grade servants. On election night in 1864, Lincoln's friend Ward Hill Lamon stationed himself in front of Lincoln's bedroom door and stood guard, armed with several pistols and bowie knives.[27]

George Washington Gayle (1810–1875), a lawyer residing in Cahaba, Alabama, placed the following advertisement in the Selma, Alabama, *Morning Dispatch* on December 1, 1864:

> One Million Dollars Wanted, to have peace by the 1st of March.
>
> If the citizens of the Southern Confederacy will furnish me with the CASH, or good securities for the sum of one million dollars, I will cause the lives of ABRAHAM LINCOLN, WILLIAM SEWARD and ANDREW JOHNSON to be taken by the first or March next. This will give us peace, and satisfy the world that CRUEL TYRANTS can not live in a "land or liberty." If this is not accomplished, nothing will be claimed beyond the sum of FIFTY THOUSAND DOLLARS, IN ADVANCE, which is supposed to be necessary to reach and SLAUGHTER the THREE VILLAINS.
>
> I will give, myself, ONE THOUSAND DOLLARS TOWARDS THIS PATRIOTIC PURPOSE.
>
> Every one wishing to contribute will address box X, Cahaba, Ala.
>
> X
>
> Dec. 1, 1864.

This ad was introduced by the prosecution at the trial of the assassination conspirators to show the climate of opinion in the South leading to the murder of Lincoln.

A nephew by marriage of William Rufus de Vane King (1786–1853), who was U.S.

senator from Alabama, 1819–1844 and 1848–1852, and vice president of the U.S. in 1853, Gayle served in the Alabama legislature, becoming chairman of the Alabama House Ways and Means Committee, and was appointed U.S. attorney for the southern district of Alabama by President Martin Van Buren (1782–1862) in 1840. Attending a hunting party with some prominent citizens of Selma in November 1864, Gayle challenged them to back up their expressed desires about the Union leaders with money. No money was collected, but two printers for the *Dispatch* named Gayle as the man who had run the ad. Arrested, Gayle was taken to Fort Pulaski, near Savannah, Georgia, and indicted for conspiracy to murder Lincoln, and for aiding the rebellion. Held for a year and a half, Gayle petitioned President Andrew Johnson for a pardon. After his petition was endorsed by the governor, the president of the state senate, and speaker of the house, along with twenty-five senators and sixty-eight representatives, Gayle received his pardon on April 27, 1867.

Gayle had protested to the authorities that he had not been serious in making his offer, but in view of the timing, and his having named the targets of Booth's conspiracy, it is no wonder that Gayle's protests were ignored.[28]

There were also rumors that an attempt would be made to disrupt the inauguration on March 4, 1865. Extra security was arranged, and, as had been the case in 1861, there was a heavy military presence supplementing the metropolitan police. Special Capitol policemen were posted in and around the Capitol building to deal with emergencies and assist in crowd control. As Lincoln and other officials passed through the rotunda on their way to the east front inaugural platform, a man attempted to push through the police lines. Officer John W. Westfall grabbed hold of the man and they struggled. Other policemen quickly came to Westfall's aid, and the man gave up his attempt to break through. After the assassination, Westfall and the other officers identified the man they had briefly detained that day as John Wilkes Booth.[29] Booth himself later stated that he had had an excellent chance to kill Lincoln on inauguration day. Showing a pass obtained from former senator John Parker Hale (1806–1873), he attended the ceremonies anyway, although this time purely as a spectator.[30] Claims that many of Booth's co-conspirators were also there are based upon comparison photos, with most of the match-up photos being very uncertain. Other arrests were also made that day for threats against the president.[31]

In late March, 1865, Lincoln visited the army at City Point, Virginia, and conferred with Generals Ulysses S. Grant (1822–1885) and William T. Sherman (1820–1891). The military arranged security for the trip, but not without some problems. Lincoln eventually went up the James River from City Point to see Richmond, which was captured by federal forces at the beginning of April. Obstructions in the river prevented the use of a large boat, thus limiting the size of the party aboard. Lincoln and his son Tad, were accompanied by Rear Admiral David D. Porter (1813–1891), Army Captain Charles Bingham Penrose (?–1895), and twelve sailors with carbines, who arranged themselves with six in front of the president and six behind. Army cavalry troops that were to rendezvous with the president's party were late arriving, leaving the president underprotected. William H. Crook, the police guard, who claimed to have been present, described how he interposed himself in front of Lincoln to foil the aim of a would-be sniper at a window, though no one else mentioned such a dramatic incident, and Crook's stories are probably fabrications.[32]

April 13, 1865, was the date set for a grand illumination of buildings all over Washington. The war was all but over, and there was to be much celebrating that night. David Homer Bates (1843–1926), who worked in the military telegraph office, later wrote of that night, "Extra precautions were taken by the authorities to protect the President and Lieutenant-General [Grant] against expected attempts to kidnap or kill them, because of Secret Service reports that plans had been made to accomplish such evil designs during the excitement of that occasion."[33]

Warnings or predictions came from individuals without specific information. A Colonel Goodwin of 104 W. 40th Street, New York City, wrote on October 2, 1864, "I have strange presentiments which I am compelled to believe." Writing again on November 8, 1864, "...Your death is premeditated before the first of January next. It will be wise for you to be on your guard as you may be assassinated. Look to your household." And on January 4, 1865, "I warned you of a conspiracy November 18, 1862, and I am now compelled to inform you that your days are numbered. You will be a dead man in less than six months." This final warning proved to be accurate, but Col. Goodwin was never charged or suspected of being involved in an assassination plot. Even public officials talked openly of the danger to the president, as in this quote from a speech of Edwards Pierrepont (1817–1892), who would later be a prosecutor of John Surratt: "If the President abused this power for despotic purposes, let him be impeached, denounced, deposed, even assassinated, if they would have it so, and it becomes necessary."

In the South, of course, numerous plans and threats were reported during the course of the war. J. S. Parramore, of Georgia, wrote to Jefferson Davis on September 12, 1861, "the best plan would be to dispose of the leading characters of the North." H. C. Durham, of Co. I, 63rd Regiment of Georgia Volunteers, wrote Davis on August 17, 1863, proposing to organize a company of three hundred to five hundred men, "to go into the United States and assassinate the most prominent leaders of our enemies. For instance, Seward, Lincoln, Greeley, Prentice, etc."

After Lincoln's assassination had become a fact, others came forward. The following, from a letter of P. R. D. Hite of Liberty County, Texas, to President Andrew Johnson, on June 11, 1866, is representative.

> Some six or eight days before he [Lincoln] was assassinated I met a Mr. Woolf, formerly, I believe, German Consul at Galveston.... He said to me, "you will receive glorious news in a few days — from Washington. It may surprise you." ... He said it will shock the world.... I ... overheard a conversation between this man Woolf and Judge Cleavland in which Cleavland said — "When Abraham, Andrew, ... the Speaker of the House and Seward are all out of the way the Constitution makes no further provision.... I learn that proposition have been made at Richmond by parties to do the work, provided should they succeed to receive ... four hundred thousand dollars." ... Judge Cleavland gave Woolf a shake by the hands, saying, 'consider me a subscriber for several thousand."[34]

So many references to Lincoln's being in danger, so many warnings of his potential end were received, that one wonders, reading of them today, why more was not done to protect the president. Yet all presidents receive threats, and no one is endowed with perfect foresight.

5. Presidential Health

> Ah, no one knows what it is to live in constant dread of some fearful tragedy ... I tremble for him on every public occasion.
>
> Mary Lincoln

Abraham Lincoln lived in a time when the practice of medicine was a good deal less refined than it is today. Although he suffered from illnesses throughout his life, one cannot accurately describe him as sickly, or that his health problems were all that unusual for his time.

As a boy he had been kicked in the head by a horse and was unconscious for a short time. His bouts of depression became serious enough to alarm his friends. Lincoln had written of his "hypochondrism" as a young man, apparently not fully understanding the nature of this psychological condition. He began to improve after meeting Dr. Anson G. Henry (1804–1865), who remained a family friend until his death, shortly after Lincoln's own.

Illnesses or medical conditions that affected Lincoln included chronic constipation, malaria, varioloid (a mild form of smallpox), strabismus, "habitual low blood pressure," and hyperopia (far sightedness). Lincoln's visual problems do not seem to have been serious or unusual. He did not wear glasses until he was forty-eight years old. His left eye deviated upward slightly, which could have caused headaches and even mental depression.

When visiting his dentist in Washington, Dr. G. S. Wolf, whose office was on New York Avenue, Lincoln brought his own supply of chloroform. Prescriptions for the president and his family were filled at Thompson's, located across from the Treasury building.[1]

Mary Lincoln's time as First Lady was

Mary Todd Lincoln. Lincoln's wife was not such a shrewish burden to him as some authors would have us believe. She was afflicted with a suspicious, jealous nature, and had serious emotional problems made worse by the loss of family members (Library of Congress).

difficult for her, and not always because of her personality. Political opposition to her husband's policies could manifest itself in social slights. Mary soon became a target for criticism. The way she dressed, her love of giving elegant parties (which some questioned as inappropriate during wartime), and even her chronic headaches and other illnesses became subjects for gossip and criticism. But all of that faded into insignificance beside the tragedy that struck the Lincolns less than a year after their entry into the White House. In early February, eleven-year-old Willie Lincoln came down with a fever. For two weeks he suffered while his parents tried to get on with their public duties. At the time Willie's illness was called "bilious fever," or perhaps malaria, but it was very likely typhoid fever, caused by the contamination of the Potomac River with bacterial waste. The Potomac was the principal source of water for the White House. On February 20, 1862, the struggle ended. Typhoid fever had claimed the life of the little boy who was said to have been his father's favorite.

It has been noted that Lincoln had a lifelong struggle with depression, often taking a dark view of life. The death of Willie brought on depression and grief so severe that for weeks Lincoln was overcome on each Thursday after Willie's death, which happened on a Thursday. "It is hard, hard to have him die," Lincoln said as he looked upon his son's lifeless form. "He buried his head in his hands, and his tall frame was convulsed with emotion.... His grief unnerved him, and made him a weak, passive child," said Mrs. Keckley, Mary Lincoln's seamstress. Twice Lincoln had his son's coffin opened to look at him again.[2]

Willie Lincoln. The Lincolns' third child, said to be his father's favorite, was bright and talented. His death in the White House in 1862 brought on severe grief for his parents (Library of Congress).

With oldest son Robert away at school, Mary had only her husband and her youngest son, Tad. Hyperactive and a slow learner, with his cleft palate making him difficult to understand when he spoke, Tad was a great concern to his parents, who indulged and spoiled him, especially after Willie's death. In her grief, Mary turned to spiritualism, which had long been popular, and in which she had shown an early interest. Mary's seamstress, Elizabeth Keckley (c.1818–1907), was also a believer, and had attended séances after the death of her son, George. Already developing a close friendship with Keckley, Mary attended séances, trying to communicate with her sons, as well as with others, such as family friend Edward D. Baker (1811–1861), who had been killed in the battle of Ball's Bluff.

There were other tragedies for the family, growing out of the national calamity of the war. As with many American families, the Todds of Kentucky had been divided by the war. Mary's half-brother Samuel B. Todd (1831–1862), a Confederate, was killed at Shiloh in April 1862. Another half-brother, David H. Todd (1832–1863), died at Vicksburg. Yet another half-brother, Alexander Todd (?–1863), was killed in battle in Louisiana. She grieved for her family members, but could not express her grief openly, for these men had been rebels. When Mary's half-sister, Emilie Todd Helm (1836–1930), lost her husband, Confederate General Benjamin Hardin Helm (1831–1863), at Chattanooga, the Lincolns took Emilie in at the White House in December 1863. Although Mary found some consolation with her sister, their differences over the war, reflecting those of the nation as a whole, brought about hard feelings. It did not help that others publicly criticized the Lincolns for entertaining a "traitor" at the White House.

Carriage accidents were commonplace, Mary being frightened on June 22, 1861, when her horses began running at an alarming pace, requiring nearby soldiers to come to the rescue of the First Lady and her guests. President Lincoln experienced a similar incident on April 20, 1862. Neither of the Lincolns were injured in these incidents. Mary Lincoln was injured in an accident in the middle of 1863, taking a ride in her carriage near the Mount Pleasant Hospital. The driver's seat came loose and the coachman was thrown off. The horses were startled by this, and began to run. Mrs. Lincoln jumped from the carriage, suffering severe bruises and a bleeding wound at the back of her head. Doctors from the nearby hospital ran out and immediately tended to the injured First Lady. It was determined that her injuries were not serious, and no bones were broken. Mrs. Lincoln was taken to the White House in another carriage. An infection of the head wound complicated her recovery, and at one point Lincoln was concerned enough to send for Robert, attending college at Harvard. Early in 1864, as Mary and Tad were riding in a closed carriage, a fourteen-year-old boy ran out and was hit by the White House carriage. The boy's leg was broken, but it healed, and he later visited the White House and met the President.[3]

Fiercely protective of her husband, Mary formed strong dislikes for several of the powerful and ambitious men around him. She distrusted the presidential ambitions of William Henry Seward and Salmon Portland Chase. Lincoln's assistant secretary John Milton Hay, and Commissioner of Public Buildings Benjamin Brown French, both aware of her extravagances in White House redecorating, became her adversaries. General George Brinton McClellan, her husband's opponent in the election of 1864, and General Ulysses Simpson Grant, whom she called "an obstinate fool and a butcher," and Grant's wife Julia, were also objects of her quick temper and harsh judgment. Her dislike of Vice President Andrew Johnson (1808–1875) was so great that she believed him to be involved in the conspiracy which killed Lincoln.

As with her dislikes, she also developed strong likings for certain individuals, such as Mrs. Keckley. Senator Charles Sumner, R-MA, was one of Mary's favorites. The handsome and learned Sumner made use of Mary's friendship to influence her and the president toward the cause of abolition. Sumner's presence at the deathbed of Lincoln offered the grieving widow and her son Robert what little consolation there was to be found.[4]

In recent times some have suggested that Lincoln had Marfan's Syndrome, a fatal disease that would have taken his life within a year of the date of the assassination. Not described until 1896, Marfan's Syndrome is named for the French physician Bernard-Jean Antonin Marfan (1858–1942). The disease affects the connective tissue and causes unusually long limbs, especially fingers and toes, which tend to be abnormally flexible, or double-jointed. Overgrown ribs can lead to deformities of the chest. Marfan sufferers tend to be unusually tall and thin. More serious complications can involve visual problems, as the connective tissue holding the eye's lens is affected. Worst of all, Marfan's Syndrome can cause cardiovascular problems such as defective heart valves and aneurysms (ballooning out) of the aorta, the large artery leading out of the heart. Rupture of the aneurysm results in sudden death.[5]

In 1962, Dr. Abraham M. Gordon of Louisville, Kentucky, suggested Lincoln seemed to have many of the characteristics of a Marfan patient. Aside from his long arms and legs, large hands and feet, large ears and small, deep-set eyes, Lincoln's voice was described as rather high-pitched and his eyes seemed to deviate (not to focus together). "Most Marfan Syndrome sufferers are above average in intelligence and are original and unique in their way of looking at things," Dr. Gordon stated.[6]

Taking up from Dr. Gordon, Dr. Harold Schwartz of Huntington Park, California, further developed the theory of Lincoln as a Marfan victim, even finding a contemporary reference to Lincoln's "spider-like legs," a description that closely parallels the language of Dr.

Elizabeth Keckley. Mrs. Lincoln's dressmaker was a former slave whose talents enabled her to earn money with which to purchase her freedom. Mrs. Lincoln grew very close to Mrs. Keckley and confided in her (Library of Congress).

Marfan. Schwartz pointed to a photograph of Lincoln taken in 1863, showing him seated, with one leg crossed over the other. The toe of the boot not resting on the floor is slightly blurred, suggesting involuntary movement caused by pulsing arteries. Dr. Schwartz further cited references to Lincoln's fatigue, and to chronic coldness in the hands and feet, indicating circulatory problems.[7]

Only one of Lincoln's sons lived a normal lifespan. Dr. Schwartz said that this could be because of inherited Marfan's Syndrome. His second son, Edward Baker Lincoln, described as tall for his age, died at age four. The third son, William Wallace Lincoln, had an "inward turning eye," and held his head to one side when reading. Though Willie's death was attributed to "bilious fever," Dr. Schwartz believed the pain and fever were not inconsistent with congestive heart failure. The fourth son, Thomas "Tad" Lincoln, had been nicknamed "Tadpole" at birth because of the largeness of his head. He was difficult to understand because of his malformed palate. Like his brother Willie, Tad suffered a serious illness at an early age, described as "lung fever," which left him in delicate health thereafter.

"Tad" Lincoln and his father. The Lincolns named their fourth child Thomas, after the president's father. Tad had health troubles and was a slow learner, earning a reputation for wildness. The Lincolns spoiled him even more after his brother Willie's death (Library of Congress).

Soon after his eighteenth birthday, Tad had an attack of water on the lungs, combined with, in the words of his doctor, "dropsy of the chest." Unable to breathe, he died. Dr. Schwartz has identified Marfan characteristics in a number of Lincoln's ancestors and descendents.[8]

Marfan's Syndrome affects about one in ten thousand Americans today, making it rare, but still involving a significant number of people. Although it has long been known to be transmitted genetically, it has only been recently that researchers have begun to identify the defect with some precision. Two suspects, collagen and elastin, part of the substances that form connective tissue, are no longer thought to be involved. The protein fibrillin was noted to be significantly deficient in most of the Marfan patients tested.[9] It was only in the summer of 1991 that the particular gene involved was identified. Researchers observed a variation in defects of the gene between patients, accounting for different symptoms and degrees of severity among them.[10]

Dr. John K. Lattimer (1914–2007) of Columbia University, New York, a well-known authority on the medical aspects of Lincoln, stated flatly that Lincoln did not have Marfan's Syndrome. His evidence is both varied and convincing. Pointing to plaster casts of Lincoln's hands made in 1860, he noted the thick bones and strong muscles. A life mask of Lincoln's face shows no sign of the elongation associated with the disorder. If anything, Lincoln's head was on the small side for a man of his height. Lincoln did wear glasses, but they were reading glasses. Marfan patients are usually nearsighted, not far-sighted as Lincoln was. While president, Lincoln test-fired a rifle with notable accuracy, showing no detachment of the lenses of his eyes. In his youth, Lincoln was a highly capable wrestler, something that would have been difficult, if not impossible, if the joints of his hands had been loosened by Marfan's. One of the Lincoln autopsy doctors noted the strong bones and powerful muscles of the president, and mentioned nothing about a sunken or malformed chest. As for the blurred toe of the 1863 photo, Dr. Lattimer pointed out that the camera was focused on Lincoln's face, and his foot, being closer to the camera, would not be expected to be as clear. Furthermore, Lincoln was fifty-six at the time of his death. Marfan patients in his time usually lived no more than thirty to thirty-two years.[11] After a long and tiring day visiting the wounded of both armies, Lincoln responded to concern that he might be fatigued by picking up an axe and vigorously chopping up a log. Then, holding the end of the axe handle, he slowly raised it up and held it out level in a line with his shoulders for several minutes. None of the younger men with him could duplicate this feat.[12]

Modern DNA testing may be able to determine once and for all if Lincoln was a Marfan victim, but such tests, requiring the destruction of genetic material, have been postponed until greater accuracy can be achieved.[13]

The nation was not taken entirely by surprise by Lincoln's assassination. His friends and family had long noted his fatalism and frequent disregard for his personal safety. "Considering the many open and secret threats to take his life, it is not surprising that Mr. Lincoln had many thoughts about his coming to a sudden and violent end." His friend Noah Brooks related a curious story Lincoln told him late in 1864, reproducing Lincoln's own words as well as Brooks could remember them.

> It was just after my election in 1860.... I was well tired out, and went home to rest, throwing myself down on a lounge in my chamber. Opposite where I lay was a bureau, with a swinging glass upon it.... And, looking in that glass, I saw myself reflected, nearly at full length; but my face, I noticed, had two separate and distinct images, the tip of the nose of one being about three inches from the tip of the other. I was a little bothered, perhaps startled, and got up and looked in the glass, but the illusion vanished. On lying down again I saw it a second time — plainer, if possible, than before; and then I noticed that one of the faces was a little paler, say five shades, than the other. I got up and the thing melted away.

Lincoln described how every time he would remember this vision it would "give me a little pang, as though something uncomfortable had happened." He told his wife about it, trying to conjure the vision again, and succeeded, though Mary Lincoln could not see it. The memory of her interpretation of this vision stayed with Lincoln. "She thought it was a sign that I was to be elected to a second term of office, and that the paleness of one of the faces was an omen that I should not see life through the last term."[14]

Lincoln was no more a believer in the supernatural than anyone else of his time (or ours), but it appears from his numerous references to dreams that he thought they might somehow foretell the future. He wrote to Mary on June 9, 1863, "Think you had better put 'Tad's' pistol away. I had an ugly dream about him."[15] He was aware of the complexity of the mind, and aware, too, that the workings of the mind were largely unknown. When in his teens he had been kicked in the head by a horse and knocked unconscious, the sentence he had been speaking to the offending animal was interrupted, but upon awakening he finished the sentence, in spite of the passage of time. He afterward would relate this experience to illustrate the mysterious ways of the mind.[16]

His fatalism drove him to make many references to his own death. Upon leaving Springfield in 1861, he told his law partner, William Henry Herndon, not to take down the sign bearing his name, for "if I live I'm coming back sometime." In his farewell speech in Springfield he said, "I now leave, not knowing when or whether ever I may return."[17] To Harriet Beecher Stowe (1811–1896), visiting him in the last months of the war, he remarked, "I shall never live to see peace. This war is killing me."[18] After visiting Richmond, only days before his death, Lincoln dreamed the White House was burning.[19] On the return from this trip, Lincoln read aloud from Shakespeare to amuse his guests. His selection was "Macbeth, and in particular, the verses which follow Duncan's assassination."[20]

Ward Hill Lamon reported that he had more than once heard Lincoln recite a poem, "The Dream," by Lord Byron (1788–1824):

> Sleep hath its own world,
> A boundary between the things misnamed
> Death and existence: Sleep hath its own world,
> And a wide realm of wild reality.
> And dreams in their development have breath,
> And tears, and tortures, and the touch of joy;
> They have a weight upon our waking thoughts,
> They take a weight from off our waking toils,
> They do divide our being.[21]

It was Lamon, too, who wrote down Lincoln's description of a dream he said he had a few nights before his assassination.

> There seemed to be a deathlike stillness about me. Then I heard subdued sobs, as if a number of people were weeping. I thought I left my bed and wandered downstairs. There the silence was broken by the same pitiful sobbing, but the mourners were invisible.... I kept on until I arrived at the East Room, which I entered. There I met with a sickening surprise. Before me was a catafalque, on which rested a corpse wrapped in funeral vestments. Around it were stationed soldiers who were acting as guards; and there was a throng of people, some gazing mournfully upon the corpse, whose face was covered, others weeping pitifully. "Who is dead in the White House?" I demanded of one of the soldiers. "The President," was the answer; "he was killed by an assassin." Then came a loud burst of grief from the crowd, which awoke me from my dreams.[22]

On April 14, 1865, Lincoln met with his Cabinet, and related to them the last of his dreams.

> The President remarked it [news from General Sherman] would, he had no doubt, come soon, and come favorable, for he had last night the usual dream which he had proceeding nearly every great and important event of the war. Generally the news had been favorable which succeeded this dream, and the dream itself was always the same.... He seemed to be in some singular, indescribable vessel, and that he was moving with great rapidity towards an indefinite shore. That he had this dream preceding Sumter, Bull Run, Antietam, Gettysburg, Stone River, Vicksburg, Wilmington, etc.... "I had," the President remarked, "this strange dream again last night, and we shall, judging from the past, have great news very soon." Great events did, indeed, follow, for within a few hours the good and gentle, as well as truly great, man who narrated his dream closed forever his earthly career.[23]

William Henry Crook, one of Lincoln's police guards, related that the president seemed to sense the danger of assassination, speaking about it with his usual sense of fatalism to the guard. On the evening of April 14, 1865, as he left for the theatre, Crook said Lincoln, who had always before told him "good night," this time said "good bye."[24]

We cannot entirely trust the literal truth of these stories. Most, if not all of them, were written after Lincoln's death, some long after. Of those which are not total fabrications, we cannot say how much comes from Lincoln himself and how much is embellishment by those seeking to make a good Lincoln story a little more interesting. At least one of Lincoln's dreams or visions can be explained by quite ordinary non-supernatural means. When Lincoln saw his double image in a mirror he was probably experiencing the effects of strabismus, the inability of the eyes to properly focus together. This is a common disorder, affecting about one out of every ten people. A few of the photographs of Lincoln seem to show one eye deviated upward, not properly aligned with the other. The famous Gardner photograph of November 8, 1863, probably best shows this effect. The deviation is very slight, and therefore open to question, but one can see the suggestion of it elsewhere, as in one of the Gardner photographs of April 10, 1865.[25] Lincoln admitted, in telling about his double-image vision, that he was tired that day and that he only saw the vision when relaxing on a couch. When he got up and changed position the double image vanished, and his wife could not see it even when he could. Everything he said about the incident is entirely consistent with the deviated-eye explanation — everything, that is, except Mrs. Lincoln's dark interpretation of what it might mean.

Lincoln got his first pair of glasses in 1857, probably a simple magnification lens, purchased in a Bloomington, Illinois, jewelry shop for 37½ cents. One pair of spectacles known to have been used by Lincoln shows an exceptionally strong correction, though this may be an over-compensation. The slight deviation of his left eye could have caused eyeaches and headaches, perhaps even bouts of mental depression, though Lincoln's melancholic personality was noted by his friends well before he began to wear glasses.[26]

Just before his trip to Gettysburg, in November 1863, Lincoln, tired from anxiety over Tad's illness, began to feel unwell himself. "At first Dr. [Robert K.] Stone [1822–1872], the physician of the White House, thought that Mr. Lincoln had symptoms of jaundice, then scarlatina [scarlet fever], and at last unmistakable signs of varioloid [a mild form of smallpox] manifested themselves. This interfered sadly with the preparation of the message [the Gettysburg Address], though it has scared away the politicians, and the parlors of the White House are deserted."[27]

This photograph, taken in mid–November 1863, best shows the tendency of Lincoln's left eye to fail to align with the right, especially when he was tired. The wandering eye is only slightly indicated here, so it is not certain that Lincoln suffered from strabismus (Library of Congress).

Any illness reported became a cause for alarm in Washington. "It is said that any president who is personally honest is certain to be killed by some secret assassins in Washington." Stories of the supposed poisoning of previous presidents Harrison, Taylor, Buchanan were revived and circulated whenever Lincoln was reported to be ill.[28] Often, Lincoln's illness was simple fatigue. Crowds of office seekers constantly pestered him and deprived him of rest.[29] Appearing at Washington's National Hotel, where a captured rebel flag was presented to him, "President Lincoln appeared quite unwell, and after receiving the greetings of a few personal friends in the parlor of the hotel, returned to the Executive Mansion."[30] "President Lincoln has been worn down with fatigue for the last two days, and was still obliged to deny himself to visitors today. He has no serious bodily ailment, and if his friends will allow him a little wholesome rest he will soon recover his strength and health."[31] "Although the President is yet quite feeble he is slowly gaining strength, and yesterday afternoon he took a short ride, appearing upon the avenue in his carriage, accompanied by his son, master

Tad. If the thousands of office seekers who are here besetting him upon every side would allow him to obtain a few days relaxation he would doubtless speedily recover his usual health; but not withstanding the President's indisposition and the fact that this is Cabinet day, the White House was thronged again this morning with parties eager to obtain an interview."[32] It would be many more years before the adoption of the civil service system relieved the president of having to personally appoint individuals to thousands of offices.

His recovery was welcome, but could not entirely relieve his friends' anxiety for him. "The recent illness of the President does not necessarily indicate that the public have reason to be under immediate apprehension, but we have the best reasons, founded upon the general observation of those who, like ourselves, have been familiar with his personal health and appearance for many years, for stating that Mr. Lincoln's physical powers have been tested beyond their capacity of endurance, and that if this ordeal is to continue, his naturally strong constitution must, at no distant day, give way.... Many who saw him at his inauguration, where the opportunity for noting the change in his personal appearance was better than in his office or at the White House, were painfully impressed with his gaunt, skeleton-like appearance."[33]

Dr. John Sotos (1957–) has recently proposed that Lincoln was afflicted with a rare genetic condition: multiple endocrine neoplasia type 2b, or MEN 2B. He believes this condition was responsible for many of the president's health problems and physical characteristics, including his unusual height.

A California cardiologist, Dr. Sotos has done a thorough investigation of Lincoln's health history. He believes Lincoln had cancer, an effect of MEN 2B, and would have died within a year, had he not been assassinated. Sotos even speculates that Lincoln's mother may have had the same disorder. She died at age 34. Also, MEN 2B may have been responsible for the disorders and early deaths of three of his four children. Dr. Sotos sees lumps on Lincoln's lips and on a life mask, and he cites these as evidence of MEN 2B, which can be characterized by such bundles of nerve tissue on the face and elsewhere, including in the intestines, which Dr. Sotos notes could have accounted for Lincoln's constipation problems.[34]

While it is interesting to speculate on what medical problems Lincoln had, or might have had, we should remember that the burden of proof must lie with those who make the claims. Obviously, no doctor living today has examined Lincoln, and most doctors are reluctant to express an opinion about a "patient" they have not themselves examined. No objective, reliable medical records of Lincoln — or anyone else of his time — exist. The diagnoses and treatment of disease and injuries of that era rarely agree with modern methods. It should also be noted that although Lincoln was very tall (6' 4", an unusual height even today), being tall is not evidence of disease. Many who have achieved positions of leadership throughout history have been taller than average. George Washington was 6' 2" and weighed 175 pounds. Thomas Jefferson was 6' 2½." Andrew Jackson was 6'1". Presidents James Monroe, John Tyler, and James Buchanan were all six feet tall. When Lincoln served in the Illinois legislature in the 1830s, he was a member of a group of men who were known as "the Long Nine," because all nine of them, serving in the same time and place, were at least six feet tall. Another of Lincoln's Illinois friends, Leonard Swett, was very tall, and even Mary Lincoln believed him to closely resemble her husband.[35]

Lincoln continues to fascinate his countrymen long after his time. It is likely that fascination, and speculation about the man, will continue into ages yet to be.

6. Reelection

> I am struggling to maintain government, not to overthrow it. I am struggling especially to prevent others from overthrowing it. I therefore say that if I shall live, I shall remain President until the fourth of next March; and that whoever shall be constitutionally elected therefore in November, shall be duly installed as President on the fourth of March; and that in the interval I shall do my utmost that whoever is to hold the helm for the next voyage, shall start with the best possible chance to save the ship.[1]
>
> Abraham Lincoln

Like most political leaders, past and present, Lincoln hoped to win a second term as president, both for his personal gratification and because he believed that the Union had to be restored, and he felt himself to be the man who was most determined and dedicated to achieving that reunion.[2] Lincoln faced multiple problems in seeking a second term. He had won in 1860 only because the Democratic Party had broken apart several ways as the nation divided at the onset of the secession crisis. Lincoln, the nominee of the new Republican Party, had found almost no support in the southern states. No Lincoln votes had been recorded in the states of Alabama, Arkansas, Florida, Georgia, Louisiana, Mississippi, North Carolina, Tennessee or Texas. He won only 23 percent in Delaware, less than 1 percent in Kentucky, 2.5 percent in Maryland, 10.3 percent in Missouri, and 1.1 percent in Virginia. In the final national vote count, Lincoln had 39.82 percent of the popular vote, but obtained 180 of the total of 303 electoral votes. Thus, he had decidedly been a minority candidate. He received the support of 1,865,908 voters, while 2,819,653 had voted for someone else. Only the three-way split of his opposition had made his first victory possible.[3] It was obvious to Lincoln and other Republican Party leaders that they needed to build up their party's strength. Well before the election of 1864, the idea of a Union Party had been urged, a party that would unite former Whigs and conservative Republicans with pro–Union Democrats. This strategy advocated making the restoration of the Union the fundamental issue of the party, rather than the abolition of slavery. The party name was already changing from Republican to Union Party at the local and state level, and became official for the national level at the 1864 convention.[4]

Unity among the leaders of the party was a problem throughout the Lincoln administration. The Democrats had made major gains in the mid-term elections of 1862, especially in the key states of Illinois, Indiana, New Jersey, New York, Ohio, Pennsylvania, and Wisconsin. Major Lincoln administration actions, such as the Emancipation Proclamation, the suspension of the writ of habeas corpus, the draft, and seeming lack of progress on the battle fronts, contributed to the overall picture of poor Republican prospects. Major voices in opposition to the president and his administration included Henry Ward Beecher (1813–1887), Salmon P. Chase, Henry Winter Davis (1817–1865), Benjamin F. Wade, and Horace Greeley.[5] There was also the lack of a tradition of reelecting presidents.

Five of the first seven presidents of the United States had been reelected and served second terms. Both of the two who did not had sought reelection unsuccessfully. So, from 1789 to 1832, it had been commonplace for presidents to seek second terms. But following the two-term presidency of Andrew Jackson (1767–1845), a long three decades had passed without a single successful reelection of a president. Van Buren had failed to achieve reelection in 1840; Tyler had not even been nominated in 1844; Polk, in failing health, stood by his word not to seek another term in 1848; Fillmore lacked support in 1852; Pierce was glad to leave after one term in 1856, as was Buchanan in 1860. There were those who felt that a single-term of four years was enough.[6]

Another factor clouding Lincoln's reelection prospects was the divisions within his own party. Alternate candidates seeking to compete with the president were Secretary of the Treasury Salmon P. Chase, Generals John C. Frémont, and Benjamin F. Butler, and perhaps others less prominent waiting to step forward should the better-known candidates falter. However, Lincoln's prospects for renomination were by no means hopeless, as he controlled more patronage than any of his rivals, and he had a decided advantage among the common people. Chase, never so popular, found his campaign collapsing by March 1864. When the post of chief justice of the U.S. Supreme Court fell vacant, Lincoln appointed Chase, thus conferring an honor upon his rival while at the same time eliminating him as a candidate for the presidency. Frémont, popular among westerners and abolitionists, lacked the support of influential leaders throughout the country. Frémont, the Republican nominee in 1856, was actually nominated as a third-party candidate in 1864, but his candidacy lost momentum when the Union Party adopted an abolition amendment in their party platform. Frémont withdrew and threw his support to Lincoln. Butler apparently believed that he could not be a credible candidate for president unless he had achieved notable battlefield victories.[7]

Salmon P. Chase. Lincoln's secretary of the treasury was also a rival for the presidency, both in 1860 and 1864. When an opening on the U.S. Supreme Court occurred, Lincoln appointed Chase chief justice, thereby eliminating him from the presidential race (Library of Congress).

Lincoln's ambition had to be tempered by political realities. The war seemed stalled, and Lincoln's steadfastness in support of leaders and policies that did not seem to be going anywhere cast a shadow over his prospects. Fully aware of this, Lincoln sounded out alternative candidates, expressing his willingness to step aside in favor of others whom he saw as strong prospects. Foremost among these was William H. Seward, former governor and U.S. senator from the crucial state of New York. Seward had been bitterly disappointed in 1860 when he had failed to gain the Republican nomination for president. Accepting the post of secretary of state in the Lincoln Cabinet, he had gradually gained respect for Lincoln as he got to know him, and by 1864 they had become good friends. To Lincoln's offer, Seward replied, "No, that is all past and ended. The logic of events requires you to be your own successor." Seward felt that if Lincoln could be reelected, the Southern rebellion would collapse. Lincoln had also sounded out another New Yorker, a curious choice. In 1862 he suggested that Governor Horatio Seymour (1810–1886) might be the man to unite pro–Union Democrats with conservative Republicans into a winning combination. Seymour, a Democrat, at first promised support for the Lincoln administration, but by January 1863, he denounced Lincoln's suspension of the writ of habeas corpus. By the summer of 1863 Lincoln had made up his mind to seek reelection.[8]

As alternatives to Lincoln fell by the wayside, Lincoln could concentrate upon his major opposition, the Democratic Party. As we have observed, the Democrats lost in 1860 because of divisions among their supporters. Although the Southern states, the traditional base of the Democratic Party, would not participate in the election of 1864, that did not mean that the Democrats were without hope. The party was strong throughout the North, and had made major gains in the elections of 1862. Democrats ridiculed Lincoln, calling him "the indecent joker." They particularly denounced the suspension of individual liberties, and emphasized the widely held war-weariness. The Democrats were also encouraged by the divisions among Republicans early in 1864. Among possible Democratic candidates, General George B. McClellan (1826–1885) emerged early as the favorite. McClellan was popular with the soldiers, encouraging the Democrats to believe that he might successfully challenge Lincoln for the soldier vote. McClellan was pro–Union. He did not take the stance that the war should be suspended and Southern independence conceded. Lincoln sized up the Democratic problem this way: "They must nominate a peace Democrat on a war platform, or a war Democrat on a peace platform; and I personally can't say that I care much which they do." The Democrats postponed their convention until August 29, to take advantage of the public discontent with the course of the war. Meeting in Chicago, they nominated McClellan for president and George H. Pendleton (1825–1889) for vice president. This was a compromise between the factions, not entirely dissimilar to the divisions that Republicans had faced. McClellan, a Union general who had taken a public stand for victory and the preservation of the Union, was running on a peace platform with a running mate associated with that faction.[9]

Lincoln's choice for the vice presidency had also been surprising. His vice president for his first term, Hannibal Hamlin, was dropped in favor of someone who could bring in pro–Union Democrats, enhancing the party's chances. Lincoln had sounded out General Benjamin F. Butler, but the general had turned him down, jokingly stating, "I would not ... be Vice President, even with himself as President, unless he will give me bond with sureties, in the full sum of his four years' salary, that he will die or resign within three months after his inauguration." Butler must have had cause to shake his head over this statement, in light of the tragic events that followed. Butler also indicated his low regard for the

Benjamin F. Butler. Gen. Butler, who was interested in becoming president, not vice president, unknowingly passed up an opportunity to be Lincoln's successor (Library of Congress).

Andrew Johnson. Chosen as Lincoln's new vice president to add pro–Union Democratic strength to the Republican ticket in 1864, Johnson inherited a troubled presidency in the immediate postwar years. He avoided being removed from office by a single vote (Library of Congress).

office of vice president, describing it as "being made to sit as presiding officer over the Senate, to listen for four years to debates more or less stupid, in which I can take no part or say a word, nor even be allowed a vote." Butler clearly had high ambition, but no foresight in being able to see that this was the closest he would ever come to achieving his dream. With Butler out of the running, Lincoln turned to Andrew Johnson, a Democrat from Tennessee. Johnson had opposed secession, and had been the only U.S. senator from a seceding state to refuse to go with his state out of the Union. Lincoln had rewarded Johnson's loyalty by appointing him military governor of Tennessee. It took some sharp political skills to get his party to reject an able New Englander and nominate a Democrat from a rebel state, but Lincoln was a masterful politician who knew which strings to pull to get what he wanted. Through sometimes heavy-handed tactics, Johnson got the nomination.[10]

1864 was the first time a presidential election had been held during wartime since 1812. The Civil War was a far larger conflict than that earlier war, with many more soldiers involved. Few states made provisions for the soldiers voting. There were no such things as absentee votes. If any soldiers were going to vote they would have to be sent home on leave on election day. At that time election day was determined by the states, and not all voting was done the same day, as is practiced in modern national elections. This helped, since clearly it would have been impossible to send most of the soldiers home at the same time in the middle of a war. Although the Democratic nominee, General McClellan, was popular among the soldiers, President Lincoln was also very popular, both with soldiers and civilians. Many soldiers were literate, and kept up with the news, and the political debates, as reported in the press. Journalistic standards of 1864 were often questionable, even when compared with today. Newspapers' political orientation tended to be reflected in their reporting, even more than is now common. There were fears in some quarters that opposing attitudes on the issues, especially emancipation, might split the army into factions, possibly resulting in the soldiers fighting each other. There was also talk of one or more of the generals attempting to seize political power. When such rumors reached Lincoln, he wrote his famous response to General Joseph Hooker (1814–1879), saying, "I have heard, in such a way as to believe it, of your recently saying that both the army and the government needed a dictator.... Only those generals who gain successes can set up dictators. What I now ask of you is military success, and I will risk the dictatorship."[11]

With so much at stake, both sides resorted to questionable methods to try to achieve their goals. Republican leaders in Congress tried to suppress pro–Democratic newspapers from getting into the hands of the soldiers. With the writ of habeas corpus suspended, arbitrary arrests, sometimes in order to promote the Republican cause, were made. Lincoln's plan for the organization of pro–Union governments in captured portions of the Confederate states, when only 10 percent of the people took oaths to support the Union, brought cries from Democrats that this was a scheme to add electoral votes to the Republican side, ensuring their victory. Soldiers from Vermont, passing through Indiana on their way home, were allowed to vote in the Indiana elections, strengthening the Republican ticket. Lincoln may have been aware of some, if not all, of these practices, and although personally honest, he was devoted to winning the war and restoring the Union above all else.[12]

Gen. George B. McClellan. He was Lincoln's Democratic opponent in the election of 1864. Although they were both pro–Union, there was a clear difference between the two. When Union victories began occurring in the fall of 1864, McClellan's chances fell sharply (Library of Congress).

Secretary of War Stanton ordered all Democratic literature barred from the army. Government employees, including contractors and laborers, had to pay fees, the money being funneled into the Union Party campaign. The government's power to extend or withhold patronage and advertising was often effective in influencing newspapers to support the reelection effort. In January 1863, a Republican congressional caucus voted to prevent the enfranchising of soldiers, believing they would be likely to support McClellan. Many officers, being politicians in civilian life, spoke to the men of their commands on behalf of the political cause. The United States Christian Commission distributed eight million pamphlets among the soldiers, most of them Republican oriented. Some officers banned the distribution of Democratic material among the soldiers. Word was passed to ambitious officers that support for McClellan for president would have a negative effect on the officers' chances for promotion.[13]

The rebels realized that they had an important stake in the outcome of the elections in the North. They were well aware that the reelection of Lincoln would mean that the war would go on, while a Democratic victory, in spite of McClellan's pro–Union position, would encourage the pro-peace and war-weary side of the North, offering hope for the success of the South. Secret Confederate operations in Canada and the North were partially intended to affect the elections. Confederate agents in Canada met openly with Northern pro-peace leaders, gathering information on Northern politics as well as suggesting action that might influence the elections.[14]

Lincoln-Johnson election poster. The name of the party was changed from Republican to Union Party, to attract pro–Union voters. Johnson, a southern Democrat, replaced Hannibal Hamlin, Lincoln's vice president in his first term (Library of Congress).

Another campaign tactic used by the Republicans came to be known as the "bloody shirt" issue. Republicans suggested that the Democrats, especially the pro-peace faction, were offering aid to the Southern rebels, and thus committing treason. "Waving the bloody shirt" was a way to remind voters that to vote for Lincoln was to support the Union, and thus to resist the "traitorous" rebels. This emotional appeal helped to obscure the campaign issues and threw the Democrats onto the defensive. "Waving the bloody shirt" became a campaign standard in elections for decades after the Civil War had ended. It didn't convince every voter, but it undoubtedly helped.[15]

In the end, all the distortion and misrepresentation of issues did not decide the election one way or the other. What made the difference was the sudden change in "no news or bad news" about the war. Lincoln received General Sherman's message on September 4. It read, "Atlanta is ours, and fairly won." On September 19, General Philip Henry Sheridan (1831–1888) informed the president, "We have just sent them [Gen. Early's Confederate army] whirling through Winchester [Virginia], and we are after them tomorrow." These victories, coming on the heels of Admiral David Glasgow Farragut's (1801–1870) capture of Mobile, Alabama, on August 4, clinched the election for the Union Party. When the votes were counted, Lincoln won 2,218,388, or 55.02 percent, to McClellan's 1,812,807, or 44.96 percent, of the popular vote—212 to 21 in the electoral vote. Lincoln had won a solid, decisive victory, if not a "landslide." He had carried every state except Delaware, Kentucky, and New Jersey.

McClellan, in a letter to his brother, reacted to his defeat, saying, "I was fully prepared for the result and not in the slightest degree overcome by it. For my country's sake, I deplore the result but the people have decided with their eyes wide open and I feel a great weight removed from my mind." Lincoln told his cheering supporters, "My gratitude is free from any taint of personal triumph. I do not impugn the motives of anyone opposed to me. It is no pleasure to me to triumph over any one, but I give thanks to the Allmighty for this evidence of the people's resolution to stand by free government and the rights of humanity." John Wilkes Booth wrote his thoughts about the election, as well. "For four years have I waited, hoped and prayed, for the dark clouds to break, and for a restoration of our former sunshine, to wait longer would be a crime. All hope for peace is dead, my prayers have proved as idle as my hopes. God's will be done. I go to see, and share the bitter end."[16]

7. Confederate Secret Service

> It can be shown that the Confederates had the knowledge and technical skill to mount an operation against President Lincoln, that they engaged in a number of activities in 1864 and 1865 that could have been related to planning such an operation; that John Wilkes Booth was in contact with known Confederate agents, and that the course of the war developed in such a way that an attack on Lincoln was a logical amendment to the original plan to capture him.
>
> Tidwell, Hall, and Gaddy, Come Retribution

The Confederate Secret Service was not a unified organization under a single leader, but a collection of groups whose overlapping activities gradually pulled them together. The groups and agencies most involved were the State Department Secret Service, under the supervision of Secretary of State Judah P. Benjamin (1811–1884); the War Department Secret Service, whose agents were often detailed to work directly with army field commanders; the War Department Signal Bureau and Signal Corps, which operated the "secret line" of safe houses and drops between Washington and Richmond, under the leadership of Major William Norris (1820–1896); the Provost Marshal of Richmond, responsible for counterespionage and internal security in the Richmond area, as well as prisoner of war camps, all under the supervision of Brigadier General John Henry Winder (1800–1865); the War Department Torpedo Bureau, commanded by Brigadier General Gabriel James Rains (1803–1881), which devised and planted mines, both on land and under water; the Navy Submarine Battery Service, also attempting to prevent ships from entering the harbors and rivers by placing mines; the War Department Strategy Bureau, which sent agents behind the lines with explosives; the Greenhow Group, a Washington-based spy ring, including the famous Rose O'Neal Greenhow (1815–1864), known as "Rebel Rose"; Cavalry Scouts, an extension of the cavalry's traditional role in gathering information; and Operations in Canada, an ambitious effort to destabilize the North through well-financed agents based in neutral Canada.

Major Norris' Signal and Secret Service, as it came to be called, established and maintained the "secret line," a route through the back country of Virginia and Maryland, enabling agents to move between Washington and Richmond while employing the aid of Southern sympathizers. Some of the people involved in the "secret line" are familiar to students of the assassination. Dr. Samuel A. Mudd was said to have made his house available to visiting Confederates. Thomas H. Harbin (1833–1885), who helped John Wilkes Booth in the planning of the Lincoln capture plot, is known to have been a rebel agent. Joseph N. Baden (?–1874) of the Confederate Signal Corps worked with Harbin. William Rollins (1833–1901), who met Booth at the Rappahannock River crossing, was also an agent of the Confederate

Signal Corps. Thomas A. Jones, who hid Booth and helped him cross the Potomac River, was in charge of a signal station and had been recruited for that duty by Norris himself. It was not by coincidence that Booth, in his flight from the scene of the assassination, followed the "secret line."[1]

Judah Philip Benjamin was one of the most influential leaders of the Confederate government, holding three Cabinet posts and described by friend and foe alike as "the brains of the Confederacy." The part he played in the direction of Confederate secret operations and the assassination of Lincoln is still a subject of controversy.

Benjamin's family roots go back to Spain, then to England by way of the Netherlands. His parents sailed for the New World in 1811, and Judah was born in Saint Croix, British West Indies, on August 11, 1811. Moving to Fayetteville, North Carolina, in 1813, and to Charleston, South Carolina, around 1821, the family found acceptance in Charleston's relatively tolerant attitude toward Jews. Benjamin entered Yale University in 1825, but left in 1827, giving economic problems as his reason, though others have hinted at something more scandalous, possibly involving gambling. Determined to start over, and looking for greater opportunity, Benjamin went to New Orleans, Louisiana, in 1828, where his rise was rapid and spectacular. Hired to teach English to the daughter of a wealthy Creole businessman, Benjamin learned French as he taught his pupil, Natalie St. Martin (1816–?), who became his wife on February 12, 1833. Having studied law in a notary's office, Benjamin was admitted to the bar on December 11, 1832. His intelligence and energy soon made him not only successful but also celebrated. By the early 1840s Benjamin had bought a large plantation and entered politics. Although he owned slaves himself, he won national attention and the applause of abolitionists by successfully defending mutinous slaves. Elected to the Louisiana legislature as a Whig in 1842, he attended the state constitutional convention in 1844, was an elector for the Whig presidential ticket in 1848, and again in 1852 was elected U.S. senator from Louisiana.

With the demise of the Whig Party, Benjamin became a Democrat in 1856. The power of his mind and the eloquence with which he spoke for Southern rights won him the friendship of other Southern leaders, especially Jefferson Davis (1808–1889).

Withdrawing from the U.S. Senate on February 4, 1861, Benjamin was appointed Confederate attorney general by President Davis, and took office May 5, 1861. When it became

Judah P. Benjamin. Called the "brains of the Confederacy," as Confederate secretary of state, Benjamin controlled the undercover operations in Canada, which appear to have been involved in plans to kidnap or assassinate Lincoln (Library of Congress).

obvious that Confederate Secretary of War Leroy Pope Walker (1817–1884) was incapable of providing the organizational abilities needed to raise and supply the huge forces required, Davis turned to Benjamin, naming him acting secretary of war as of November 21, 1861. When Roanoke Island, North Carolina, fell to Union forces in February 1862, Benjamin was blamed for failing to properly supply the garrison. He had to shoulder the blame, for he knew it would harm the South to admit the real reason, that he simply had not had the means to assist the defenders. Confederate Congressman Henry Stuart Foote (1804–1880) was especially harsh in his criticism of the man he called "Judas Iscariot Benjamin," and decried the "tight and terrible President Davis–Jew Benjamin alliance." Davis, who had had serious altercations with Foote before, confounded his own and Benjamin's critics by promptly naming Benjamin to the newly vacant office of secretary of state. Benjamin assumed his new duties on March 18, 1862, and held this office through the end of the war.

As secretary of state, Benjamin sought to try to persuade Britain and France to support the Confederacy, something that was made difficult by their opposition to slavery. Benjamin even urged his friend Davis to consider emancipating slaves who were willing to fight for the South.[2]

As Confederate secret operations based in Canada came under foreign policy, Benjamin assumed overall control, second only to Davis, of the South's most important and ambitious covert operation. Benjamin selected Confederate operatives such as Jacob Thompson (1810–1885) and Thomas Henry Hines (c.1840–1898), for the Canada assignment. Thompson, who was the senior Confederate operative in Canada, reported directly to Benjamin. Although Benjamin destroyed his records at the end of the war and left no subsequent account, the recollections of others and a few key documents confirm his position as one of the central figures in the rebel undercover organizations.

Jacob Thompson received the following letter:

> Richmond, Va., April 27, 1864
> Sir: Confiding special trust in your zeal, discretion and patriotism, I hereby direct you to proceed at once to Canada; there to carry out the instructions you have received from me verbally, in such manner as shall seem most likely to conduce to the furtherance of the Confederate States of America which have been entrusted to you.
>
> Very respectfully and truly yours,
> Jefferson Davis.[3]

Born May 15, 1810, in Leasburg, North Carolina, Thompson attended public school and Bingham Academy, Orange County, North Carolina. His father wanted him to enter the ministry, but Thompson decided on a law career upon his graduation from the University of North Carolina at Chapel Hill in 1831. After teaching at UNC from 1831 to 1832, Thompson studied law in Greensboro and was admitted to the bar in 1834. He began his law practice in Pontotoc, Mississippi, in 1835. Moving to Oxford, Mississippi, he married the daughter of a wealthy farmer. Although defeated for state attorney general in 1837, Thompson was elected the following year to the U.S. House of Representatives, where he served from March 4, 1839, to March 3, 1851, and was chairman of the Indian Affairs Committee. Denied an appointment as U.S. senator in 1845, and losing his House seat in the election of 1850, Thompson remained active in politics, being a delegate to the Democratic National Conventions of 1852 and 1856. Having turned down a consular post in Havana, Cuba, in 1853, Thompson ran for U.S. senator in 1855, losing to Jefferson Davis. Appointed secretary of the interior by President James Buchanan, Thompson served from March 6, 1857, to January 8, 1861. Improving the efficiency of his department, he also became very influential as an advisor to the president.

Initially opposed to Southern secession, though a strong advocate of states' rights, Thompson urged a moderate, pro-peace attitude for the federal government, but when Buchanan sent supplies to reinforce Fort Sumter, Thompson resigned from the Cabinet. Entering the Confederate army as a lieutenant colonel, Thompson became an aide to General Pierre Gustave Toutant Beauregard (1818–1893). In 1862, Colonel Thompson became inspector general of the Confederate army. Captured after the siege of Vicksburg, he was soon released and elected to the Mississippi legislature.[4]

To assist Thompson in his new assignment to Canada were Clement Claiborne Clay (1816–1882) and William Walter Cleary (1831–1897). They would make contact with others already in Canada, and welcome still more who would follow them from the South. The mission was very well financed, for Thompson was provided $1,000,000 initially, with more to follow, and he was given the widest discretion in how the money was to be spent, no receipts or financial reports being required.[5]

Jacob Thompson. Head of the Confederate Secret Service operations in Canada, Thompson remains controversial to this day over the question of whether he took large amounts of Confederate money with him when he fled to Europe (Library of Congress).

Initially, Thompson sought to make contact with secret organizations in the North that were opposed to the war. These included the "Sons of Liberty" and "Knights of the Golden Circle." Thompson met with the leader of the "Sons of Liberty," former congressman Clement Laird Vallandigham (1820–1871), whose vigorous opposition to the Union war effort had resulted in his arrest and banishment to the South. Vallandigham told Thompson there were hundreds of thousands of people in the states of Ohio, Indiana, Illinois, and other parts of the area known as the Old Northwest who were willing to resist the Lincoln administration's war policies. What was needed was leadership and money, and Thompson promised both. Sending Confederate agents into these areas, Thompson and his aides devised plans to use a pro-peace uprising to storm prisoner of war camps and release thousands of Confederate soldiers, who would be armed and in a position to wreak havoc behind Union lines, forcing the North to send thousands of troops to the rear, giving Confederate armies in the South a chance to regroup and gain new advantages.[6]

Other Confederates in Canada, or soon to arrive, included Thomas Henry Hines,

Robert M. Martin (1839–1901), John William Headley (c.1840–1930) — all cavalrymen who had seen action with some of the South's leading cavalry commanders — and James Philimon Holcomb (1820–1873). Thompson controlled the funds for the Canada mission, and supplied money in vast amounts for every project undertaken. Captain Hines estimated this money as in excess of two and a half million dollars.[7]

In a letter to Secretary Benjamin, dated December 3, 1864, Thompson described in general terms what he and the men of his mission had been doing. An attempt was being made to capitalize on anti–Lincoln and pro-peace sentiment. Large numbers of Confederate prisoners of war were being held in camps such as Johnson's Island in Lake Erie, and Camp Douglas in Chicago. With the Democratic National Convention scheduled to meet in Chicago on July 29, 1864, it seemed the perfect time for rebel agents to meet with their local collaborators for the attack on Camp Douglas. When the time came, however, heavier security had a discouraging effect upon the "Knights," and too few of them showed up to make an attack possible. Another plan, to capture the steamer U.S.S. *Michigan*, the only Union gunboat on the Great Lakes, fell apart when the rebel agents were betrayed and nearly captured.

Other plans included an attempt to set fires in New York City hotels in reprisal for what Union General William T. Sherman (1820–1891) and his army were doing in the South. An incendiary chemical known as "Greek fire," which burst into flame when exposed to air, was used. On November 25, 1864, rebel agents set afire ten hotels, Barnum's Museum, and ships docked at wharves. The "Greek fire" proved to be disappointing, and the raiders were betrayed by counterspies. The damage, though serious, was quickly contained.

The town of St. Albans, Vermont, was raided, people killed, money stolen from banks, and buildings set afire. The raiders returned to Canada, where they claimed the protection of the British authorities. Thompson denied any involvement with the St. Albans raiders, though he knew them all.[8]

Another member of the Confederate mission in Canada, George N. Sanders (1812–1873), had been urging bank robbery as a means of supplementing the funds available to Thompson. Born in Lexington, Kentucky, on February 21, 1812, Sanders was the third of nine children. Young George went to school in Owingsville and helped with his father's horse business at the family farm, "Grass Hills." George married Anna J. Reid on November 29, 1836, and they had four children.

Sanders' business concerns often coincided with his political activity. His interest in the "Young America" movement, which encouraged the nation's growth westward, also brought him into contact with similar movements in Italy, Ireland, and Germany. He attempted to arrange for the sale of American muskets to French revolutionaries in 1848. Moving to New York City in 1845, he was involved in a variety of business deals, and he became an agent of Hudson's Bay Company. He also represented eastern speculators in real estate in Chicago, being associated with August Belmont (1816–1890) and George Law (1806–1881). Prominent in Democratic Party politics, Sanders was a strong supporter of the presidential ambitions of Stephen Arnold Douglas as early as 1852. Sanders was active in journalism as well, being publisher of *Democratic Review* beginning in 1851.

President Franklin Pierce (1804–1869), seeking favor among Southerners, appointed Sanders U.S. consul in London in 1853. In February 1854, Sanders hosted a gathering of revolutionaries at his home in London. Among his guests were Lajos Kossuth (1802–1894) of Hungary; Giuseppe Garibaldi (1807–1882) and Giuseppe Mazzini (1805–1872) of Italy; Aleksandr Ivanovich Herzen (1812–1870), Russian revolutionary; and Arnold Ruge (1803–1880),

German philosopher and politician — all prominent in revolutionary European politics. Sanders' imposing appearance and pleasant manner allowed him to be at ease with almost anyone. Revolution was not the only thing on Sanders' mind, for he was also eager to promote American products, portraying his mercenary interests as patriotism. His pro-revolutionary activity proved embarrassing to his supervisor in London, American Minister James Buchanan, who succeeded Pierce as president in 1857. Sanders had openly advocated the assassination of French Emperor Louis Napoleon (1808–1873), "by any means and in any way." His friend August Belmont used influence to help keep Sanders out of serious trouble, though his enemies in the Senate, particularly Senator William H. Seward, were able to prevent his confirmation as consul, to the regret of his revolutionary European friends. Appointed navy agent at the port of New York in 1857, Sanders continued his political activity, campaigning for Senator Douglas for president in 1860.

When the Civil War began, Sanders went south, but soon returned to Europe, by way of Canada, as an agent of the Confederacy. Unsuccessful in attempting to have ironclad blockade runners built in England, Sanders returned to Canada. By February, 1863, Sanders was again on his way to England, now as a bearer of Confederate dispatches.[9]

Again in Canada in early 1864, Sanders became a member of the official Confederate espionage effort there, headed by Jacob Thompson. Thompson seems to have been concerned about having Sanders as a member of his team, because of his prominence and well-known views, but Sanders had the support of no less than Confederate President Jefferson Davis. Sanders' zeal as an agent of the Confederacy was strengthened when he learned that his son Reid, a major in the Confederate army, who had been captured while on a clandestine mission for his father, died on September 5, 1864.

Sanders was instrumental in setting up a peace conference in the summer of 1864 at Niagara Falls. The Confederacy was represented, besides Sanders, by Clement Claiborne Clay and James Philemon Holcomb. Meeting with them, though without any official connection with the Lincoln administration, were newspaperman Horace Greeley, and John M. Hay. Even before the conference failed, Sanders suggested to Confederate agent Thomas H. Hines that robbing banks in northern cities would divert Union troops from the war fronts. Forging Clay's signature, Sanders masterminded the raid on St. Albans, Vermont, which took place on October 19, 1864. When the raiders were arrested and put on trial in Canada, Sanders obtained $6,000 to pay for their defense. He also saw to it that those on trial were comfortably housed and well fed. Attending the trial, Sanders made full use of his personality and presence, seeming at times to have influence over court officials. He "leaked" news to the local papers, nothing more than rumors and often false ones at that, in an effort to win Canadian sympathy for the raiders and the Southern cause. The raiders were ultimately released.[10]

When John Wilkes Booth visited Montreal, Canada, in October 1864, he met with Confederates operating there on behalf of their cause. It appears that Sanders was one of those spending time with Booth. Sanders was away October 23–25, but upon returning to Montreal he stayed at the St. Lawrence Hall, the same hotel where Booth was then staying. While in Montreal, Booth opened a bank account at the Ontario Bank. Upon returning to Washington in mid November, he made another large deposit in a bank there. Sanders had access to Confederate funds through Clay, as shown by his lavish spending in the St. Albans raid. Clay's letter of September 12 refers to "Mr. Sanders" as then on his way to Richmond. Benjamin met with Confederate Secretary of War James Alexander Seddon (1815–1880) in

Richmond between September 12 and 15 to plan the Lincoln abduction plot headed by Captain Thomas N. Conrad (1837–1905). Conrad's plot very closely resembled Booth's. If we cannot prove Sanders was instrumental in encouraging Booth, at least it remains a strong possibility.[11]

Thomas Nelson Conrad was born at Fairfax Court House, Virginia, on August 1, 1837, son of Nelson Conrad, a wholesale merchant in Baltimore, and Lavinia Thomas Conrad. He attended Dickinson College in Carlisle, Pennsylvania, from 1853 to 1857. Upon graduation, he taught at a private school in Georgetown, DC, later becoming the founder of the Georgetown Institute.

Arrested on August 2, 1862, by Washington Provost Marshal William E. Doster, who later served as a defense lawyer at the trial of the Lincoln assassination conspirators, Conrad was held in the Old Capitol Prison for a time. Exchanged for prisoners of war, Conrad headed south, joining the Confederate army and becoming a cavalryman in the command of General James E. B. Stuart (1833–1864). As chaplain of the Third Virginia Cavalry, Conrad held the rank of captain, serving in William C. Wickham's (1820–1888) brigade of Fitz Lee's (1835–1905) division. Although a chaplain, he also served with the cavalrymen in battle, his intense Southern patriotism answering any questions he may have had about the compatibility of his two occupations.

His earlier years in the Washington area made Conrad well suited to be a scout, which soon led him into the world of espionage. Old friends and Southern sympathizers in Washington helped Conrad set up a spy network. He knew War Department clerks and even had a spy planted in Lafayette Baker's (1826–1868) detective force. Conrad made use of people who traveled, especially two country doctors from Maryland, who would deliver his messages. Conrad often stayed at the Van Ness Mansion in Washington, the home of Thomas Green (c.1800–?) and his wife Anne Green, whose sons were serving with Conrad in the Confederate cavalry. Learning of the route Union General Ambrose E. Burnside (1824–1881) planned to take toward Fredericksburg, Conrad personally delivered the information to General Robert E. Lee's headquarters, information that greatly contributed to Lee's stunning victory.

By early 1864, Conrad was appointed to the Confederate Secret Service Bureau, but was arrested as a suspected spy and confined at Point Lookout, Maryland. When smallpox broke out, Conrad pretended to be sick and was placed outside the camp with other sick prisoners. When the opportunity presented itself, he escaped.

In the summer of 1864 Conrad was ordered to Richmond for special duty. By mid-September Conrad was involved in a plot,

Thomas N. Conrad. One of the best of the Confederate scouts, or spies, Conrad had a plan to kidnap Lincoln that very closely resembled Booth's plan (courtesy of Surratt House Museum/MNCPPC).

organized by Confederate leaders at the highest level, to kidnap President Lincoln and bring him south, to be exchanged for Confederate soldiers in Northern prison camps. Conrad later related that he had been given the idea by a group of Confederate officers from Maryland. Suggesting the scheme to Secretary of War Seddon, Conrad was given the go-ahead to develop the plan. His team members included Daniel Mountjoy Cloud (1837–1871), John J. Norton, Lemuel H. Henry, and Gabriel Edmondson (1840–?), all Confederate army veterans. They were to have the assistance of Lieutenant Colonel John Singleton Mosby (1833–1916) and his famous cavalry raiders, and of Lieutenant Charles H. Cawood, in charge of Confederate Signal Corps operations in northern Virginia. Although it is not known whether Conrad met with Booth, the actor was beginning to organize his own very similar plan at about the same time. Furthermore, Conrad was a friend of the Surratt family and had visited them at the tavern in Surrattsville, Maryland, several times before the war. John Surratt (1844–1916) would later become a member of Booth's gang.

During the latter part of 1864 and the beginning of 1865, Conrad made several trips between Richmond and Washington, met with high Confederate officials, and received money for his expenses. The expenditure was personally authorized by Jefferson Davis. Conrad's plan, like Booth's, was to capture Lincoln as he rode out to the Soldiers Home, or any other location outside the city. Observing Lincoln's movements from Lafayette Park, across the street from the north side of the White House, Conrad may have been close to an actual attempt in September 1864, only to be surprised by Lincoln having a cavalry escort.

Conrad remained in Washington until mid–November and then was needed elsewhere. It appears that he was called upon to oversee covert operations and maintain lines of communication through northern Virginia. His primary activity in the final months of the war was rooting out and discouraging pro–Union spies in the area between the Potomac River and Richmond. He was also instrumental in placing "torpedoes," or mines, in the waterways of Virginia. Conrad was, however, still maintaining contact with Confederate agents in Washington, and he made another trip to Washington in early February, bringing money for the agents. Since we know Booth was in Washington until February 9, 1865, it is tempting to speculate that Conrad may have been in contact, directly or indirectly, with him. We have already observed that Conrad knew John Surratt, and he was, through his contacts with Mosby's men, acquainted with or knew of all three of the Confederate soldiers who helped Booth in the final days of the assassin's escape: Absalom Ruggles Bainbridge, Mortimer Bainbridge Ruggles, and William Storke Jett.[12]

John Wilkes Booth became associated with the Confederate underground possibly as early as the spring of 1863. Always pro–Southern, Booth may have joined a secret organization, such as the Knights of the Golden Circle, even before the war. He told his sister Asia Booth Clarke (1835–1888) that he was involved in smuggling quinine into the South. At about this time Booth became friends with David Edgar Herold (1842–1865), then a drug store employee and later a trusted member of Booth's gang of conspirators. Booth registered at the Parker House hotel in Boston on July 26, 1864. His name in the hotel register appears preceded and followed by four others, whose real identities cannot now be traced. It is tempting to speculate that these men may have been Confederate agents. Three of them gave Canadian addresses, and the other listed Baltimore. It was around this time that Booth began to organize his conspiracy to abduct President Lincoln. Although his acting engagements fell off to practically none, he had access to large sums of money. Could some of that money have come from Jacob Thompson? Booth signed the register of Montreal's

St. Lawrence Hall on October 18, 1864. Whether or not Booth met with Thompson, he certainly saw known Confederate agents while in Canada. Booth arranged to ship his trunk, containing his theatrical wardrobe and other belongings, with the blockade runner Patrick Charles Martin (1817–1864), and Booth was seen in the company of George N. Sanders. Although he spent several days in Montreal, Booth had no professional engagements there. Opening a bank account at the Ontario Bank in Montreal, Booth deposited $455.

Patrick Martin was born in New York and made a living selling liquor, first in Pittsburgh, and after 1850 in Baltimore. By 1860, Martin and his wife Mary had five children. His pro–South activities necessitated moving himself and his family to Montreal, about in 1862. In Montreal he associated with former Baltimore police chief George Proctor Kane, trying to organize an assault on Johnson's Island, a federal prisoner of war camp in Lake Erie, in 1863. That scheme fell through.

When Booth came to Montreal he was introduced to Martin by the other Confederates. Opening an account at the Ontario Bank on October 27, Booth was accompanied by Martin. Booth received from Martin a letter of introduction to Dr. William Queen (1789–1868), of Charles County, Maryland. Queen put Booth in touch with other Confederate agents and sympathizers in southern Maryland, where Booth planned to escape. Booth also arranged for Martin to ship his theatrical trunk to Nassau, Bahamas. Martin chartered a schooner, the *Marie Victoria*, a 73-footer, built in 1858. When a storm drove the ship aground near the town of Bic, Quebec, all aboard, including Martin, were drowned. Booth's trunks were recovered from the wreckage, but by then the owner was dead and their contents water damaged. They were sold at auction for far beneath their value. Martin's family stayed on in Montreal.[13]

Confederate secret line agent Thomas A. Jones later wrote, "Sometime in December, 1864, I heard that there was 'a big scheme' afoot to abduct President Lincoln and take him a prisoner." After describing the abduction plan in some detail, Jones stated, "There were quite a number of persons in this abduction conspiracy; prominent among whom were the actor John Wilkes Booth, and his friend, John H. Surratt." Jones was to become deeply involved in Booth's escape.[14]

Confederate Brigadier General Bradley Tyler Johnson (1829–1894) was set to abduct Lincoln from the Soldiers Home. Johnson's mission was to have been a part of General

Gen. Bradley Tyler Johnson. Johnson was set to kidnap Lincoln during the Confederate raid on Maryland and the District of Columbia in 1864, but his part in the raid was called off at the last minute (Library of Congress)

Jubal A. Early's raid on Washington in July 1864, but the Johnson raid was cancelled at the last minute. Both the Johnson raid and the Conrad abduction plot were to make use of the "secret line," as Booth also intended to do.[15]

Union spies alerted their superiors that Confederate "peace commissioners" in Canada were suggesting Lincoln be assassinated as part of a plot to disrupt the 1864 elections. The authors of *Come Retribution* say, "The Confederate peace commissioner who advocated assassinating Lincoln ... could only have been George Sanders."[16]

One of the earliest instances of the use, or attempted use, of biological warfare was a scheme of the Confederate underground in Canada that has come to be called the "Yellow Fever Plot." Yellow fever, also called "Yellow Jack," is an infectious disease caused by a virus, and transmitted by the mosquito *Aedes aegyptae*, though its cause was not known in 1865. Yellow fever epidemics caused thousands of deaths in the United States, especially in the South, beginning around 1820.

Confederate agents in Canada were informed by a Kentucky doctor, Luke Pryor Blackburn (1816–1887), that he would obtain clothing of yellow fever victims in Bermuda and ship the clothes to Halifax, Nova Scotia, Canada. An agent could then take the clothes into the United States and distribute them to Union soldiers and civilians in Northern cities.

In mid–December 1863, the Rev. Stuart Robinson introduced Dr. Blackburn to Godfrey Joseph Hyams in Toronto, Canada. Blackburn promised Hyams $100.000 if he would take several trunks full of infected clothing to Washington, DC; Norfolk, Virginia; and wherever concentrations of Union troops were to be found. Hyams agreed to the scheme, waiting in Toronto until June 8, 1864, when he received a letter from Robinson, who claimed not to know anything about the scheme except that Hyams was to proceed to Montreal, and from there to Halifax, where he would get in touch with Blackburn. Hyams took possession of eight trunks and a valise, following Blackburn's directions. Hyams was willing to take the clothes south, as instructed, but he balked at sending the valise to the White House, where it was to have been donated to President Lincoln.

Hyams arranged to have the trunks smuggled into Boston and shipped from there to Philadelphia, from whence he took them to Baltimore. After changing trunks to conceal his work, he took the trunks to Washington, where he arranged to have them sold by the auctioneers W. L. Wall & Co. Hyams used the alias J.W. Harris in his dealings with Wall, receiving an advance of $100 against the sale of the clothing and trunks. 96 shirts were purchased by Stingler & Siege, 9 coats by Walker, 3 trunks by William Smith, and 2 trunks by Hand, realizing a total of $142.90 for Hyams, minus the auctioneer's fee and taxes of $14.29.

Upon his return to Canada, Hyams said he was directed by Blackburn to apply to Jacob Thompson for funds. Thompson, according to Hyams, paid him $50, and promised another $50, but wanted proof that Hyams had done what he said he had. Hyams wrote to Wall, asking for a statement of his account, which he received. Hyams' efforts to obtain more money came to nothing. Blackburn shunned him, and none of the Confederate commissioners gave him any more of the huge sums he had been promised.

Hyams came to the attention of Lafayette Baker's detectives. He provided Baker with much information on the Confederate operations in Canada. Dr. Blackburn was arrested by Canadian authorities in Montreal on May 18, 1865, and tried in connection with the raid on St. Albans, Vermont. The story of the Yellow Fever Plot came out at Blackburn's trial, but since there was insufficient proof against him, Blackburn was acquitted. Hyams testified at the trial of the conspirators, as part of the government's efforts to link Confederate leaders with the assassination of Lincoln. Hyams' story was considered of little value, and although Confederate leaders were named along with the defendants on trial, the cases against them were allowed to fade quietly away.[17]

Just after the fall of Richmond, a former Confederate soldier, who said he had served in the Torpedo Bureau, had heard of a plot against President Lincoln. He didn't know the details, but his story sounded credible. After the assassination, George Atzerodt (1835–1865) stated, "Booth said he had met a party in New York who would get the Prest. Certain. They were going to mine the end of the Pres. House near the War Dept. They knew an entrance to accomplish it through." Thomas Frank Harney (1837–?) was an explosives expert from the Torpedo Bureau. Records show Jefferson Davis authorized $1,500 for "Secret Service" on April 1, 1865, and Harney left Richmond around that date.[18]

Another Confederate agent who was in Richmond just before the city fell was John H. Surratt, Jr. A trusted member of Booth's conspiracy, Surratt received $200 in gold from Secretary Benjamin personally. Although Surratt denied any Confederate involvement in Booth's conspiracy, he readily admitted spying for the South and being paid for it shortly before Lincoln's assassination.[19]

As the Confederates looked for a way to deal the North a blow heavy enough to set back the war effort, the lightly guarded figure of President Abraham Lincoln became all too obvious a target.

8. John Wilkes Booth

> How many ages hence
> Shall this our lofty scene be acted over
> In states unborn and accents yet unknown!
>
> William Shakespeare, *Julius Caesar*, Act 3, scene 1

John Wilkes Booth was born May 10, 1838, on his parents' farm in Bel Air, Maryland. His father, Junius Brutus Booth (1796–1852), was one of the most famous and celebrated actors of the American stage. His mother, Mary Ann Holmes (1802–1885), was not legally married to Junius until 1851. John Wilkes was the ninth of ten children. His sister Asia, later wrote that their mother had had a vision that John Wilkes would not live a long life. Four of her children had died in the six years before John Wilkes' birth, a fact that may have influenced such a dark premonition.[1]

Dividing his time between "the Farm," as they called the Bel Air property, and a house in Baltimore, at 62 North Exeter St., John Wilkes acquired an education not inferior to most Americans of his time and better than many. Like his older brother Edwin (1833–1893), he attended a school run by Martin J. Kerney in Baltimore, also on Exeter St. Wilkes' younger brother Joseph (1840–1902) attended Kerney's school, as did Asia's future husband John Sleeper Clarke (1833–1899). Neighborhood friends in Baltimore included the O'Laughlen family, and John Wilkes became a close friend of T. William O'Laughlen (1838–1915) and his younger brother Michael (1840–1867), who would later become one of Booth's fellow conspirators.[2]

Asia described her brother John Wilkes

John Wilkes Booth. Lone assassin or Confederate conspirator? The government made an effort to prove rebel involvement in the assassination at the time, and more recent scholarship suggests a connection with the Booth conspiracy (Library of Congress).

as "not quick at acquiring knowledge, he had to plod, progress slowly step by step, but that which he once attained he never lost.... He possessed a tenacious rather than an intuitive intelligence like his brothers.... He had great power of concentration, and he never let go a subject once broached until he had mastered it or proved its bareness.... His feelings were ardent and impulsive, in a moment of devotion or enthusiasm he would grant or give anything he possessed, while in time of danger his quick eye took in the situation regardless of his own safety.... He was never known to throw off a friend, or to slight an acquaintance."[3]

From 1849 to 1852 John Wilkes attended the Milton Academy in Cockeyesville, Maryland. In 1852 he entered St. Timothy's Hall at Catonsville, Maryland, a military school requiring uniforms and emphasizing discipline. His schoolmates nicknamed him "Billy Bowlegs," after a slight bow-leggedness that he bore throughout his life. Here he met Samuel Bland Arnold (1834–1906), another of his later co-conspirators. Leaving St. Timothy's after a year, John Wilkes' formal schooling came to an end. His father died in 1852, and, with his older brothers already embarked on acting careers, John Wilkes was needed back on the farm. Hard times had come to the Booth family. Junius Sr.'s debts had to be paid, but the life of a poor farmer held no appeal for young John Wilkes. He had spoken to childhood friends of a desire to do great things, to become famous through some spectacular act.

During his early years at the farm he developed his skill with horses, and also as a marksman, skills he would exploit later. His social and political views also developed along the lines of rural Maryland. He became interested in the American Party, also known as the "Know Nothing" Party (due to the secretiveness of its members). A wave of immigration swept over America during the 1850s, with the arrival of large numbers of Catholics. The Know Nothings felt threatened by the growing strength of the foreign born. The thousands of Irishmen and Germans also provided an alternative to slave labor, thus threatening the Southern way of life to which John Wilkes was increasingly devoted.[4]

John Wilkes Booth entered the acting profession in 1855, appearing as Richmond in *Richard III* at Wheatley's Arch Street Theatre in Philadelphia, on August 14. His inexperience and stage fright made his debut an embarrassment, and it was two years before he returned to the stage. On August 15, 1857, he again appeared at the Arch Street Theater, and performed dozens of times that season, being on stage almost every night, often in two different plays in the same evening. Some of the plays in which he appeared during the 1857 to 1858 season included *The Belle's Stratagem, Charity's Love, or the Trials of the Heart, Richard III, The Lady of Lyons, The Hunchback, Jane Shore, Romeo and Juliet, Much Ado About Nothing, The Merchant of Venice, The Apostate, Hamlet, Othello, Jack Cade, Macbeth, My Neighbor's Wife, Civilization, Julius Caesar, The Queen of Spades, Rob Roy, Richelieu, London Assurance, Still Waters Run, Deep, The Last Days of Pompeii, She Stoops to Conquer, Lucretia Borgia, King Henry IV, King Lear*, and many others. He also met and began friendships with other actors and theatrical people. John Wilkes was a member of the stock company, playing supporting parts and not receiving star billing, at a salary of $8 a week. So as not to focus undue attention on the still-inexperienced actor, and to make a reputation independent of his famous father and brothers, he used the name "John Wilkes," saving the "Booth" for later, when he would be more worthy.[5]

Theatrical practices in nineteenth-century America were very different from those of today. Plays were often rewritten or modified to suit local audiences. Sensationalism was encouraged. Exaggerated, flamboyant gestures were the rule, especially with John Wilkes, who became known for his vigorous, athletic portrayals. The major American theatrical centers included New York, Philadelphia, Charleston, St. Louis, New Orleans, Boston, and Chicago. Any suitable building could be rented for a season, with a stock company built around one or more stars, and plays presented. Although the Civil War hurt the theatrical business at first, soon the need for diverting entertainment brought a surge of new business. Actors did far better in the North than in the South, where wartime economizing was much more drastic. The shortage of manpower in Southern armies led to the closing of Richmond's theatres in 1864; the actors had been drafted.[6]

As his career matured, Booth joined the ranks of the celebrated stars, which included Adah Isaacs Menken (1835–1868), Charlotte Cushman (1816–1876), Joseph Jefferson (1829–1905), Edwin Forrest (1806–1872), and Laura Keene (1826–1873), as well as members of his own family.

Following his season in Philadelphia, John Wilkes became a member of the company of the Marshall Theatre in Richmond, Virginia, beginning September 4, 1858, and continuing through May 1860. Again, he played a very large variety of roles, often appearing six days a week. He was also able to put in limited appearances in Lynchburg, Virginia; Petersburg, Virginia; Columbus, Georgia; Montgomery, Alabama; and even Boston, Massachusetts. It was while he was performing in Richmond that abolitionist John Brown (1800–1859) carried out his raid on the federal arsenal at Harpers Ferry, Virginia. When the governor called up troops to preserve order at Brown's trial in Charlestown, Virginia, John Wilkes Talked his way onto the train carrying Company F of the Richmond Grays, borrowing a uniform from the soldiers. Present at Brown's hanging on December 2, 1859, Booth was inspired by Brown's dignity and defiance, but sickened by the sight of death.[7]

During the 1860–1861 season, John Wilkes toured widely, performing in Rochester and Albany, New York, and Portland, Maine, and during the 1861–1862 season, Buffalo, New York; Detroit, Michigan; Cincinnati, Ohio; Louisville, Kentucky; St. Louis, Missouri; Chicago; Baltimore; New York; again in St. Louis; Boston; and back to Chicago and Louisville. He was now a featured player, performing leading roles in plays as where he had previously been just a supporting player. He would continue to be compared, often unfavorably, to his father and his brother Edwin, and by general agreement, did not match their talents, but by the 1862–1863 season John Wilkes Booth had become a star in his own right.[8]

Performing his own stunts, including making great leaps and falls as well as fighting with swords and knives, could be dangerous. He suffered bruises and a serious knife wound. On October 12, 1860, Booth was accidentally shot, by his manager, Matthew W. Canning (1830–1890) of Philadelphia, who handled Booth's career from 1860 to 1863. Canning told his wife that the wound was serious and left the actor scarred. In February, 1861, Booth fell upon his knife and suffered a wound that immobilized his right arm for a time. He suffered other wounds, not in the line of duty. Actress Henrietta Irving, in a fit of jealousy, tried to stab him, the knife leaving a scar on his arm. A wound on his neck, the result of the removal of a tumor, was opened again and did not heal properly, leaving a scar which was used to identify his remains at his autopsy. Other actors occasionally suffered injury when performing with John Wilkes, especially during swordfight scenes.[9]

The season of 1862–1863 saw John Wilkes performing in Lexington and Louisville, Cincinnati, Chicago, St. Louis, Boston, Philadelphia and Cleveland. He appeared in Washington, DC, for the first time on April 11, 1863, as Richard in *Richard III*, at the National Theatre. He performed again on April 13–18 at the same theatre, in a different play each night. Moving to the Washington Theatre on April 27, he appeared there through May 9, almost every night, again in a different role each night. The following season, 1863–1864, was another busy one for John Wilkes. He was in demand and traveled widely, from Boston, Providence, Hartford, Brooklyn and New Haven to Washington, Cleveland, St. Louis, Louisville, Nashville, Cincinnati, New Orleans, and back to Boston again. Appearing at the new Ford's Theatre on November 9, 1863, playing Raphael in The Marble Heart, he appeared before President Abraham Lincoln, who occupied boxes 7 and 8. When Lincoln sent word he wanted to meet the actor and congratulate him on his performance, John Wilkes refused.[10]

John Wilkes Booth had many friends and was highly regarded as a man as well as an actor. Anne Hartley Gilbert (1821–1904), an actress, said of him, "The most perfect Romeo, the finest I ever saw, was ... Wilkes Booth. He was very handsome, most lovable and lovely. He was eccentric in some ways, and he had the family failings [meaning a touch of insanity], but he also had a simple, direct and charming nature. The love and sympathy between him and his mother were very close, very strong."[11] Another actress friend, Clara Morris (1848–1925), described his appearance. "His coloring was unusual—the ivory pallor of his skin, the inky blackness of his densely thick hair, the heavy lids of his glowing eyes were all oriental, and they gave a touch of mystery to his face when it fell into gravity—but there was generally a flash of white teeth, behind his silky moustache, and a laugh in his eyes."[12] Joseph Hazelton (1853–1936), only a boy at the time of the assassination, had a chance to meet and observe John Wilkes, and wrote of him years later: "He was not without his vanities, his artificialities, and his petty foibles, but he was intensely human.... He would stop on his way in or out of the theatre in the evenings to speak with me, or if we chanced to meet upon the street.... I do not recall that he was either popular or unpopular with the players at Ford's. He and they were of the same mold, but his intimacies were reserved for the stage crew, a few truckmen, and a mechanic or two from other walks of life."[13]

Much has been written about Booth's motives for the assassination, including some rather far fetched ideas. It is impossible for anyone today to truly understand the crime without a knowledge of its context. The Civil War, which had been raging for four years, had aroused strong passions on both sides. It was much more than a dispute over slavery. The North and the South had developed very differently, and each was concerned it would be politically dominated by the other. The South was a land of agriculture, with crops such as tobacco, sugar, and cotton, requiring a large labor force. The North, though also having much agriculture, was increasingly becoming dominant in manufacturing and trade, interests that conflicted with the protection-minded South. A long-standing and sincere disagreement about the nature of the American Union existed, with Southerners believing that the states were supreme and had the right to withdraw from the Union, since they had voluntarily entered into it. Contrary to that idea was the belief that, once established, the federal government was supreme over the states, an idea that was championed by Abraham Lincoln.

Not all Southerners wanted secession. Many, such as Alexander Hamilton Stephens (1812–1883) of Georgia and Robert E. Lee of Virginia, initially opposed it. Some Southerners, such as Andrew Johnson of Tennessee, were so opposed to secession that they went north and stayed with the Union. Some Northerners opposed a long and violent war to keep the South in the Union. Clement Laird Vallandigham, an Ohio congressman, actively supported the Confederate cause, while others, such as newspaperman Horace Greeley, though supporters of the Union, felt that the war was too bitter and costly and sought peace rather than victory, a position at odds with the Lincoln administration.

John Wilkes Booth was a Marylander, a state torn between the two sides, both geographically and philosophically. Marylanders fought as soldiers in both the Northern and Southern armies. Booth, though, was never in doubt about where his loyalties lay. Contrary to many of his friends and even to his own family, he supported the South. "I have ever held the South were right," he wrote. "The very nomination of Abraham Lincoln four years ago, spoke plainly — war, war upon Southern rights and institutions. His election proved it." "He [Lincoln] is made the tool of the North, to crush out, or try to crush out slavery by robbery, rapine, slaughter and bought armies." Booth's words could have been copied from anti-administration editorials and tracts, Northern as often as Southern, but his sentiments were real and sincerely held.[14]

Booth appeared on Northern stages much more often than Southern, though that was due to the fact that far more money could be made in the North. Although he talked about it, he never enlisted in the Confederate forces to fight for the South. While Booth did not wear a rebel uniform, his eagerness for the success of the Southern cause led him to undertake missions for the South. He told his sister that he was a smuggler of quinine, a drug needed to treat malaria. After the assassination, it was widely believed in the North that Booth and his compatriots were active agents of the South, and that Southern leaders, including Confederate President Jefferson Davis, were the real brains behind the assassination. Denied for decades, in recent years this idea has been revived, and a closer look has been taken at the many clues pointing to Confederate involvement.[15]

By the end of the 1863–1864 season, as Booth became more and more involved in his kidnap plot, his acting appearances dwindled to only a handful in the 1864–1865 season.

National Hotel, Washington, D. C.

National Hotel. One of the major Washington, DC, hotels in Lincoln's day, the National was a favorite of John Wilkes Booth. Clues to his conspiracy were found in his room there (courtesy of Surratt House Museum/MNCPPC).

He performed for the first and only time on stage with his brothers, Junius, Jr. (1821–1883), and Edwin, in *Julius Caesar* at the Winter Garden Theatre in New York City, on November 25, 1864, with John Wilkes taking the part of Marc Antony. It is significant that Booth appeared in this play, dealing with the assassination of a ruler, during the period he was planning the kidnapping of Lincoln, but there is no support for the idea that Booth was obsessed with the play and that it played a part in motivating him to commit his crime. This was the only recorded time when he appeared in a complete performance of *Julius Caesar*, and he had no part in selecting this particular play for this performance.

His last two performances were in Washington, DC, on January 29, 1865, at the National Theatre, as Romeo in *Romeo and Juliet*, and on March 18 at Ford's Theatre, as Pescara in *The Apostate*. After having boasted that his income was as high as

Booth brothers on stage. The only occasion when the three acting Booth brothers appeared together on the same stage, November 25, 1864, at New York's Winter Garden Theatre, in Shakespeare's *Julius Caesar*. Left to right, they are John Wilkes, Edwin, and Junius Brutus, Jr. (Library of Congress).

$20,000 the previous season, John Wilkes must have made very little in his short final season. His New York performance with his brothers was a benefit to raise money for a statue of Shakespeare, and his investments in Pennsylvania oil fields consumed $6,000 without earning anything. His money in the last months of his life appears to have come from his association with the Confederate Secret Service.[16]

"Kidnap President Lincoln! I said. I confess that I stood aghast at the proposition ... I was amazed — thunderstruck — and in fact, I might also say, frightened at the unparalleled audacity of this scheme." This is how John H. Surratt, Jr., described his initial reaction to John Wilkes Booth's plan to seize the president of the United States, spirit him away into rebel territory, and hold him for the exchange of Confederate prisoners of war.[17] How such a plan might work was recalled by another Booth conspirator, Samuel B. Arnold. "Often Abraham Lincoln, attended by no one except his carriage driver, visited the hospital over the Anacostia bridge. He [Booth] proposed to intercept him on one of these visits, take him, coachman and all, drive through the lower counties of Maryland, place him in a boat, cross the Potomac to Virginia and thence convey him to Richmond."[18]

In a deposition taken in February 1866, John H. Patten stated that he had had a conversation with Confederate President Jefferson Davis in July 1863, in which Davis said, "he did not wish that the life of Lincoln should be taken unless absolutely necessary; that if he should be brought a prisoner alive it would serve the country equally well and perhaps better than to kill him.... Davis said we should be furnished through General [John Henry] Winder [1800–1865] with all the funds necessary." Patten and a friend named Lamar collected money from Winder and engaged men for the kidnap attempt. After about two weeks, "A man named McCulloh, who had been engaged by Lamar to aid in the enterprise, had been arrested for disclosing the plot and sent to Castle Thunder" (the Confederate prison in Richmond, used for political prisoners). Urging that the kidnappers act immediately, so as not to be thwarted by Union spies, "Mr. Davis then said, 'Gentlemen, you will not misunderstand your instructions; it is my wish that you capture and bring Mr. Lincoln within our lines without harming a hair of his head, if possible; but if after making the capture you find there is danger of his being retaken, you will take care that he does not return to Washington alive.... Remember that he is your enemy and Commander-in-Chief of the Northern armies, and that you have the right, and that it is your duty, to cut him down the same as any other officer or soldier belonging to those armies.'" Patten said that by that time the conspiracy had fallen through and its members scattered.

Patten's statement could be pure fabrication. Although held in custody for two years after the war, Jefferson Davis was never prosecuted. Some of the testimony at the trial of the conspirators was determined to be false, without foundation or unproven. Patten did not testify at the trial, and his statement is dated after the trial had ended.[19]

Booth's kidnap plan got under way "about the latter part of August or the first part of September, 1864," according to Samuel Arnold. Booth met with Arnold and Michael O'Laughlen in Baltimore to explain to them how it would be possible. Booth wanted to capture Lincoln in a theatre. "First I [Arnold] was to rush in the box and seize the President whilst [George A.] Atzerodt ... and J. Wilkes Booth were to handcuff him and lower him on the stage whilst — Mosby [Lewis T. Powell, 1844–1865] was to catch him and hold him until we all got down. Surrat [sic] and unknown to be on the other side of bridge to facilitate escape, afterward changed to Mosby and Booth to catch him in box throw him down to me on stage. O'Laughlin [sic] and unknown to put gas out."[20]

As they thought about it, this plan did not seem feasible to Arnold and O'Laughlen. A heated argument ensued, with violent threats made by both sides. While Arnold and O'Laughlen considered pulling out of the conspiracy, Booth found out that Lincoln was to attend a performance at Campbell Hospital on Seventh Street, close to the Soldiers Home. On March 17, 1865, the conspirators had a rendezvous at a restaurant near the hospital. Present were Booth, Atzerodt, Powell, and Surratt. David Herold had been sent down to Surrattsville to stash arms and equipment at the Surratt tavern. While his fellow conspirators waited, Booth went to the hospital, where he met fellow actor E. L. Davenport, who told him that Lincoln would not be coming. Booth and his gang returned to Washington, with Surratt, Powell, and Booth meeting at Mrs. Mary Surratt's (1823–1865) boarding house, where boarder Louis J. Weichmann (1842–1902) observed them "much excited." "At a signal from Booth the three men went upstairs into the little back attic where Payne [Powell] slept, and must have remained there, I judge, about thirty minutes. Then they left the house without saying a word to me."[21]

Rumors of rebel kidnap plots abounded by 1864. Secretary of War Edwin M. Stanton and his feared chief detective, Colonel Lafayette C. Baker, were well aware of these rumors and did what they could to improve Presidential security. In his "Sam" letter, Arnold wrote to Booth on March 27, 1865, "You know full well that the G ––– t [government] suspicions something is going on there; therefore the undertaking [kidnap plot] is becoming more complicated." Louis Weichmann had informed upon the Surratts to a coworker, Captain Daniel H. L. Gleason (1841–1917). "I even said something about capture to Mr. Gleason, and asked him if he thought such a thing could be effected … Gleason and I talked over the matter a good deal; he told me to keep a watch on them [Booth's conspirators, who sometimes met at Mrs. Surratt's house] and if anything again occurred of a serious nature we would report it at once to the Secretary of War." But, according to Weichmann, nothing happened subsequently to bolster his suspicions. Gleason may not have believed Weichmann, or he may even have felt some suspicion toward him. In a letter to Weichmann dated November 23, 1865, Gleason told him, "When I last saw you my feelings were anything but true, friendly ones, as you must know, but the course you pursued, the testimony you gave, which I assure you was critically read by me, has a long time since completely changed my opinion, and I beg your pardon for all unjust suspicions which I have ever entertained toward you."[22]

We shall see how Booth's plan to kidnap Lincoln was transformed into a plot to assassinate the president, and how that decision affected all concerned, including subsequent generations.

9. Conspiracy

> If there was any other man at the head of the government ... the revolution would immediately cease so far as the South is concerned.
>
> Dr. Samuel A. Mudd[1]

John Wilkes Booth's conspiracy began as a plan to kidnap the president, not assassinate him. The conspirators he recruited all joined him toward that end. Some of them confessed that they had conspired with Booth only to kidnap Lincoln, and denied any share of guilt for his murder. This argument made little impression on the military commission that tried those accused of conspiring with Booth.

Eight defendants were tried at the conspiracy trial in May and June 1865. they were Samuel Bland Arnold, George Andrew Atzerodt, David Edgar Herold, Samuel Alexander Mudd, Michael O'Laughlen, Lewis Thornton Powell, Edman Spangler, and Mary Elizabeth Surratt. One other conspirator, John Harrison Surratt, Jr., was tried separately in 1867.

Samuel Bland Arnold was born in Georgetown, DC, on September 6, 1834. Arnold went to school at Georgetown College, now Georgetown University, until his family moved to Baltimore. He met Booth at St. Timothy Hall in Catonsville, Maryland, where they were students. In 1852, Arnold's father had to be called in when young Sam participated with Booth in an armed standoff with school authorities. Later described as "a restless and wayward youth, inclined to bad associations," Arnold joined other young men from the Baltimore area heading south to serve in the Confederate army. He served in Company C, First

Samuel Arnold. The only one of the Booth conspirators to have left a lengthy written account, Samuel Arnold spent four years at Fort Jefferson for his part in the conspiracy (Library of Congress).

Maryland Infantry, receiving a disability discharge. Returning home by early 1864, Arnold drifted between the homes of his parents in Baltimore and his brother William Stockton Arnold (1845–?) in Hookstown, Maryland. He was without employment when word came that his old friend Booth wanted to see him.[2]

Meeting with Booth at Barnum's Hotel in Baltimore, Arnold and Michael O'Laughlen became recruits in Booth's scheme to capture President Lincoln, carry him off to the South and demand to exchange him for thousands of Confederate prisoners in northern P.O.W. camps. When Booth again met Arnold in late 1864, he had him take charge of numerous weapons.

Telling his parents he was in the oil business with Booth, Arnold went to Washington with O'Laughlen around the beginning of January 1865. The two men stayed at the Lichau House on Pennsylvania Avenue, making frequent trips back to Baltimore, where Arnold stayed with his parents. One of Booth's horses was put in Arnold's name to avoid questions about why Booth had more than one horse.[3]

Arnold's part in the conspiracy came to a head in a meeting with Booth and other conspirators at Gautier's Restaurant in Washington on March 15, 1865. Arnold later wrote that this was the first time he met George A. Atzerodt, Lewis T. Powell, and David E. Herold. Booth and Powell would seize Lincoln in the theatre box, Arnold helping them as they lowered the president to the stage. Herold was to turn off the gas lighting. Arnold objected that not only was the plan impractical, in his view, but also unnecessary, as prisoner of war exchanging had been resumed. As they argued, Booth threatened to shoot Arnold, who responded, "Two could play at that game." Both men cooled down, and Arnold was to have participated in the attempt by the Booth conspirators to stop Lincoln's carriage on March 17, an attempt that could not be carried out because Lincoln changed his plans.[4] Giving up the conspiracy after this, Arnold returned to his parents' home, where he continued to look for employment. It was at this point that he wrote the letter now known as the "Sam" letter.

Dated March 27, 1865, the letter expressed Arnold's misgivings about the kidnap conspiracy. The importance of this letter is obvious for the government's case against Arnold. In the letter, Arnold acknowledged his membership in the conspiracy with Booth, and also mentioned "Mike" (Michael O'Laughlen), likewise implicating him.

But beyond these obvious points, Arnold made two statements in the letter that are highly intriguing in their implications. Referring to Booth's request that he rejoin the conspiracy and come back to Washington (Arnold had returned to Baltimore), he says, "You know full well that the G———t suspicions something is going on there." "G———t" was a common abbreviation for government. Arnold seems to be referring to knowledge of the Booth plot by the authorities in Washington. If Booth and other conspirators believed that the government was aware of their plot, it would have been very dangerous for them to go ahead with it. But how would the government have known, and how would the conspirators have known that they knew? Was there a double agent in the conspiracy? Arnold does not explain this remark. Another passage reads, "Do not act rashly or in haste. I would prefer your first query. 'Go and see how it will be taken at R———d.'" This part is the most sensational in the letter, as it seems to suggest that Booth was, or planned to be, in touch with Confederate authorities. Much recent research has focused upon this possibility, which the government tried to prove at the trial of the conspirators. But did Arnold mean that? Arnold put the statement beginning "Go and see..." in quotation marks, and he preceded it with "your first query." This leaves us confused as to exactly who is suggesting to whom that he "go and see how it will be taken at R — — — d." Was Arnold quoting someone, and if so, was it Booth or someone else?

The letter was found in Booth's trunk in his room at the National Hotel in Washington. It was considered a prime piece of evidence and was introduced as such at the trial of the conspirators. The intriguing questions it raised were not dealt with either by the prosecutors or the defense attorneys, nor have historians delved very deeply into these questions since 1865.[5]

Meeting with Booth for the last time on March 31, Arnold was told that the kidnap plan had been abandoned. On April 2, Arnold began work for John W. Wharton, who had a store at Old Point Comfort, Hampton Roads, Virginia. Samuel Arnold was arrested April 17, 1865, at Wharton's store.[6]

Johann Heinrich Atzerodt (1800–?), a blacksmith and maker of edged weapons, and his wife Victore Friedrike Hahn Atzerodt (1805–?) were living in the little town of Dorna, in the small state of Thuringia, part of the German confederation, when, at 5:30 in the morning of June 12, 1835, their fourth child, and second son, was born. They named him Georg Andreas Atzerodt. Johann had learned his trade from his father, but business was poor, requiring him to move about in search of work. The family resided in Dorna from 1830 to 1839, then moved to Seebach. With five children born between 1826 and 1842, one of whom died in infancy, and with economic prospects being poor, the family left for America in 1844, part of a wave of German immigration in the nineteenth century that numbered in the hundreds of thousands.[7]

Following common practice of immigrants at that time, Atzerodt anglicized his name from Georg Andreas to George Andrew, while his brother Johann Ernest Christian Atzerodt (1830–?) became John C. The two brothers established a carriage repair business in Port Tobacco, Maryland, in the 1850s. John was better at repair work, and George would paint and varnish. After a while, John moved to Baltimore and married.

Becoming involved with a widow named Rose Wheeler (c.1830–?), George fathered a child by her but refused to marry the woman. She said she loved Atzerodt, though he was not the only man she entertained. From 1863 onward, Atzerodt suffered from "consumption," which usually meant tuberculosis, often fatal at that time.[8]

Port Tobacco, from 1658 to 1895 the county seat of Charles County, Maryland, is situated on the Potomac River south of Washington, DC, and became a convenient station between North and South. Once the

George A. Atzerodt. Speaking with a thick German accent, Atzerodt was also known as "Port Tobacco," after the town where he lived. His assignment was to kill Vice President Johnson. Only Atzerodt's lack of nerve saved Johnson's life (Library of Congress).

war began, Atzerodt found he could make money by helping the blockade runners and Confederate agents passing back and forth. His knowledge of the area, and his skill at handling boats, became valuable to the rebel cause.

In mid–January 1865, Confederate Secret Service agent Thomas Henry Harbin introduced Atzerodt to Booth conspirator John H. Surratt, Jr., who was looking for a boatman who could be trusted to ferry the conspirators across the Potomac with their captive, President Lincoln. Atzerodt was brought into the conspiracy. John Surratt purchased a boat from two of Atzerodt's neighbors near Port Tobacco, Richard Mitchell Smoot (1833–1906) and James Brawner (1835–1886). Atzerodt was to see that the boat was hidden and to make it ready on short notice.[9]

Atzerodt made several visits to Mrs. Surratt's house and even boarded there for a short while. As the residents had trouble pronouncing his name (AT-zer-ott), they usually referred to him as "Port Tobacco" or "Plug Tobacco." His coarse manners and heavy accent did not make him popular, and Mrs. Surratt evicted him from her house, claiming she found liquor in his room. When Atzerodt attended the meeting of Booth and his fellow conspirators at Gautier's Restaurant, his role was described as assisting Surratt in guiding the others in their escape, especially in crossing the Potomac River. Another variant of the plan had Atzerodt assisting Booth in the theatre box, handcuffing Lincoln and lowering him down onto the stage, where Powell would be waiting. On March 17, Atzerodt was one of the conspirators poised to capture Lincoln on his way to attend a play at Campbell Hospital, near the Soldiers Home. Booth told his helpers that the president had not attended, after all.[10]

Adam George Herold (1803–1864) and Mary Porter Herold (1810–1883) had ten children in all, but David Edgar was the only one of three boys to survive childhood. David was born June 16, 1842, at the family house at the corner of 8th and I Streets, SE, in Washington, DC. His father worked at the Washington Navy Yard, rising to the position of chief clerk during his service of over twenty years. Father and son frequently went hunting away from home for as long as a month and ranging southward into Virginia. Stories of David's early life describe him as lazy, frivolous, and trifling, but if those words are accurate, they do not seem to fit the young man who had a better than average start in life. After early schooling, David entered Georgetown College in the fall of 1855. He studied to be a pharmacist, leaving Georgetown in April 1858, then going to work for a Dr. Bates at the corner of 7th and I Streets, SE, near the family home. David next found employment at William S. Thompson's drug store at Pennsylvania Avenue and 15th Street, only a block from the White House. David worked for Thompson until October 1863, then became an employee of Dr. Francis S. Walsh at Walsh's drug store, 608 8th St., SE, and lived at Walsh's house, in the neighborhood of the Herold family home.[11]

Herold's behavior began to change around the time he became acquainted with Booth. The frivolity mentioned by those who knew him became more noticeable. He spent more time in the woods and pathways leading south. One doctor later testified that he heard Herold might mislabel a prescription as a joke. Adam Herold seems also to have thought of his son as unreliable, for his will forbade David a role in settling the estate, "under no circumstances."[12]

By the time Samuel Arnold became involved in Booth's kidnap scheme, Herold was already a member of the inner circle. According to Arnold, he and O'Laughlen were met by Herold as they were leaving Rullman's Hotel on Pennsylvania Avenue late in the evening of March 15, 1865. Herold took both men to Gautier's Restaurant nearby. There Booth and several of the other conspirators discussed their plans. Arnold later wrote that Herold was to extinguish the gas lights in the theatre while Booth and Lewis Powell would seize the president, bind him and lower him to the stage, where Arnold would help to rush the captive out the rear door. Objections to the feasibility of the plan led to a new idea — to capture Lincoln as he rode out to the Soldiers Home or one of the hospitals around the edges of Washington. Herold was involved in hiding two carbines, a box of ammunition, length of rope, and a monkey wrench in the Surratt Tavern in Surratsville, Maryland. In between these dangerous escapades, Herold lived at home with his mother and sisters, doing chores such as collecting rent for his mother's properties.[13]

Herold may have been with Booth and Powell the evening of April 11, when they stood in front of the White House listening to Lincoln's speech. Booth urged Powell to try to shoot the president then and there, and swore before his two partners, "That will be the last speech he ever makes!"[14]

David E. Herold. Herold played the fool at his trial, but it appears that he was far from the childlike tool of Booth that he has been portrayed as being. Of all the conspirators in Booth's plot, Herold was the one who was with him at the end (Library of Congress).

Michael O'Laughlen was born in Baltimore, Maryland, in 1840. His family lived at 57 N. Exeter Street, across from the Booth home. After attending school in Baltimore, Michael learned the trade of making ornamental plaster decoration. Around 1857, Michael's brother William joined the Knights of the Golden Circle, a secret organization sympathetic to the South. It is likely that Michael also joined the Knights. When the war began, Michael served briefly in the Confederate army, returning to Baltimore in the summer of 1862. According to a friend, "he came home somewhat sick." After returning home, Michael took the oath of allegiance to the Union. For about a year he worked with his brother in the produce and feed business in Washington. When William closed the Washington store and returned to Baltimore, Michael stayed on in the capital taking orders and collecting debts for his brother, though he also made frequent trips back to Baltimore.[15]

When O'Laughlen joined Booth's conspiracy is uncertain. Samuel Arnold said that he was brought into the plot in "the latter part of 1864." Booth met with Arnold and O'Laughlen at Barnum's Hotel in Baltimore on August 9, 1864. Arnold suggested that O'Laughlen had already been enlisted for the kidnap plot prior to this meeting, and that he and O'Laughlen had been drinking when they agreed to Booth's plot. Arnold also stated that at that early date he and O'Laughlen were the only other members of Booth's conspiracy. Booth told his two old friends that they would capture Abraham Lincoln some time before the election in early November. Although this timetable proved impossible, Arnold and O'Laughlen remained active participants in Booth's conspiracy over the following months. In January 1865, Booth asked Arnold and O'Laughlen to help him transport equipment and weapons to Washington. He also told them about his oil dealings, and how that would be used as a cover for their plot. By February 10, Arnold and O'Laughlen were in Washington, staying at 420 D Street. Their landlady said the two told her they were in the oil business. Booth was a frequent visitor.[16]

Although Booth told them he was enlisting others in the plot, Arnold and O'Laughlen did not meet most of them until the meeting at Gautier's Restaurant on March 15. O'Laughlen joined Arnold in dissent over the feasibility of the plan. The argument with Booth was settled peacefully, but it led to Arnold and O'Laughlen both assuming an inactive role. Booth still hoped to have their participation, and he sent messages to them, but both men were now highly skeptical and probably had already decided to take no further active part in Booth's schemes. O'Laughlen

Michael O'Laughlen. An old school friend of Booth's from Baltimore, O'Laughlen paid the ultimate price for his friendship. Sentenced to life at Fort Jefferson, he died in the yellow fever epidemic (Library of Congress).

returned to Baltimore, living with his brother-in-law, P. H. Maulsby, at 57 North Exeter Street.[17]

On April 13, O'Laughlen went to Washington in company with three companions, Bernard J. Early, Edward Murphy (a plumber), and James B. Henderson (a navy lieutenant). O'Laughlen left Early waiting as he went into the National Hotel, returning to his companion after about five minutes. Rejoining Henderson, the four men made the rounds at several eating and drinking places. Joined by another friend, Daniel Loughran, they stayed up until about two A.M. The following day, April 14, the friends resumed their amusements. Murphy later testified that O'Laughlen was in good spirits all the time, not anxious or worried. When news of the assassination reached them, "O'Laughlen seemed surprised, and said he had been in Booth's company very often, and people might think he had something to do with it."[18]

Although he used several aliases (such as Payne, Paine, Mosby, and Wood), the real name of the big, silent conspirator was Lewis Thornton Powell. Born April 22, 1844, in Alabama, he was the youngest son of a Baptist minister. Following financial difficulties, the Powells moved to Florida. Although Lewis showed a winning personality to family and friends, he seems to have undergone a hardening as a result of the war. He saw action in the Confederate army at Yorktown, Seven Pines, Gaines Mill, Second Manassas, Antietam, Fredericksburg, and Gettysburg, where, as a member of the 2nd Florida Brigade, he was wounded in the right wrist and taken prisoner on July 2, 1863. Recovering, he served as a hospital orderly first at Gettysburg, then at Baltimore. Making his way through the lines, he joined John Singleton Mosby's Rangers in late 1863. Leaving Mosby's men around the beginning of 1865, he made his way back to Baltimore.[19]

There is a story that Powell had met John Wilkes Booth as early as 1861, and that Booth happened to notice him four years later as they passed on a Baltimore street. It is far more likely that Powell was recruited for the position of aide to Booth by Booth's Confederate collaborators. David Preston Parr (1819–1900), who ran a china shop in Baltimore, was active as an

Lewis T. Powell. Big and silent, Powell was perhaps the most deeply involved of all the Booth conspirators. His attack on the Seward household left five men wounded, and nearly killed the secretary of state and his son (Library of Congress).

agent of the Confederate Secret Service. Parr, in contact with Powell, probably introduced him to John Surratt. Powell used Parr's china shop as a meeting place and conferred several times with Surratt in early 1865. The Confederate underground may also have put Powell in touch with the Branson family, who ran a boarding house in Baltimore, at 16 North Eutaw Street. The Branson sisters, Mary (1835–?) and Margaret (1832–?), were known to the authorities as "notorious rebels." Powell may have had a romantic interest in Mary Branson. He stayed at the Bransons' house upon his return to Baltimore. When Powell was arrested for assaulting a maid at the Branson house, he gave the authorities the impression he was very limited intellectually, though an officer interrogating him suspected he was a Confederate spy. Upon his release, Powell became a trusted and important part of Booth's scheme to capture, and later to kill, President Lincoln.

Although Powell would be described, both at the time and later, as a big, inarticulate brute, it appears that Booth told him more of his plans than any of the other accomplices. In one of his few final statements, Powell also suggested that he was more closely involved with Booth than any of the others.[20]

Samuel Alexander Mudd was born December 21, 1833, of a family that had already been in America for two centuries. Young Sam went to college in Frederick, Maryland, and studied Latin and Greek at Georgetown College in the District of Columbia. His studies also included music, and soon he was proficient on the piano, flute and violin. After a year and a half of medical schooling, at the University of Maryland in Baltimore, he married his childhood sweetheart, Sarah Frances Dyer (1835–1911), on November 26, 1857. They settled on two hundred acres of farmland near Beantown, Maryland, which Sam's father had given them. As the young doctor's practice was not very rewarding in the rural back country of southern Maryland, the farm became their main source of income.[21]

Booth visited southern Maryland in November 1864, telling people he was looking for horses to buy. Frances Mudd said that this was the only time he visited with the Mudds prior to the assassination. Booth talked with Dr. Mudd one afternoon, staying fairly late into the evening, but didn't stay over. He had a bed for the night at a neighbor's, Dr. William Queen (1789–1868). He was back at Mudd's for breakfast the next morning, bought a horse, then left.[22]

Dr. Samuel A. Mudd. Because of his education and obvious "gentlemanly" nature, Dr. Mudd was treated less harshly than the others. He did not have to wear heavy chains and stiff shackles at the trial, but harsh punishment followed his escape attempt from Fort Jefferson (Library of Congress).

Two days before Christmas in 1864, Louis Weichmann said he and his friend John H. Surratt, Jr., were walking down a Washington, DC, street when they heard Surratt's name being called. Weichmann identified the man calling as Dr. Mudd, who said he wanted to introduce Surratt to his friend, "Mr. Boone." Boone invited the other three to have a drink with him in his room at the National Hotel. According to Weichmann, Mudd asked Boone out into the hallway and conversed with him for several minutes. Then they asked Surratt to join them. When they returned to the room they apologized for leaving Weichmann by himself for so long. They then continued conversing in low tones just out of Weichmann's hearing. Boone took an envelope from his pocket and drew lines on it, while Mudd and Surratt studied it carefully. They remained together for some time. Dr. Mudd, in parting company, said he was returning home the next day. When Weichmann and Surratt were alone Surratt told Weichmann that the man they had called "Boone" was actually John Wilkes Booth.[23]

Edman Spangler was tried and convicted, along with seven others, but his shorter sentence can be taken as an acknowledgment by the government that the case against him was much weaker than that of the others.

Edman Spangler. Even the military court that tried Spangler must have had doubts about the extent of his involvement with Booth's conspiracy, for they gave him the lightest sentence, six years at hard labor (Library of Congress).

Spangler, born in York County, Pennsylvania, on August 10, 1825, had learned the carpenter's trade. He became acquainted with the Booth family while still a child. In 1854 Spangler worked on the Booth family home, Tudor Hall, in Bel Air, Maryland. Beginning in 1853 Spangler worked in Baltimore's Holiday Street Theatre and the Front Street Theatre, with theatre manager John T. Ford (1829–1894). When Ford opened a theatre in Washington, Spangler went to work there. Much of his leisure time was spent fishing for crabs.[24]

On April 14, 1865, Spangler was busy at Ford's Theatre. Special decorations had to be put up, especially around the front of boxes 7 and 8, where President and Mrs. Lincoln and their guests would be sitting that night. Spangler was very familiar with Ford's Theatre, sleeping there each night. He took his meals at the boarding house of his fellow theatre employee, Jacob Ritterspaugh (1840–1926): Mrs. Scott's, at Seventh and G Streets. Spangler kept a valise at the boarding house as well. During the performance, Spangler was at the back of the stage, near the door to the alley. Ritterspaugh's testimony at the trial of the conspirators was most damaging to Spangler, for he described how, after Booth ran out, Spangler slapped Ritterspaugh's face, telling him, "Don't say which way he went." When Ritterspaugh demanded an explanation, Spangler replied, "For God's sake, shut up."[25]

John Harrison Surratt, Jr., born April 13, 1844, and his brother Isaac (1841–1907) were sent to school at St. Thomas Academy at Bel Alton, Maryland, in 1855. The school was run by Father Bernardin F. Wiget (1821–1883), and had been chosen by John's mother, Mary Surratt, with the low boarding cost in mind. In 1859, fifteen-year-old John entered the preparatory college of St. Charles Borromeo in Howard County, Maryland. Here he met another new student, Louis J. Weichmann.[26]

Weichmann described John, Jr., as "tall, erect, slender, and boyish, with a very prominent forehead and receding eyes. His nose was sharp, thin, and aquiline; his face bore an unusually keen and shrewd expression.... He was neatly dressed, and I remember he provoked the risibilities of the older students by wearing a white necktie." The students were allowed almost no contact with the outside world, where momentous events were pushing the nation toward civil war.[27]

With the death of his father, and his brother's entry into the Confederate army, John had come home by the fall of 1862 and assumed his father's duties as postmaster, also helping keep the family's tavern going.

John Surratt was well placed to become involved in the activities of the Confederates. Even before his father's death, the tavern at Surrattsville was a regular stop for Southern spies traveling between Washington and Richmond, and John was soon involved as a carrier of dispatches for the Confederate Signal and Secret Service. Confederate spies such as Thomas Nelson Conrad became regular visitors at the Surratt Tavern and got to know the family well. John enjoyed his dispatch riding activities, easily evading Union forces with the help of pro–South sympathizers.

The Surratt family was increasingly in financial difficulties. Much of their land had to be sold. With interest accumulating, on top of the death of her husband and departure of her older son for war service, Mrs. Surratt could not seem to get anywhere. John, Jr., even lost his position as postmaster on November 17, 1863, dismissed because of "disloyalty." There was one hope for the family. Among his many deals, John, Sr., had acquired a house in Washington. His widow decided to lease the tavern, move the family to the H Street house and earn badly needed money by renting its extra rooms. By the end of 1864 the move was complete.[28]

It is possible that John Wilkes Booth and John H. Surratt, Jr., were brought together by Confederate secret agent Thomas H. Harbin. Harbin knew Surratt through their clandestine work, and Harbin met with Booth at the Bryantown, Maryland, tavern in late December 1864. He may have given Surratt's name to Booth as someone who knew the route through southern Maryland and on to Richmond.[29]

John Surratt later said he was at first suspicious of Booth and his kidnap plot. Soon Surratt and Booth were visiting southern Maryland together, undoubtedly scouting their escape route. In January, Surratt bought three boats from a Charles County, Maryland, farmer, Richard M. Smoot, paying him $125, money he likely obtained from Booth. The boats were large enough to hold fifteen people each, and Surratt concealed them at Kings Creek.

Booth was by now a regular visitor at the Surratt boarding house, and there may have been a kidnap attempt planned around mid-January, which came to nothing. There is no doubt that Surratt was deeply involved in Booth's conspiracy to kidnap Lincoln and exchange him for Confederate prisoners held in Northern P.O.W. camps. Samuel Arnold stated that "most of his [Booth's] time was spent with him [Surratt]," and described Surratt's familiarity with the proposed escape route. Atzerodt said Surratt and Herold had recruited him for the conspiracy.[30]

Mary E. Surratt. Controversy still surrounds the conviction of Mrs. Surratt. Was she the centerpiece of the conspiracy or an innocent woman, as she claimed? She became the first woman to be executed by the United States government (courtesy of Surratt House Museum/MNCPPC).

John M. Lloyd, who had rented Mrs. Surratt's tavern, was also involved, probably through John Surratt. Also showing up at Mrs. Surratt's house in February and March 1865 were two known Confederate agents, Sarah Antoinette Slater (1843–c.1880) and Augustus Spencer Howell (1837–1869).[31]

On Wednesday, March 15, 1865, Weichmann returned to his room at the Surratt house to find Powell and John Surratt together. "I beheld [them] seated on a bed surrounded by brand new spurs, bowie knives, and revolvers. The moment the door was opened they almost unconsciously threw out their hands as if trying to conceal the articles." That evening, Surratt and Powell went to Ford's Theatre, in company with Surratt house boarders Honora Fitzpatrick (1846–1896) and Apollonia Dean (1855–1894). Booth had given them tickets. They occupied the box President Lincoln would have on the fateful night a month later. While the play was on, Booth came in the box and Surratt and Powell spoke with him for several minutes, standing at the box door so the young girls would not hear them.[32]

As Booth's gang began fragmenting, John Surratt returned to his espionage activities.

On March 24, Sarah Slater arrived at Mrs. Surratt's house, bringing Confederate dispatches for Richmond. The following day John accompanied his mother and Mrs. Slater, intending to go only as far as the Surratt Tavern at Surrattsville, where Slater would join Augustus Howell for the trip to Richmond. When they arrived at Surrattsville they found that Union troops had raided the area the night before and Howell had been arrested. John offered to escort Mrs. Slater and, after a stopover at Brawner's Hotel in Port Tobacco, Maryland, they headed on to Richmond, arriving on March 29. John registered at the Spotswood Hotel, using the alias "John Sherman." At the hotel Surratt was informed that the Confederate secretary of state, Judah P. Benjamin, wanted to see him. "He asked me if I would carry some dispatches to Canada for him. I replied 'yes.' That evening he gave me the dispatches and $200 in gold with which to pay my way to Canada. I left Richmond on Saturday morning [April 1, again accompanying Mrs. Slater] ... and reached Washington the following Monday at 4 o'clock P.M., April 3rd, 1865." Surratt stated he learned that Union detectives knew about his trip and were looking for him. Eluding the detectives, he encountered one of the Booth conspirators on Seventh Street, and offered his opinion that now that Richmond had fallen (on April 2) the abduction plot should be abandoned. Surratt left the morning of April 4 with Mrs. Slater. They parted company in New York City, with John heading on to Montreal, Canada. Arriving there on April 6, he registered at the St. Lawrence Hall, using the alias "John Harrison." He gave Benjamin's dispatches to the new Confederate representative, General Edwin Gray Lee (1836–1870).[33]

John H. Surratt, Jr. Son of Mary and close confidant of Booth, Surratt was a known agent of the Confederate underground. He claimed innocence of the assassination plot, and he became the only one of Booth's conspirators to avoid prison or the gallows (Library of Congress).

Lee enlisted Surratt for a spy mission. At Elmira, New York, there was a large prisoner of war camp housing as many as 45,000 men. In hopes of organizing a mass break-out of Confederate prisoners, Lee wanted Surratt to go to Elmira, look over the prison and note how it was laid out and guarded. Surratt was in Elmira from April 13 to 15. Learning of the assassination of Lincoln on April 15, Surratt left for Canandaigua, New York. On Monday, April 17, he read the details of the assassination in the New York newspapers. There he discovered that he was suspected of being the attacker of Secretary of State William H. Seward and that there was a reward on his head. Dressing in clothing of the Canadian fashion, he managed to get across the border and arrived in Montreal on April 18.[34]

John Surratt's mother was born Mary Elizabeth Jenkins in 1823 on Calvert's Manor, Prince George's County, Maryland. She was the middle child of Archibald Jenkins (c.1780–1825) and Elizabeth Ann Webster (1794–1878), having an older and a younger brother. Her father died when she was only two, leaving an estate large enough to include eleven slaves.

Surratt House, Washington, DC. At her boarding house, Mrs. Surratt entertained such visitors as John Wilkes Booth and some of his fellow conspirators. The house still stands, though it is a Chinese restaurant today (Library of Congress).

9. Conspiracy

Although her parents were Protestants, young Mary was enrolled at a Catholic school in Alexandria, Virginia, around 1835. Converting to Catholicism, she began using the name Eugenia, after the saint, in place of her real middle name.

John Harrison Surratt, Sr. (c.1813–1862), married Mary Jenkins in 1840. Their children were Isaac Douglas Surratt, Elizabeth Susanna Surratt (1843–1904); called Anna, and John H. Surratt, Jr. Mary's husband worked for a time as a contractor on the Orange and Alexandria railroad. Richard Neale, a family friend who may have been related to John Surratt, provided the young family with land, eventually leaving John his property. Though John Surratt owned as much as four hundred acres, built a tavern in 1852, and became a leading citizen of his community, he piled up considerable debts, which would have a substantial impact upon his family.

By 1854, Surratt's tavern had become a polling place and post office. The village forming around it became known as Surrattsville (now named Clinton), Maryland. Because of her husband's drinking, Mary had to do most of the postal work. A transaction in 1853 traded some of the Surratt's Maryland land for property in Washington, DC, including a house, 541 (now 604) H Street, NW. For the next twelve years the Surratts rented out this house.[35]

The Civil War was to have disastrous consequences for the Surratt family. Like most of their neighbors in southern Maryland, they sided with the South. The older son, Isaac,

Surratt Tavern. Mrs. Surratt's home before moving to Washington, the tavern stands at a crossroads in southern Maryland, originally named Surrattsville. The tavern is still standing, and has been restored and is open to visitors (National Park Service).

left for Texas to join the Confederate army. On August 25, 1862, John H. Surratt, Sr., suddenly died. The slaves began running away and Mary became hard pressed to try to settle her husband's debts.[36]

In 1864 Mary decided to move to Washington and rent out the tavern at Surrattsville. The H Street house would serve both as a family residence and boarding house. Anna moved to the city on October 1, 1864, with Mary following in November, while John, Jr., stayed behind until December 1, when John Lloyd took over the tavern.[37]

It is probable that Mrs. Surratt's house was a Confederate "safe house," as her tavern had been. Booth met with his fellow conspirators at the house, but he and they also spent time talking with Mary. Mary later claimed that all such conversations were entirely innocent and that she had no particular interest in politics.[38]

Events that would later help to incriminate Mrs. Surratt included her son's storing weapons at the Surrattsville tavern and her own visit to Lewis Powell, who was staying at the Herndon House in Washington by late March 1865.

On the afternoon of April 14, 1865, Mrs. Surratt and Louis J. Weichmann left Washington to make the one-and-a-half-hour trip to Surrattsville. She claimed that she went there to discuss land business with a Mr. John Nothey. Failing to find Nothey, they had started back when John Lloyd stopped to talk with Mrs. Surratt. She stated after her arrest that Lloyd asked her if she had eaten, saying that he had fish and oysters. She denied saying anything about "shooting irons," and further denied knowing that any weapons were stored at the tavern. John Lloyd told a very different story. He said he met Mrs. Surratt on Tuesday, April 11, and on that occasion she asked him about the articles stored at the tavern. When he didn't understand her, "she came out plainer and asked me about the 'shooting irons.' ... She told me to get them out ready; that they would be wanted soon." He speculated that she seemed to want to hide her meaning from the others who might overhear them. Meeting her again on April 14, Lloyd said she again told him to have the "shooting irons" ready that night. Both Lloyd and Mrs. Surratt agreed their meeting on Friday was about five o'clock in the afternoon.[39]

It can be seen that Booth's conspiracy, while loosely organized, was real and included numerous members, and the claim that the rebel government in Richmond was involved was more than a mere possibility.

10. A Night of Horrors

> Assassination is not an American practice or habit, and one so vicious and so desperate cannot be engrafted into our political system.
>
> William H. Seward[1]

The presidential party arrived at Ford's Theatre at about 8:30 in the evening of April 14, 1865. The comedy *Our American Cousin* was already in progress. The party consisted of President Abraham Lincoln; Mrs. Mary Todd Lincoln; Colonel Henry Reed Rathbone (1837–1911); Rathbone's fiancée, Miss Clara Hamilton Harris (1834–1883); the president's footman, Charles Forbes (1835–1895); and the police guard, John Frederick Parker (1830–1890). Coachman Francis P. Burke (1827–1887) remained outside with the carriage. Following standard procedure, Parker had come ahead and was waiting at the theatre when the Lincolns arrived. The party, led by Ford's chief usher, James R. O'Bryon, mounted the stairs to the dress circle, one floor above the street entrance, and proceeded around and down the right to the door to boxes 7 and 8, which had been converted into one box for that evening.

The play was briefly interrupted to acknowledge the arrival of the distinguished guests, the orchestra playing "Hail to the Chief," and Lincoln giving a small bow, acknowledging the audience's applause, before settling into his seat. The brief excitement over, the play resumed. Parker, the police guard, apparently left about an hour later, taking a drink at the Star Saloon next door to the theatre with Burke the coachman and Forbes the footman. It thus appears that by the time Booth arrived, the president had been left unprotected.[2]

The box normally occupied by President Lincoln when he visited Ford's Theatre was actually two boxes, numbers 7 and 8, which could be separated by a movable partition. These were the upper two boxes on the right side as one faced the stage. Boxes 7 and 8 were entered through a small vestibule from the dress circle, or first balcony. Entering the door from the dress circle, one would find two doors, one on the left, opening into box 7, and the other on the right, at the end of the vestibule, leading to box 8.

Booth was seen in the theatre on the afternoon of the day of the assassination, and it has been assumed that he made the peephole in the door to box 7, as well as the niche in the wall of the vestibule into which a bar was fitted and wedged against the inside of the door from the dress circle. When this bar was in place the door was secured and could not be opened from the outside. Booth did make use of the bar, which Colonel Rathbone had to remove before anyone could enter the box, but, according to a Ford descendant, theatre employees made these holes in the wall and the box door to enhance the security of the box after the locks on the doors were broken, some time prior to April 14. The original door to box 7, with the peephole, has survived, and is now in the collection of the Lincoln Museum at Ford's

Ford's Theatre. The scene of the assassination, Ford's has been restored in modern times, and once again is a playhouse for live theatre. A museum in the basement tells the story of the events that made this building so famous (Library of Congress).

Theatre. The other door, the one at the end of the vestibule, opening into box 8, was most likely the door through which the occupants of the box entered.

The boxes were designed to hold two persons each, or a total of four if the partition was removed, but additional chairs to accommodate up to six in each box was possible, though that would have been unusually crowded. A box could be reserved for $10, but the reservation had to be made in advance, as the theatre was often crowded during the war years. Dark red figured wallpaper covered the walls, with yellow satin draperies and Nottingham lace curtains shielding the box's occupants from the view of most of the audience. The furniture on the fateful night consisted of two armchairs, six cane chairs, a sofa upholstered in velvet, and a high-backed upholstered rocking chair.

The double box was in the shape of a parallelogram. Entering the box through the door to box 8, the stage was to the left, with the theatergoers turning left to take their seats at the front of the box. A support column divided the front of the box into two parts. On the night of the assassination, President Lincoln sat on the left (as one faced the stage), with Mrs. Lincoln sitting beside him on his right. Clara Harris took an armchair on the right side, along the side wall, with Rathbone sitting on the sofa behind her.[3]

Booth was very familiar with the theatre and may have spent some time planning the crime that afternoon. He was also familiar with the play, and had chosen the precise moment to strike. In the third act, when only one actor would be on stage, and that actor would speak a line that would produce a hearty laugh from the audience — at that exact moment Booth would fire. The laughter would help to cover the noise of his pistol shot, and the nearly empty stage would enable him to escape by jumping down from the box and running out the theatre's back door.[4]

Arriving at the rear door of the theatre, Booth called to have Edman Spangler, one of the scene shifters back stage, hold his horse. Spangler, who was needed at his post inside, turned this duty over to young Joseph Burroughs, known by his nicknames "Peanut John" or "Peanuts." As the appointed time approached, Booth, after having a drink at the tavern next door, returned to the theatre. He carried two weapons, a derringer pistol and a bowie knife, concealed by his jacket. Booth made his way to the vestibule door, presented his card to Forbes, who was sitting in the dress circle just outside the box, and went in. In the vestibule that connected the box with the dress circle, Booth secured the door behind him with a portion of a wooden music stand wedged into a hole in the wall. Booth then opened the box door and entered.

In the darkness, Booth stepped behind the president, pointed his pistol at Lincoln's head, and fired. Lincoln slumped in his chair, prevented from falling on the floor by the quick action of Mrs. Lincoln, who put out her arms and held him up. Rathbone, who had not noticed Booth until the shot was fired, rose and struggled with the assassin. Booth dropped his pistol and pulled out his knife, thrusting it at Rathbone, who parried the blow, receiving a painful three-inch long gash in his upper left arm.[5]

Assassination. Booth fired his derringer from a distance of only about one foot. At that range there was little chance that his shot might not prove fatal (*Harper's Weekly*, April 29, 1865).

Climbing over the box rail, Booth jumped down onto the stage, a distance of about twelve feet. It is assumed that he broke his ankle in jumping, after catching his spur in one of the flags that draped the front of the box. It is possible, however, that the break occurred later, on the road, when his horse took a fall. Broken leg or not, he hurried across the stage, flashing his knife and shouting "Sic semper Tyrannis!"* While showing his face to the audience, some of whom recognized him. All of this took but seconds, and few in the audience were quick enough to know what was happening. James P. Ferguson (1828–1897), sitting in an orchestra seat near the stage, climbed up and began chasing Booth even before Rathbone and Miss Harris called out, "Stop that man!"

Crossing the stage, Booth pushed his way between actors Laura Keene (1826–1873) and William Jason Ferguson (1845–1930), who were standing in the wings opposite the president's box, just out of sight of the audience. They had been rehearsing the upcoming scene when they heard the shot and saw the assassin rush toward them, bloody knife in hand. Frozen in bewilderment and terror, they offered no resistance. Orchestra leader William S. Withers, Jr. (1836–1905), standing backstage in the passageway nearby, and likewise frozen in astonishment, was unable to get out of the way of the fleeing assassin. Booth took a few swipes at Withers with his knife, slashing his coat but not inflicting any serious injuries, as Withers dropped to the floor.

Reaching the rear door to the alleyway, Booth ran to his horse, which was still being tended by "Peanut John." Climbing into the saddle as the horse skittered about, Booth gave "Peanuts" a kick to get him out of the way before spurring his horse. Theatergoers, only seconds behind Booth, burst through the door too late to grab hold of horse and rider, and had to watch helplessly as the assassin raced up the alley and disappeared around the corner, headed for the street.[7]

At nearly the same time that Booth was shooting the president, Secretary of State William Henry Seward was attacked by a knife-wielding assassin, who inflicted serious wounds on the secretary and injured four other men who tried to stop him. Only luck saved Seward and the others from death. Soon it was revealed that the would-be assassin, Lewis Thornton Powell, was a member of the conspiracy headed by John Wilkes Booth. Investigators soon learned that another of Booth's fellow conspirators, George A. Atzerodt, had been assigned to kill Vice President Andrew Johnson that same night. Rumors quickly spread throughout Washington that all the leaders of the government had been marked for death, some versions even stating that the whole Cabinet was dead.[8]

---

*The Latin phrase is translated, "Thus ever to Tyrants!" The motto of the state of Virginia, in use since 1776, emphasizes the rebellious spirit of the American Revolution, with its resistance to the "tyrant," Britain's King George III (1738–1820). On the Virginia state seal, the goddess of virtue stands over the defeated body of tyranny, who is dressed as an ancient Roman, with a crown fallen from his head. Most accounts of the Lincoln assassination have Booth shouting this after jumping down from the box, before running off the stage, although in his diary, Booth stated that he spoke the words in the box, before he fired.

Booth knew the motto and associated it with the South, but also, as an actor, he was well acquainted with William Shakespeare's play Julius Caesar, during which in Act III, Scene 1, immediately after the conspirators assassinate Caesar, Cinna says, "Liberty! Freedom! Tyranny is dead!"—words very like the common translation. Booth had appeared in a performance of Julius Caesar in New York City on November 25, 1864, well after he had begun to plan his kidnap conspiracy.

At the trial of the conspirators, a card bearing the seal of Virginia, including the motto, was submitted in evidence (exhibit 52). This was one of several cards found at Mary Surratt's house, and belonged to her daughter Anna. Booth probably did not see it there, for Anna kept her pro-South souvenirs hidden, but it does show that representations of the Virginia seal were commonly available.[6]

10. A Night of Horrors

Booth's flight from the theatre. Jumping down from the box, Booth ran across the stage. Most witnesses agreed that he paused to shout something like "Sic semper Tyrannis!" (*Frank Leslie's Illustrated Newspaper*, May 20, 1865).

The Sewards' houseboy, William H. Bell (c.1846–?), was on duty when Powell rang the doorbell. Powell told Bell he had a package of medicine to deliver to Seward from one of the secretary's doctors. When the houseboy told him he had orders not to let anyone up, Powell replied that he had to instruct the secretary in how to take the medicine and he must see him. They argued in the hall, Powell slowly moving to the stairs.

Bell had reason to be suspicious of the messenger. Tall and powerfully built, "he looked very rough to me," Bell recalled later. Powell's heavy footsteps prompted Bell to ask him not to make so much noise. At the top of the stairs they met Frederick William Seward, the secretary's son, who had been serving as acting secretary of state while his father recovered from a serious accident, and had earlier that day attended a Cabinet meeting at the White House. Hearing the footsteps on the stairs, Frederick Seward came from his room out to the landing to see who it was. Lewis Powell stood before him.[9]

"He repeated two or three time that he must see Mr. Seward personally. As he seemed to have nothing else to say, he gave me the impression that he was rather dull or stupid. Finally I said, 'well, if you will not give me the message, go back and tell the doctor I refused to let you see Mr. Seward.'"[10] While her brother was disputing with the stranger on the landing, Frances Adeline "Fanny" Seward (1844–1866), who had been sitting up with nurse George Foster Robinson (1832–1907) in her father's room, went to the door to see what was going

William H. Seward. Seward was confined to bed, recovering from a carriage accident, when he was attacked by Lewis Powell. Seward's daughter Fanny was in the room with her father and witnessed the attack (Library of Congress).

on. Thinking the visitor might be important, might even be the president, she opened the door and looked out, stating to her brother, "Fred, father is awake now." Her brother gave her a look that she took to mean she shouldn't have opened the door. Powell now spoke directly to her. "Is the Secretary asleep?" She turned and looked back, then answered, "Almost." Her brother then quickly pulled the door shut.[11]

Fred Seward now once again insisted that Powell leave. "He replied, 'very well, sir, I will go,' and turning away, took two or three steps down the stairs. Suddenly turning again he sprang up and forward, having drawn a navy revolver, which he leveled, with a muttered oath, at my head, and pulled the trigger." The pistol failing to fire, Powell struck Fred Seward several times on the head, breaking the ramrod under the barrel of the pistol. Though stunned, Seward grappled with his assailant as Powell made for the door of the secretary's bedroom. The frightened William Bell, who witnessed this attack, turned and ran down the stairs and out the front door, shouting, "Murder!"

Fanny Seward, hearing the sound of blows out in the hall, asked the nurse, Sergeant Robinson, to go out and see what was the trouble. The two of them both reached the door at the same time. Robinson had no sooner opened the door than he received a blow on the head from Powell's knife handle, knocking him down. Coming through the door were two men, struggling. The nearer of the two Fanny recognized as her brother Fred, "his face was covered with blood, the rest very pale, his eyes full of intense expression.... On his right hand was the assassin.... In the hand nearest me was a pistol, in the right hand a knife. I ran beside him to the bed imploring him to stop. I must have said 'Don't kill him,' for father wakened, he says, hearing me speak the word kill, and seeing first me, speaking to some one whom he did not see — then raised himself and had one glimpse of the assassin's face bending over, next felt the blows — and by their force (he being on the edge of the bed, where fear of hurting his broken arm, had caused him to lie for some time) was thrown to the floor."[12]

All of this was happening very fast, faster than it takes to read about it. George Robinson, knocked off balance, got back up and grabbed Powell, pulling him away from the bed. Powell turned to Robinson and took him by the throat.[13] Fanny's screams awakened another brother, Major Augustus Henry Seward (1826–1876), who hurried to his father's room. Thinking at first that his father was attacking the nurse in a delirium, Augustus grabbed the struggling figure, quickly realizing from his size that this was not his father. Still confused, it occurred to him that perhaps the nurse had become delirious from his long hours by the bedside. Powell, struggling to get away from Major Seward and Sergeant Robinson, struck at them repeatedly with his knife, wounding both men. As they grappled together, Augustus Seward heard Powell say "in an intense but not strong voice, the words, 'I'm mad! I'm mad!'" Having dropped his pistol, Powell felled Sergeant Robinson with a blow of his fist, then wrenched himself away from Augustus and ran for the stairs.[14]

A messenger from the State Department, Emerick W. Hansell (1817–1893), who had been sleeping in a room upstairs, became frightened and started down the stairs at that moment. Powell rushed from the bedroom, knife in hand, and ran into Hansell. A quick thrust of the knife caught the unfortunate messenger in the back, hardly slowing down the fleeing assassin. Frederick's wife Anna Wharton Seward (1835–1919) and the senior Seward's wife Frances (1805–1865) had been roused by the noise and had seen Powell struggling with Augustus as he escaped from the bedroom. Asking Fanny what was happening, she questioned them in return, "Is that man gone?" to which they could only reply, "What man?"[15] Augustus, seeing Powell start down the stairs, hurried to his room and began searching through his carpet bag for his pistol. Finding it at last, he ran downstairs to stand guard, still not comprehending everything that had happened. People were beginning to gather before the house. Augustus deputized some of them as guards and sent others for doctors. He realized his own forehead was bleeding from Powell's knife blows.[16]

Frederick W. Seward. The son of William H. Seward was assistant secretary of state. He was severely beaten on the head by his father's would-be assassin and nearly died (Library of Congress).

One of those walking in Lafayette Square that night was Alfred Cloughley. He heard shouts coming from the Seward home and saw Powell riding away. Entering the house, he found a chaotic scene. Frederick Seward was still conscious at that time, in spite of the severe injuries dealt to his head by Powell's revolver. Cloughley sent word to the presidential guard, then headed over to Ford's Theatre to tell the president of the attack upon the secretary of state. Men he met in the street informed him that Lincoln, too, was the victim of an assassin.[17]

Meanwhile, Fanny Seward, who had followed the struggling men out of the room, turned and ran back, shouting, "Where's Father?" The secretary had slid off the bed and was lying on the floor. As she attempted to help him, her "feet slipped in a great pool of blood." Sergeant Robinson, hurrying to her aid, examined the secretary, found him still alive, and began immediate treatment of his wounds. Enlisting Fanny, he instructed her in how to help, applying cloth bandages to stop the bleeding. Fanny's fears for her father's life were eased a little when she heard him speak to her, not only saying that he was not dead, but also issuing instructions to her to close the house, have a guard posted, and to send for the doctors.[18]

The Seward family physician, Tullio Suzzaro Verdi (1829–1902), had left the Seward home around nine, his patient resting comfortably. An hour and a half later he was summoned by William Bell to return. Frances Seward met him at the staircase of her home. "Look to Mr. Seward!" she implored him in an agonized tone. The secretary was lying on the bed, covered with blood. There was blood everywhere in the room. Seward's right cheek was bleeding badly and a great flap of his flesh hung loosely. Verdi thought at first that the jugular vein had been cut, but he was able to check the bleeding with ice water, and his worst fears were not realized.

Seeing to the other casualties, Dr. Verdi examined Mr. Hansell, the messenger who had been stabbed on the stairway. He found a gash over the sixth rib, to the right of the spine. Hansell was conscious and able to speak to the doctor. Probing the wound, Verdi determined that it had not penetrated any vital organs, but was deep and bleeding. Frederick Seward was also conscious; he recognized the doctor, but could only speak hesitantly. As Verdi examined the wound of the forehead, Frederick gestured toward the back of his head, where a more serious injury could be seen. The doctor attempted to reassure his patient, who lost consciousness after a while. Regaining his senses briefly, Frederick Seward aided his helpers in getting him to bed.

Dr. Joseph K. Barnes (1817–1883), the surgeon general, arrived shortly after Dr. Verdi, and examined Secretary Seward and Frederick Seward, assisting in their treatment. Barnes looked in on Augustus, but did not participate in his treatment. He was needed elsewhere: an urgent summons had come from Ford's Theatre.

Dr. Verdi hurried back and forth, treating Augustus, who had two cuts on his forehead and one on his right hand. Sergeant Robinson also had been wounded in the shoulders by the assassin's knife.[19]

Coming downstairs to get more ice, Fanny Seward found a rapidly growing crowd forming. Reporters pestered her, and other members of the household, for more information on what had happened. Many had proceeded upstairs and were milling about on the landing just outside the bedrooms. Fanny posted herself at her father's door and refused admittance to everyone, unsure whom she could trust. Relieved of that duty, she watched at her father's bed while another doctor, Basil Norris, closed the wounds with sutures. She feared that her father must be in great pain, but he later told her that, while the process awakened him, it was not painful.

Most of the household sat up throughout the night and early morning hours, wondering and worrying. Fanny described the scene.

> I was in constant apprehension of some fatal turn in [Secretary Seward's] symptoms.... As we sat through those long dark hours the thoughts they brought were almost overwhelming. The thought that such cruel and inhuman beings, as the man who had attacked my father and brothers, existed, made me wish myself dead and out of such a world anywhere seemed better. The anxiety of the condition of father and Fred was fearful. Although a guard sat in the entry, I could not reason away a feeling that the assassin who had wounded so many might return and finish his attempt.... "I have supped full on horrors," rang over and over in my mind — and I retraced the dreadful scene — and remembered the moment when I felt almost beside myself.... Blood, blood, my thoughts seemed drenched in it — I seemed to breathe its sickening odor. My dress was stained with it — Mother's was

drabbled with it — it was on everything. The bed had been covered with blood — the blankets and sheet chopped with several blows of the knife.... The gray light of morning came ... that light should come and the sun rise and the birds sing and the green leaves rustle in the trees, seemed strange in such a world.

Secretary of War Edwin M. Stanton, who had visited the previous night, returned to the house about nine the next morning. Mrs. Seward asked him if he had heard anything more about the president's condition. Stanton told her the terrible news and Mrs. Seward communicated it to her husband: "Henry — the President is gone." Seward remained calm.[20]

It has often been reported that Seward was wearing a special collar or neck brace that had interfered with the assassin's knife, but there is no confirmation of this. The collar with which Seward was fitted was applied around early May, over two weeks after the assassination attempt. Seward was treated by a dentist experienced in jaw fractures, Dr. Thomas Brian Gunning, who had to improvise complicated splints that Seward was required to wear until October, a full six months. He was unable to chew solid food for five months. Both Seward and his son Frederick were permanently scarred. Although the other three victims of Lewis Powell had all been injured, they, like the Sewards, recovered.[21]

News of Abraham Lincoln's assassination spread rapidly, and nearly everywhere was met with surprise and shock. James P. Ferguson (1828–1897) had been sitting opposite the presidential box and was looking into it when he saw the flash and heard the shot. His first reaction was fear. "As he [Booth] came across the stage facing me he looked me right up in the face and it alarmed me and I pulled the lady who was with me down behind the banister."[22] Dr. Charles S. Taft (1835–1900) wrote of hearing the shot: "While it startled everyone in the house, it was evidently accepted by all as an introductory effect preceding some new situation in the play."[23] Actor Harry Hawk (1837–1916) was standing on the stage with his back to the presidential box. Turning, he saw Booth "rushing towards me with a dagger and I turned and ran."[24]

Not everyone sat impotently. "Two men sprang for the stage, a Mr. Stewart and myself [James S. Knox, 1840–1892]. Both of us were familiar with the play, and suspected the fearful tragedy. We rushed after the murderer.... The shrill cry of murder from Mrs. Lincoln first roused the horrified audience, and in an instant the uproar was terrible. The silence of death was broken by shouts of 'kill him,' 'hang him,' and strong men wept and cursed, and tore the seats in the impotence of their anger, while Mrs. Lincoln, on her knees uttered shriek after shriek at the feet of the dying President."[25] Ticket taker John Edward Buckingham (1828–1909) noted, "Horror and excitement ... took possession of that audience. Everybody jumped to their feet, ladies screamed and fainted, men cried 'stop him!' and several jumped to the stage in their endeavor to prevent Booth's escape."[26]

Seaton Munroe, hearing of the shooting, ran to

Secretary of War Edwin M. Stanton. Stanton took control of the government on April 14, 1865, directing the hunt for the assassins. Concern that he might be an intended victim did not prevent him from rising to the occasion (Library of Congress).

Ford's Theatre and witnessed the chaos. "The seats, aisles, galleries, and stage were filled with shouting, frenzied men and women, many running aimlessly over one another; a chaos of disorder beyond control."[27] Watching Lincoln being carried out of the theatre, Roeliff Brinkerhoff (1828–1911) observed, "His face was very pale, and the stamp of death upon it, which once seen rarely deceives us."[28]

Chief Justice Salmon Portland Chase (1808–1873) described his hearing of the news of the assassination. "My first impulse was to rise immediately and go to the President, whom I could not yet believe to have been fatally wounded; but reflecting that I could not possibly be of any service and should probably be in the way of those who could, I resolved to wait for morning and further intelligence. In a little while the guard came — for it was supposed that I was one of the destined victims — and their heavy tramp-tramp was heard under my windows all night.... It was a night of horrors." Thus did Chase carefully phrase his reason for being one of the few prominent officials who did not visit Lincoln's bedside on the night of the assassination. Later the next day, Chase administered the oath of office to the new president, Andrew Johnson.[29]

> Instantly the news spread through the city. At eleven o'clock I [the Marquis de Chambrun] was myself standing before the house in which Mr. Lincoln was lying. The crowd was rapidly increasing; squads of soldiers were coming, too, and soon formed in line on the pavement. At that moment all were silent, and no one exactly knew what had happened. Suddenly I heard Booth's name muttered by the crowd: he was the assassin, it was said. A few minutes later we heard that Mr. Seward had been murdered at his house, and soon after rumors were current of similar deeds perpetrated upon Mr. Stanton and General Grant. Then the aspect of the crowd changed all of a sudden. Until then it had seemed panic-stricken; all at once it became infuriated. Everyone thought himself in the presence of mysterious enemies hidden in the darkness of the night, and from whose murderous steel it became incumbent to save those who were yet alive.[30]

Louis J. Weichmann described the scene in Washington the morning after. "Where all had been rejoicing [over the end of the war], all was now grief and terror. Excited groups of angry men could be seen everywhere on the streets discussing the terrible calamity. The news boys were unable to hand out the papers fast enough to meet the demands for the latest editions. The poor colored people were especially affected, and the tears running down their cheeks were mute witness of their sorrow over the loss of their best friend. As rapidly as possible all private residence and public buildings were put in mourning, and before nightfall the whole city was shrouded in black; Lincoln's portrait was placed on many houses and such mottoes as 'we mourn our loss' 'Our Father,' 'Our Saviour,' were numerous."[31]

Elsewhere reaction to the assassination was just as strong as in the capital city. Poet Walt Whitman, visiting his family in New York City, described the scene. "Mother prepared breakfast — and other meals afterwards — as usual; but not a mouthful was eaten all day by either of us. We each drank half a cup of coffee; that was all. Little was said. We got every newspaper morning and evening, and the frequent extras of that period, and pass'd them silently to each other." Crossing from Brooklyn to Manhattan, Whitman saw the closed shops now draped in black, and everywhere the "strange mixture of horror, fury, tenderness & a stirring wonder brewing." In the sky above were "long broad black [clouds] like great serpents slowly undulating in every directrion."[32]

As word spread into the South, reaction was mixed, and it is difficult to judge the true feelings of many Southerners, most of whom displayed the appropriate sorrow in order not to antagonize occupying Northern forces. For some, though, there was genuine shock and concern. Confederate General Joseph E. Johnston (1807–1891), negotiating the surrender of his army to General William T. Sherman, was described by Sherman as he received the news. "The perspiration came out in large drops on his forehead and he did not attempt to conceal his distress. He denounced the act as a disgrace to the age, and hoped that I did not charge it to the Confederate government." Confederate Secretary of the Navy Stephen Mallory (c.1812–1873) wrote of his discussion of the assassination with President Jefferson Davis. "I expressed my deep regret, expressing among other views, my conviction of Mr. Lincoln's moderation, his sense of justice, and my apprehension that the South would be accused of instigating his death. To this Mr. Davis replied sadly, 'I certainly have no special regard for Mr. Lincoln; but there are a great many men of whose end I would much rather [hear] than his. I fear it will be disastrous to our people and I regret it deeply.'" Many Southerners expressed fear for the thought of the South now being subjected to the governance of Andrew Johnson, a Southerner who had long been despised by the South's former ruling class, and who had felt equal contempt for the secessionist cause. William J. Minor, a prominent Louisiana farmer, wrote in his diary upon hearing of Lincoln's death, "This is ... one of the greatest misfortunes that could have befallen the country ... a great loss to the whole country & especially to the South.... Oh! My poor country—what have you yet to suffer."

But for every genuinely sorrowful Southerner there were just as many who were cheered by the news. In towns not occupied by federal troops there were shouts of joy and dancing in the streets. Mrs. Cornelia McDonald of Virginia wrote in her diary that the assassination of Lincoln was fitting for him who "had urged on and promoted a savage war that had cost so many lives."[33]

For many, especially in the North, sorrow and grief gave rise to anger and fury. All over the country those expressing joy for the act and sympathy for the assassins were seized and beaten, stabbed, shot, and hanged. Hundreds died at the hands of enraged mobs or even individuals. No one was safe from the maniacal outrage of the mobs. Franklin Pierce, former president of the United States, had to face such a crowd on his doorstep in Concord, New Hampshire. They demanded he show a flag as proof of loyalty. Pierce was able to calm the mob and convince them that he was, after all, a patriotic American. Mud and ink were thrown at the Buffalo, New York, home of former president Millard Fillmore (1800–1874), who lay inside the home, sick in bed. Women, known or believed to have expressed anti–Union sentiments, were terrorized and roughly treated.[34] In Cincinnati, Ohio, a man who expressed his approval of Lincoln's death was "shot ... dead on the spot," while another "was literally cut to pieces." The mayor of Philadelphia announced that the city police would not protect anyone who was not displaying signs of mourning. Cities on the opposite coast experienced similar violence, as homes and businesses of Democratic Party members were vandalized and burned in San Francisco and Los Angeles. Not only those who had supported Lincoln's opposition were victimized. Anyone with a longstanding rivalry, or real or imagined grievances against others, took advantage of the widespread breakdown of authority to settle scores. Many victims were very likely entirely innocent. No similar outbreak of violence and lawlessness on so wide a scale can be found in all of American history.[35]

Order was gradually restored, of course, but the sincere grief felt by so many shielded most of them from being held responsible for the damage and misery unleashed upon a whole nation. In spite of democratic institutions and other civilizing influences, people are still people, and no one is entirely immune to irrational outbursts, given sufficient provocation.

11. Cause of Death

> The history of surgery fails to record a recovery from such a fearful wound.
> Dr. Charles A. Leale

On the night of April 14, 1865, the first priority of the doctors was to examine their patient and determine the extent of his injuries. The first doctor to enter the box was Dr. Charles Augustus Leale (1842–1932), an army surgeon who had been seated nearby. Before he had even reached the president he asked that brandy and water be brought. Mrs. Lincoln was holding her husband up, preventing his falling from his chair. Dr. Leale checked for a pulse but at first could find none. While moving the unconscious Lincoln to the floor of the box, Leale discovered a blood clot near the left shoulder. Cutting the president's coat and shirt from neck to left elbow revealed no wounds. Next, Leale opened Lincoln's eyelids and saw the pupils were fixed and dilated, indicating a brain injury. Running his fingers through Lincoln's hair, Leale located the wound behind the left ear. Removing a blood clot from the wound resulted in some improvement, so for the rest of the evening the doctors kept the wound open. Dr. Leale was under no illusions about the nature of the wound. He later wrote, "The history of surgery fails to record a recovery from such a fearful wound and I have never seen or heard of any other person with such a wound and injury to the sinus of the brain and to the brain itself, who lived even for an hour."

Dr. Leale was born in New York City, on March 26, 1842. After studying science, receiving medical instruction in diseases of the heart and lungs (with Dr. Austin Flint, Sr.), in surgery and gunshot wounds (with

Dr. Charles A. Leale. The first physician to attend the dying president, Leale had only very recently completed his medical studies. His quick actions prolonged Lincoln's life for several hours (Library of Congress).

Dr. Frank H. Hamilton), and at Bellevue Hospital Medical College in New York, Leale graduated early in 1865. Simultaneously with his medical studies, Leale served as an army medical cadet and completed his one-year course on February 17, 1865. He was commissioned in the volunteer corps on April 8, 1865, and was placed in charge of a ward for wounded officers at Washington's Army General Hospital, Armory Square. He worked long hours treating the huge number of casualties of the war.

Dr. Leale was in the crowd at the White House on the evening of April 11. Impressed with the president, he decided to try to see him again, and, changing to civilian clothes so as not to be challenged for not having a pass (he had obtained permission to be off duty), Leale went to Ford's Theatre on April 14. Arriving at 8:15 P.M., Leale was disappointed that he could not obtain an orchestra seat, and had to settle for one in the dress circle, "near the front on the same side [as the President's box] and about forty feet from the President's box." The young surgeon was thrilled a short time later to see the president and his party arrive. Lincoln passed by him "a few feet behind me." "I had the best opportunity to see distinctly the full face of the President, as the light shone directly upon him.... His face was perfectly stoical; his deep-set eyes gave him a pathetically sad appearance. The audience seemed to be enthusiastically cheerful, yet he looked peculiarly sorrowful, as he slowly walked with bowed head and drooping shoulders toward the box. I was looking at him as he took his last walk."

Describing "a disturbance at the door of the President's box," Leale suggests that there was someone at the door leading from the dress circle into the box vestibule, whom he called a "guard," who spoke with Booth before letting him in. Hearing the shot, Leale saw Booth jump down to the stage and cross it into the wings. Jumping over seats and pushing his way through the crowd, Leale arrived at the box door. Again he said there was someone at the door, whom he called an "usher," who allowed him in when told Leale was a doctor. Upon entering the box, Leale was ordered to stop by Rathbone, who, upon learning he was a doctor, asked him to tend to his wounded arm. A quick look at Rathbone determined that he was not in immediate danger. Leale then responded to Mary Lincoln's entreaties that he help her husband.

For the next several hours Leale and other doctors did what they could to prolong Lincoln's life, aware that, as Leale said upon first examination, "his wound is mortal; it is impossible for him to recover."

Dr. Leale had been joined by other doctors from the audience, who assisted in the treatment. Artificial respiration was administered, first by the standard method of the time—chest pressure and arm pulling—and when this was unsuccessful, Leale performed mouth-to-mouth breathing, at that time little known. Finally, breathing and detectable heart action resumed. At this point a little brandy was given and swallowed.

When Lincoln had improved slightly, the doctors decided to move him out of the theatre. It was thought that the White House was too far away, that he would not be able to stand the journey, so he was taken to a house across the street. Carrying Lincoln from the theatre to the house, Dr. Leale held the president's head. Lieutenant John T. Bolton of the 7th Regiment, Veteran Reserve Corps, drew his saber and cleared a path through the crowd.

Laid diagonally across the bed, which was not long enough to accommodate his 6'4" body, Lincoln was thoroughly examined and found to have no other injuries. The wound was probed with a finger, but the ball could not be felt. It had passed deep into the head. More brandy was administered, but Lincoln was losing his ability to swallow, so this had

Petersen House. The boarding house stood — and still stands — across the street from Ford's Theatre. Lincoln was carried there because the doctors believed that he could not survive being taken to the White House. Lincoln died in the small back bedroom of this house (*Frank Leslie's Illustrated Newspaper*, May 20, 1865).

to be discontinued. The left upper eyelid was observed to be swollen and darkened from internal bleeding. After a short time the same was observed in the right eye, with the eye beginning to protrude. Mustard plasters were applied, which served both to warm Lincoln and stimulate the nerves.

Dr. Leale sent word to other doctors, government officials, members of the Lincoln family, and clergy to come to the Petersen House. When other doctors arrived, especially the Lincoln family physician, Dr. Robert King Stone (1822–1872), and Surgeon General Joseph K. Barnes, Leale explained his treatment to them and they approved.[1]

The facial muscles on Lincoln's left side began twitching at about 11:30 P.M., over an hour after the shooting, and it was noticed that the president's mouth was drawn toward the left. Blood and brain tissue oozed from the wound from the time Lincoln was placed on the bed until 5:30 A.M., when the oozing stopped. Whenever the free passage from the wound became obstructed the patient's vital signs began to suffer, so the doctors kept the wound clear and draining. Probing the wound to locate the ball was a standard practice before the invention of x-raying, and this was done, first with a silver probe. A bone fragment, driven in by the ball, was felt, but the probe, about six inches long, was of insufficient length to do more. A longer instrument, a Nelaton probe, of rubber with a porcelain tip, was obtained. The wound was probed again, locating a second hard substance that the doctors decided must be another bone fragment. The wound was probed one more time, and the doctors were satisfied that they had located the ball.[2]

All that could be done now was to wait and observe. Lincoln's breathing became more labored and irregular, seeming to cease for as long as a minute, only to burst forth again and continue the struggle a little longer. Leale took Lincoln's right hand in his and held it, as he explained, to let the president know "that he was in touch with humanity and had a friend.[3]

Dr. Joseph K. Barnes. Surgeon general of the army, Dr. Barnes was called to the Seward house first, where he helped with the treatment of the five wounded men there. Word came to him that the president had been shot, and he hurried to the Petersen House. Barnes remained at Lincoln's side until the president's death (Library of Congress).

Muscle contractions were noted about 1 A.M., and both pupils were seen to be widely dilated and fixed. This is what we would now call brain death. The labored breathing continued, to the amazement of the doctors. Breathing and the feeble pulse finally ceased, and Lincoln was pronounced dead at 7:22 A.M., April 15, 1865. Leale "gently smoothed the President's contracted facial muscles, took two coins from my pocket, placed them over his eyelids, and drew a white sheet over the martyr's face."[4]

In addition to Dr. Leale, other doctors present at Ford's Theatre the night of April 14, 1865, were Charles Sabin Taft, Charles D. Gatch, George B. Todd (1835–1874) of the U.S.S. *Montauk*, and Albert Freeman Africanus King (1841–1914). As the first doctor to reach the stricken president, Dr. Leale assumed the direction of medical care and remained with Lincoln until the president's death the following morning. Dr. Taft climbed on the stage and was assisted by members of the audience up to the box, which he entered by climbing over the rail. Doctors Gatch and Todd had also been sitting in the dress circle. After Lincoln was carried across the street to the Petersen House, other doctors arrived, most of them observing, rather than taking any active part in the treatment. Doctors known to have looked in were Assistant Surgeon General Charles Henry Crane (1825–1883); Edward George Curtis (1838–1912); James Crowdhill Hall (1805–1880); Charles Henry Liebermann (1812–1886); John Frederick May (1812–1891), who had also treated John Wilkes Booth; William Morrow Notson (1836–1882); Lyman Beecher Todd (1832–1902); Ashbel Woodward (1804–1885);

Deathbed vigil. Lincoln's great height required that he be laid diagonally on the bed. The doctors treated him while the room filled with his family, friends, and dignitaries. The room was small and could not hold very many at a time (*Harper's Weekly*, May 16, 1865).

11. *Cause of Death* 107

Lincoln deathbed. This photograph was taken shortly after the body had been taken out, and shows the blood-stained pillow (Library of Congress).

Charles Mason Ford (1840–1884); Willard Bliss (1825–1889), of Armory Square Hospital; Chew Van Bibbles; and William R. Neal.[5]

Six soldiers of the Army Quartermaster Corps — William Reith, John C. Weaver, Eli Morey, David Frantz, John Richardson, and Antolio Bregazzi — carried Lincoln's body in a casket to the White House and placed it in a room on the second floor, northwest corner. At noon, the autopsy was begun. Dr. Joseph Janvier Woodward (1833–1884), an assistant surgeon from the Army Medical Museum, performed the autopsy, assisted by Army Assistant Surgeon Edward George Curtis. Others present were Surgeon General Joseph K. Barnes, Assistant Surgeon General Charles Henry Crane, Lincoln family physician Robert K. Stone, Army Acting Assistant Surgeon Charles Taft, Army Assistant Surgeon William M. Notson, and Lincoln's friend, former Senator Orville Hickman Browning (1806–1881). Dr. Charles A. Leale declined to be present. Some accounts that include President Andrew Johnson and members of the Cabinet at the autopsy are in error, for Johnson was convening a meeting of the Cabinet at the Treasury building at noon that day.

Opposite bottom left: Robert T. Lincoln. The president's oldest son had been at the White House when news of the assassination reached him. Hurrying to the Petersen House, he was often overcome by grief as he waited for the inevitable end (Library of Congress). *Opposite bottom right:* Charles Sumner. Senator from Massachusetts, Sumner was a friend of the Lincolns and did his best to console Mrs. Lincoln and Robert. But his own grief overpowered him and he wept uncontrollably (Library of Congress).

The autopsy was not a complete one, as only the head was examined. The fatal wound was the only wound, so the doctors declined to do a full autopsy. The skull was opened and the brain sectioned down to the track of the wound. It was found that the pistol ball had traveled across the head and lodged in front. Bone fragments from the entry site had been driven inward by the ball, and were removed. The ball itself was removed and found to have been considerably flattened by its impact with the hard, thick bone. There was much clotted blood in the brain ventricles and in the tissue along the track of the ball. The orbits, thin bony plating behind the eyes, were fractured. The autopsy doctors decided this was the result of contre-coup, the transference of the shock of the impact to the opposite side of the skull. Doubt was expressed by some that contre-coup was involved. An article in the British medical journal, the *Lancet* (1865, Vol. I, p. 649), proposed that the fractured orbits were caused by the impact of the brain itself, driven forward by the force of the shot.

Although the precise track and final location of the ball was noted, the accounts do not agree. Dr. Woodward, Dr. Curtis, and Dr. Stone said the ball lodged behind and above the left eye, but Dr. Barnes and Dr. Taft said it was the right eye. To further confuse matters, Dr. Taft, in a later account, changed his mind and said the left eye. That the track of the ball took an upward direction after entering Lincoln's skull can be explained by a witness, James P. Ferguson, who was looking into the box at the moment the shot was fired, and saw Lincoln looking down and to the left. If this was so, the ball would likely have lodged behind the right eye.[6]

12. The Missing Guard

> I have provided men at your mansion to perform all necessary police duty, and I am always ready to perform any duty that will properly conduce to your interest or your safety.
>
> Ward Hill Lamon
> to Abraham Lincoln

Records of the Washington Metropolitan Police show that four of their officers were detailed for service at the White House, and reported for duty on November 3, 1864. They were Sergeant John R. Cronin and officers Alfonso T. Donn, Thomas Frances Pendel (1825–1909), and Andrew C. Smith. They were ordered to report to Marshal Ward Hill Lamon.[1] Lamon had assumed primary responsibility for Lincoln's protection, repeatedly expressing his exasperation when the president failed to take his warnings of danger seriously.[2] This modest detail of guards underwent several changes over the weeks leading up to the assassination. By January 6, 1865, Pendel and Donn were gone, and William S. Lewis had been added. On January 10, William Henry Crook (1839–1915) joined the others. Lewis' name was dropped by January 24, and replaced by George W. McElfresh. On February 6, Thomas T. Hurdle joined the other four officers. Official records for March and April are missing,[3] but a curious document survives that gives us an idea of when John Frederick Parker joined the White House detail.

> Executive Mansion
> Washington, April 3d, 1865
>
> This is to certify that John F. Parker, a member of the Metropolitan Police has been detailed for duty at the Executive Mansion by order of
>
> Mrs. Lincoln[4]

Thus, sometime between late February and the beginning of April 1865, John F. Parker became a White House guard. There has been uncertainty over whether the police officers were there to guard the White House rather than Lincoln's person. The evidence strongly points to the latter. Ward Hill Lamon wrote Lincoln a letter, dated December 10, 1864, in which he said, "I regret that you do not appreciate what I have repeatedly said to you in regard to the proper police arrangements connected with your household and your own personal safety. *You are in danger.*" Later in this same letter, Lamon mentions the policemen again. "You certainly know that I have provided men at your mansion to perform all necessary police duty, and I am always ready to perform any duty that will properly conduce to your interest or your safety.[5] In this letter Lamon twice directly links the policemen at the White

House with Lincoln's personal safety. Furthermore, the letter is entirely about Lincoln's personal protection. If the police officers were not there to protect Lincoln, and were not actively involved in this protection, why would Lamon mention them in that context?

Additional evidence that Parker was the police guard assigned to duty at Ford's Theatre the night of the assassination comes from two of his fellow police guards, Thomas F. Pendel and William H. Crook. Having left the police force at the beginning of January 1865, Pendel became one of the White House doorkeepers. He described speaking to Parker on the evening of April 14.

> Previous to starting for the theatre, I said to John Parker, who had taken my place, to accompany Mr. Lincoln, "John, are you prepared?" I meant by this to ask if he had his revolver and everything all ready to protect the President in case of an assault. Alfonso Dunn [sic], my old companion at the door, spoke up and said, "Oh, Tommy, there is no danger." I said, "Dunn, you don't know what might happen." ... I said, "Parker, now you start down to the theatre, to be ready when he reaches there. And you see him safe inside." He started off immediately, and did see Mr. Lincoln all safe inside the theatre, and Mrs. Lincoln, Major Rathbone and Miss Harris also reached the building in safety.[6]

William H. Crook had more to say about Parker, and much of it was extremely damaging.

> It was the custom for the guard who accompanied the President to the theatre to remain in the little passageway outside the box — that passageway through which Booth entered.... A chair was placed there for the guard on the evening of the fourteenth. Whether Parker occupied it at all I do not know — Mr. Buckingham [John Edward Buckingham, the theatre ticket taker] is of the opinion that he did. If he did, he left it almost immediately; for he confessed to me the next day that he went to a seat at the front of the first gallery, so that he could see the play. The door of the President's box was shut; probably Mr. Lincoln never knew that the guard had left his post.... Had Booth found a man at the door of the President's box armed with a Colt's revolver, his alcohol courage might have evaporated. However that may be, Parker's absence had much to do with the success of Booth's purpose. The assassin was armed with a dagger and a pistol.... The dagger, which was noiseless, was intended for anyone who might intercept him before he could fire.... Had Parker been at his post at the back of the box (he) could have managed to make some outcry.... Parker knew that he had failed in duty. He looked like a convicted criminal the next day. He was never the same man afterward.[7]

There is other evidence that Parker was assigned to guard Lincoln and that he was present at the theatre that night. In the National Archives is a document entitled "Statement of Francis Burns," dated April 25, 1865. "Burns" was actually Francis P. Burke, the president's coachman. His statement reads as follows:

> On the night of the murder of Mr. Lincoln, he [Burke] drove him to the theatre and stayed at the door until the tragedy occurred. The special police officer and the footman of the President came to him and asked him to take a drink with them, which he did.[8]

Although he does not give their names, Burke said he had a drink with the "special police officer and the footman of the President." The footman was Charles Forbes, and the special police officer was Parker.[9] We know that Forbes was sitting in the dress circle, just outside the door to the vestibule, which led into the box. McGowan saw Booth approach the vestibule door, speak briefly with Forbes, and hand Forbes a card.[10] McGowan refers to Forbes as "the messenger," a title by which Forbes was widely known.

Another witness, Helen Du Barry, described the arrival of the presidential party at the theatre.

> There was a great applause and cheering and our attention was directed from the stage to the Dress Circle — close to the wall — walked Miss Harris — Mrs. Lincoln — Major Rathbun [sic] — a gentleman[,] the President and another gentleman behind him. These two gentlemen were *watchmen* in citizens dress who have always accompanied the President since the war commenced.[11]

The term "watchmen," which Mrs. Du Barry underlined in her letter quoted above, had been in common usage since well before the establishment of a full-time professional police force in Washington.[12] Her underlining the word "always" also strengthens the argument that Lincoln had guards of some sort throughout his presidency. This description, by an eyewitness, strongly tempts us to name the two "gentlemen" as Charles Forbes and John Parker. While Mrs. Du Barry did not name them, she positively stated there were two, and that she believed them to be police guards.

Of course, we must examine this evidence carefully before we accept it all. Both Pendel and Crook made claims for themselves that have been found to be questionable. Pendel seemed to want his readers to assume that he was a White House policeman at the time of the assassination. Official records of the police indicate otherwise. There is even doubt about Pendel's claim to be a White House doorman, for he is not described that way in a contemporary document.[13]

Crook seems also to have considerably embellished his recollections of his service as a police guard. In his book, he told a vivid story of accompanying Lincoln to Richmond shortly before the assassination. Crook even stated that he courageously shielded the president from a marksman taking aim from a window. Unfortunately for Crook, no other account of these events mentions a police guard being present, or anything about a sniper at a window. John S. Barnes, commanding officer of the U.S.S. *Bat*, was following the presidential party during the walk through Richmond, and was close enough to clearly see everything that happened. He stated, "There were no private detectives guarding his [Lincoln's] person."[14] In a letter to researcher David Rankin Barbee (1874–1958), Robert Lincoln O'Brien, who served as a White House clerk in the 1890s, stated that he knew Crook at that time and found him to be "an intrinsically stupid man who lived on his pretended intimacy with Abraham Lincoln." O'Brien also dismissed the ghostwritten memoir of "the man at the door." He did not remember the "man at the door's" name, but it seems likely that he was referring to Pendel.[15]

The strongest piece of evidence that Parker was Lincoln's guard, and that his assignment on the night of April 14, 1865, was to guard the president at the theatre, is a complaint filed against Parker with the Metropolitan Police Board by the superintendent of police, Almarin Cooley Richards (1827–1907), on the charge of "neglect of duty." The specification reads, "In this, that said Parker was detailed to attend and protect the President Mr. Lincoln, that while the President was at Ford's Theatre on the night of the 14th of April last, said Parker allowed a man to enter the President's private box and shoot the President." Richards listed as witnesses himself and Forbes. We know only that the charge of neglect of duty was dropped. There are no existing records that could tell us how and why Parker was not punished.[16]

Born May 19, 1830, at Winchester, Virginia, John Frederick Parker was the firstborn of John Parker and Caroline Parker. His father was a butcher by profession. Young John eventually had five brothers. He worked first as a carpenter and later as a machinist in Washington, DC. John married Mary A. Maus on July 16, 1856. By 1860 they were living at 570 L Street, NW, and had three children, Cora, Sally, and Kate. A son, Willie, was born in 1867.

When the Civil War began, Parker enlisted in the District of Columbia militia for ninety days. Leaving the militia on July 11, 1861, Parker joined the newly formed Metropolitan Police Force, some time before the end of 1861. Parker appeared before the police board on October 14, 1862, to face charges of "conduct unbecoming an officer, in using violent, coarse and insolent language and behavior to his Roundsman." Parker was involved in a racial incident in June 1863, when he was reported to have refused to help a negro soldier who was being attacked by several men and boys. Military authorities attempted to bring charges against Parker, but there is no record that they succeeded. As a patrolman, Parker's name can be found in police records, arresting individuals who were charged with drunkenness, posing as a "bogus detective," fighting, making threats, disorderly conduct, cruelty to animals, larceny, and use of profanity (an interesting charge, considering Parker's own record for colorful speech).[17]

We often hear of Parker referred to as being of poor quality. He was brought before the police board on charges of using language to a superior officer that "was exceedingly violent and disrespectful, and, if permitted to be continued, must lead to insubordination." Parker received a reprimand and a transfer. On March 16, 1863, he was again charged with using foul language, and also with visiting a house of prostitution. No official action was taken against Parker on this occasion. Shortly thereafter, Parker was charged with sleeping on a streetcar while on duty. He was able to talk his way out of that one. Another charge having to do with bad language was dismissed about three months later.

Author Otto Eisenschiml (1880–1963), discovering the letter of April 3, 1865, stating that Parker had been detailed as a White House guard at the request of Mrs. Lincoln, observed, "What prompted the wife of the President to make this unusual request in behalf of an obscure and mediocre patrolman like Parker will probably remain a moot question."[18] An attempt to solve this mystery was made by Ver Lynn Sprague, who speculated that John was "almost certainly a kinsman" of Mrs. Lincoln, whose mother's maiden name was Parker. Sprague notes that in 1849, then Congressman Abraham Lincoln wrote to Navy Secretary William B. Preston (1805–1862), requesting the appointment of John T. Parker, Mary Lincoln's uncle, to a post in the Navy Department. Sprague openly wonders if John T. Parker was the father of John F. Parker, the police guard. The possibility is also raised in Sprague's article that no action was taken against Parker to avoid embarrassment to Mrs. Lincoln.[19] Researcher James O. Hall (1912–2007) had a more plausible explanation for Mrs. Lincoln's letter. He stated that she was seeking draft exemptions for two White House guards, Parker and Joseph Shelton, and noted that the letter about Parker "is awkwardly worded ... Parker was already on duty at the White House and Mrs. Lincoln was simply protecting 'her turf.'" The letter's text is not in Mrs. Lincoln's handwriting, though it does bear her signature.[20]

Parker may not have been an exemplary law officer, but was he as bad as many authors would have us believe? One way to answer this question is to compare Parker's record with that of his fellow officers. Sergeant John R. Cronin was tried on December 16, 1863, for "intoxication," and reprimanded. On November 9, 1864, he was tried for "improper arrest," the charges being dismissed. In the summer of 1865, Cronin got into a fight with a soldier whose loyalty he had questioned. Cronin wound up shooting the soldier, who recovered. John R. Cronin was dismissed from the police on August 2, 1865, as a result of this incident. Patrolman Alfonso T. Donn was tried on April 19, 1862, for using violent language and fighting in a police station. Less than a month before, Donn had faced charges for being absent without leave. Police records fail to show the outcome of these disciplinary actions. Patrolman William S. Lewis was tried February 27, 1867, for using "insulting language" to a citizen; there is no record of how this incident came out. Patrolman George W. McElfresh faced charges no less than seven times, and twice resigned, in 1863 and 1864, being reappointed both times. Patrolman Thomas F. Pendel was charged in July 1862 with "Unnecessary violence against a soldier." On October 25, 1862, Pendel was charged with dereliction of duty when he failed to come to the aid of other officers. Another charge against Pendel, of violence against a prisoner, was tried on June 5, 1862. Pendel left the force on January 2, 1865.[21]

We can see that Parker was far from unique in his record of service with the police. Each of the officers just mentioned served as a guard at the White House before, during, or soon after Parker's tenure. Why were such problematical men chosen for this duty? The demands of the war for manpower made it necessary for the police to make use of whatever men were available. We note, also, that Parker's records are not the only ones missing, indicating that the suggestion that his records were deliberately removed from police files is unlikely, or at any rate impossible to prove.

If we accept that Parker was assigned to guard Lincoln on the night of April 14, 1865, what can we discover about what went wrong? There is a good deal of speculation over what exactly were Parker's orders. One of his fellow police guards, George W. McElfresh, left an account that states,

> My orders were ... that when the President went to the theatre, I should get there as soon as possible, take a seat at the box door, and let no one enter without first sending in his name or card, and I often stopped people that I knew to be particular friends of the family, until I had announced them.... If the officer that took my place had carried out the orders given to me I don't think Booth could have gotten into the President's box.[22]

This is very similar to what Crook was to say, and both accounts, along with Pendel's recollections, did not appear until many years after the assassination.

Crook told us that the guard's post was inside the vestibule that connected the box with the dress circle, although McElfresh said the guard was stationed "at the box door," without specifying which door he meant — the door to the vestibule in the dress circle, or one of the two doors inside the vestibule, leading into the box. If you have visited Ford's Theatre and seen the narrow vestibule, four feet wide by ten feet long,[23] you might find it difficult to imagine a chair being placed there without it being in the way, particularly of ladies wearing the wide skirts then fashionable. Although Booth, in his diary, mentioned being stopped, he did not specify by whom or precisely where.[24] Colonel Rathbone, describing the scene with some attention to detail, made no mention of a chair in the vestibule, either upon entering or exiting. He said he "rushed to the door" of the vestibule, in a state of excitement, having wrestled with Booth and received a serious knife wound, and having just determined that the president had been seriously wounded. Rathbone probably would not have carefully picked his way around a chair in the vestibule. Had there been a chair there, the excited Rathbone would likely have run into it in the unlighted narrow hallway.[25]

In 1962, Frank Ford, son of theatre manager Henry Clay Ford, wrote, "I say again and unequivocally that John Wilkes Booth did not bore the hole in the door leading to the box President Lincoln occupied the night of the assassination.... The hole was bored by my father, Harry Clay Ford, or rather on his orders ... [to] allow the guard, one Parker, easy opportunity whenever he so desired to look into the box rather than to check on the Presidential party." This may clear up the question of who made the hole in the door, but it does not entirely explain why.

Judge Abram B. Olin (1808–1879) examined the theatre box on April 16, a day and a half after the crime. As he testified, "The passageway is somewhat dark," requiring him to

President's box at Ford's Theatre. Special decorations had been installed for the occasion of the visit of the president and his guests. The door to the vestibule leading to boxes 7 and 8 can be seen just behind the pillar on the right. The Lincolns and their guests entered the vestibule through this door and Booth did likewise later. In the resoration, the box has been re-created to look as it did on the night of April 14, 1865 (Library of Congress).

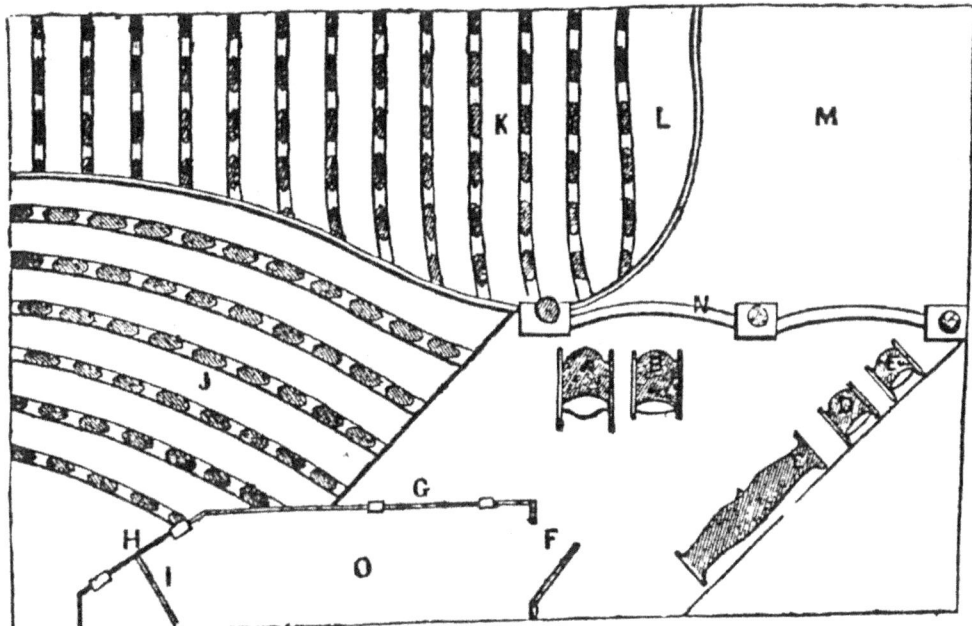

President's box — plan. One entered the box vestibule through the door on the left, marked with a letter H, and the combined boxes through door F. Lincoln sat in the rocking chair to the left, with Mrs. Lincoln to his right. Miss Harris sat in one of the chairs on the right, and Rathbone on the sofa behind her (*Harper's Weekly*, April 29, 1865).

use a light for his examination. This was when no performance was on. During the performance, with the lights dimmed and the vestibule doors closed, the little vestibule would have been almost totally dark. No one would want to spend an extended time, sitting or standing, in the dark vestibule, orders or not.[26]

The man seated in the dress circle, just outside the vestibule door, was Charles Forbes, not John Parker. Theodore McGowan, sitting nearby with a friend, described where they were sitting, and how they had to move slightly to enable Booth to pass. McGowan stated that Booth took out a "visiting card," "and then showed it to the President's messenger."[27] McGowan twice refers to the "President's messenger" in his testimony. We have already observed that Forbes was commonly known around town by that title. Newspaperman Simon P. Hanscom (1820–1876) visited the box shortly before Booth, and afterward published his observations in the *National Republican*, using the editorial "we" to describe himself.

> Upon approaching the door of the box we found the passage-way leading to it blocked by two gentlemen who were seated upon chairs, about six or eight feet from the door. We requested them to allow us to pass. They did so, and upon reaching the door we found no other person belonging to the President's household than Mr. Charles Forbes, one of Mrs. Lincoln's footmen and messengers, who was always in the habit of attending the President and Mrs. Lincoln at the theatre. As the play was progressing we requested Forbes to hand the dispatch to the President. It was the last he ever received. At that time there were no guards, watchmen, sentinels, or ushers about the door of the President, and anyone could have passed in without molestation.[28]

This statement has Hanscom giving his papers to Forbes, who then took them into the box and gave them to Lincoln. Hanscom pointedly tells us that there were no other guards outside the box but Forbes. We have Rathbone's statement that at the time of the shooting the box was occupied by the Lincolns, Miss Harris, Major Rathbone, "and no other person."[29] Taken together, Hanscom tells us that there was no police guard outside the box, and Rathbone states there was no guard inside the box, so where was Parker?

We have heard Burke's statement that he went to the saloon next door and had a drink with Forbes and Parker. Witnesses tell us that Forbes was back in the theatre, sitting outside the box vestibule door, at least twenty minutes before Booth arrived. We do not know where Burke, the coachman, was at the time of the shooting. He knew he would not be needed until the performance was over, so he may have felt free to remain in the saloon and have another drink. Did Parker remain with Burke after Forbes went back into the theatre?

If he did not, if Parker returned

The chair in which Lincoln was sitting when he was shot was a high-backed rocker and is now at the Henry Ford Museum in Dearborn, Michigan. Dark stains on the upper part of the chair are not Lincoln's blood, but grease from ushers' hair (Library of Congress).

inside the theatre, he did not take up his post, either in the vestibule or in the dress circle near the vestibule door. Crook stated that Parker told him "he went to a seat at the front of the first gallery, so that he could see the play."[30] However, Parker's boss, Superintendent Richards, said he was in the theatre when the shot was fired. In an interview given forty years later, Richards said he was sitting in the dress circle, "at the right which gave me a good view of the auditorium."[31] As we have seen, Richards brought charges against Parker, but in his later published letters and interview, he made no mention of his absent officer. Very few of his contemporaries had much to say about Parker. Considering what happened, one might expect the missing guard to be close to the center of attention of the investigation and trial of the conspirators. But not only did Parker not appear as a witness at the trial, he was not even mentioned, either by name or by title, in any of the testimony![32] Why this was so remains a mystery, and likely always will.

From the time he accompanied Burke and Forbes to the saloon until early the next morning, we know nothing about the whereabouts of Parker. He next shows up on the police records, between 6 and 8 A.M., on Saturday morning, April 15. The entry reads, "A woman named Lizzie Williams was brought in last night by officer Parker on suspn. Dismissed."[33]

On May 1, 1865, Parker was served with a formal complaint for neglect of duty for allowing Booth to enter the president's box and shoot the president. The trial before the police board was set for May 3, at one o'clock in the afternoon.[34] On that date, Parker was listed in precinct records as being "on detail at President's house.'" His name appears in the same precinct record for May 3, 4, 6, 7, 8, 9, and 10. On May 11, Parker arrested a soldier for "sleeping in street." On that date another officer, D. Hopkins, was assigned to the "President's house." It therefore appears that Parker left the White House guard detail on May 10, 1865, returning to duty with the 5th precinct.[35] On June 2, the charges of neglect of duty against Parker were dismissed by the police board. There is no transcript of a hearing, no testimony, no documentation at all except for a cryptic note of the dismissal. What Parker's defense was, or even whether a formal hearing was actually convened, must remain unknown.[36]

Mary Lincoln's dressmaker, Elizabeth Keckley, described a scene in which Mrs. Lincoln, upon hearing that the guard at the White House was the same one who was to have guarded them on the fateful night, ordered that he be brought before her. When he arrived, Mrs. Lincoln accused him of being a member of the conspiracy. The guard denied the charge, but, unconvinced, Mrs. Lincoln dismissed him from her presence. Keckley did not name the man, only described him as "the new messenger," but it would have to be Parker to whom she referred. No date is offered for this incident, but we know Mrs. Lincoln lingered in the White House until May 23, so such a confrontation could have occurred. We have here one of the earliest references to Parker's duty that night. However, as with the later accounts of Crook and Pendel, this little story is unsubstantiated. No other sources point to Mrs. Lincoln believing Parker was involved in the assassination plot.[37]

With the charges against him dropped, Parker remained with the Metropolitan Police Force at least until May 1869.[38] In 1870, the Parker family was living at 1239 8th Street, NW, moving the following year to 1241 9th Street, NW. Parker's daughter Cora was married on January 8, 1876, to Charles H. Barnaclo. The following year, his daughter Sally married Alexander Foreman. Parker returned to his trade of machinist after leaving the police force, working at the Washington Navy Yard.[39]

For many years, Parker was active in the Masons, being a member of Harmony Lodge, No. 17, in Washington. He received the degrees of Entered Apprentice on December 20, 1863, Fellow Craft on July 18, 1865, and Master Mason on August 15, 1865. To an inquiry from David Rankin Barbee in 1943, the grand secretary of the Masonic Temple of Washington, DC, stated, "It is not likely that the Fraternity would have conferred any degrees on this brother if the charges to which you referred in your letter had been true."[40]

Ill with asthma for eight months, and having developed pneumonia during the last two months of his life, John F. Parker died June 28, 1890, at his home at 816 6th Street, NW. The funeral was held at the family home the following afternoon, after which his Masonic brothers escorted the remains to Glenwood Cemetery in Washington.[41]

Although it is surprising to see how much there is to say about John F. Parker, in the end the questions with which we began are still unanswered. Where was he at the critical moment, and why did he fail in his duty? If that was his duty, why was he not punished? Why was he not called as a witness by the military commission? Though we know a lot about Parker, we do not know the answers to these crucial questions, and probably never will.

13. The Hand of the Avenger

> But if any man hate his neighbor,
> And lie in wait for him, and rise up
> Against him, and smite him
> Mortally that he die, and fleeith into
> One of these cities:
> Then the elders of this city
> Shall send and fetch him thence,
> And deliver him into
> The hand of the avenger of blood,
> That he may die.
>
> Deuteronomy 20:11–12

Fleeing into Baptist Alley behind Ford's Theatre, John Wilkes Booth mounted his horse, rode up the alley, turned to his left and headed for F Street. Reaching the street, he made a right turn and headed east. He was seen riding hard around the south side of the Capitol, heading for the Navy Yard Bridge, which crossed the Eastern Branch, or Anacostia River, immediately east of the Navy Yard, near today's 11th Street Bridge.[1]

The Navy Yard Bridge was guarded that night by several soldiers, whose leader was Sergeant Silas Tower Cobb (1838–1867) of Company F of the Third Regiment of Massachusetts Heavy Artillery. Cobb later stated that "the first [horseman] passed from twenty to twenty-five minutes of eleven…. When first seen, he was riding rapidly, and as soon as he came up I halted him, and challenged him." Cobb had orders not to allow anyone to pass across the bridge to the southeast after nine o'clock in the evening. Questioning the man, Cobb was told by the man that his name was Booth and that he was returning to his home in Charles County, Maryland. Although expressing doubt about letting Booth cross, Cobb relented and Booth rode over the bridge at a walk, calmly and coolly. A second man rode up to the bridge ten or fifteen minutes later and asked if anyone had crossed recently. Cobb asked him to describe the man he wanted. Confirming the description given, Cobb allowed the second man to cross also. The second man must have been David Herold, though Cobb was unable to positively identify him at the trial of the conspirators. A third man came riding up to the bridge about fifteen minutes later. It was stableman John Fletcher (?–1867), who was chasing Herold in order to recover the horse he had rented to him. Cobb told Fletcher he would let him cross but that he could not return that night. Fletcher turned around and headed for the headquarters of General Christopher C. Augur (1821–1898), where he provided information useful to the authorities.[2]

Booth rode through Uniontown, now called Anacostia, taking Harrison Street, now called

Good Hope Road, up Good Hope Hill toward Forts Baker and Wagner, part of the defenses of Washington. Like Sergeant Cobb, the soldiers at these forts had not yet received word of the assassination. Looking for his compatriot, Booth encountered two men, Polk Gardiner and George Doyle, and asked them if they had seen another rider along this road. They told him they had not. David Herold joined Booth at Soper's Hill, around eight miles southeast of Washington.[3]

Encountering two more travelers, Henry Butler and George Thompson, Booth and Herold inquired about a doctor. Booth had a broken fibula, the smaller bone in his lower left leg. Most accounts say that he broke the bone when he jumped on the stage at Ford's Theatre. Booth himself, in his diary, said this was what happened. However, author-researcher Michael W. Kauffman believes that Booth may have had an accident out on the road. Booth did not limp on the stage, or at least no witnesses at the time reported seeing him limp in the theatre. His trousers were stained with mud and his horse had a fresh bruise on its shoulder when he arrived at Dr. Mudd's house. Booth and Herold told several people his horse fell, including those he had already told about his crime. Sergeant Cobb mentioned nothing about Booth being muddy or in pain when he crossed the Navy Yard Bridge. If Booth's injury occurred on the road, it must have been somewhere between the Navy Yard Bridge and the Surratt Tavern.[4]

Herold and Booth arrived at the Surratt Tavern around midnight. John Minchin Lloyd (1824–1892), the tavern keeper, said, "Herold came into the house and got a bottle of whiskey, and took it out to him [Booth]." Herold told the tavern keeper, "Lloyd, for God's sake, make haste and get those things!" The "things" were two carbines, ammunition, a rope, and a monkey wrench, all of which had been hidden at the tavern several weeks before by John H. Surratt, Jr. Lloyd brought them the carbines, and Herold and Booth drank some whiskey. Herold took a carbine, but Booth was in too much pain to carry his, so Lloyd took it back and hid it inside between the upper floors. According to Lloyd, Booth told him, "I am pretty certain that we have assassinated the President and Secretary Seward." Lloyd estimated the fugitives spent only about five minutes at the tavern.[5]

Lloyd had been brought by his family to Charles County, Maryland, two years after his birth in Virginia on December 18, 1824. Lloyd worked as a bricklayer after his arrival in Washington in 1845. His marriage to Mary Elizabeth Mahorney (?–1906) took place on January 29, 1846. None of their children survived childhood. Lloyd took a job as a policeman in Washington in 1851, serving until the police were reorganized in 1861. The following year, Lloyd became a farmer in Prince George's County, Maryland. During the war, Lloyd was charged with blockade running, but was pardoned.

When Mrs. Mary E. Surratt decided she could not make enough with her tavern in Surrattsville, she rented it to Lloyd. The price agreed upon was $500 a year. John Lloyd became the tavern keeper on December 1, 1864. Like many of the residents of southern Maryland, Lloyd was a Roman Catholic and a Southern sympathizer. He was also a heavy drinker, often intoxicated. Under Lloyd's management the tavern at Surrattsville, already a way station on the Confederate "secret line," continued to be frequented by scouts and spies.[6]

From the Surratt Tavern, Booth and Herold headed for the home of Dr. Samuel Alexander Mudd, though the precise route they took is unknown. At about four in the morning of April 15, the Mudds were awakened by knocking at their door. The doctor, who was not feeling well, tried to get his wife to answer the door, but she was uneasy because of reports of guerrillas in the area, so Dr. Mudd got up and went himself. Mudd and Herold helped the injured Booth inside and the doctor treated his leg. Although the fugitives expressed the desire to continue their flight, Mudd advised them to stay, seeing that his patient was much in need of rest and healing. In the morning, Booth did not come down for breakfast. Herold ate with the family and then rode out with Dr. Mudd, who was on his way into Bryantown. Mrs. Mudd took a tray upstairs and offered food to Booth, who declined. After inquiring at the home of Dr. Mudd's father, Henry Lowe Mudd (1798–1877), to see if he could provide a carriage for Booth, and finding none available, Dr. Mudd continued into Bryantown. Herold rode part of the way with the doctor, but avoided going into town.[7]

In Bryantown, Dr. Mudd learned of the assassination from soldiers who were searching for Booth and Herold. The doctor returned home around five o'clock, Saturday afternoon, and ordered the fugitives to leave. Although Herold requested directions to the home of the Reverend Lemuel Wilmer (?–1869), he and Booth did not go there, instead heading south toward the home of William Burtles. Possibly they used Wilmer's name to confuse their pursuers, Wilmer being pro–Union and therefore unlikely to help them.[8]

Running to the south and southeast of Dr. Mudd's farm is an area called Zekiah Swamp. Although it possessed a fearsome reputation, the swamp was not particularly dangerous; the main difficulty to be encountered in crossing it, then as now, was the dense foliage. Wandering around for hours, trying not to be seen except when necessary, the fugitives came to the farm of Oswell Swann (1835–1890), a free black. Learning from Swann that they were only a couple of miles from Burtles' place, they asked Swann to take them there, offering him two dollars. On the way, Booth and Herold changed their minds, telling Swann they would give him an additional five dollars to take them to the home of Samuel Cox (1819–1880), another ten miles, bringing them close to the Potomac River. Arriving at Cox's house, "Rich Hill," around twelve o'clock in the morning of April 16, Booth and Herold had Swann wait for them.[9]

In his statement immediately after being taken prisoner, David Herold said they were not allowed into Cox's house. However, Herold, in that same April 27 statement, told several lies about his association with Booth. He further confused things by saying it was a man named "Thomas" who refused them hospitality. He probably was trying to protect Cox, as well as another man who helped them, Thomas A. Jones (1820–1895). Swann stated that Booth and Herold were greeted by Cox, who let them inside, and that they stayed three or four hours. After helping Booth into the saddle, Herold threatened Swann, "If you tell that you saw anybody you will not live long."[10] Swann returned home, only to be arrested on April 24 and held in the Old Capitol Prison until May 17.[11] Further evidence that Cox helped the fugitives comes from the fact that it was Cox who sent his foster brother, Jones, to help the assassins. Cox told Jones that the men had been at his farm at about four in the morning. This agrees with Swann's statement that they arrived around midnight and stayed three to four hours.

Jones found Booth and Herold hiding in the woods about five miles from Pope's Creek and around a mile from Rich Hill. For the next four days the pair were at the mercy of Jones, who brought them food and newspapers. Because of the danger that their horses might be seen and thus give away the fugitives' location, Jones advised them to do something about the horses. Knowing they couldn't get the animals across the Potomac, Herold led them away and shot them, hiding the bodies in the swamp. That is what Cox later told Jones, but, knowing there were Union soldiers in the neighborhood, it seems a risky thing to have fired two pistol shots. Whatever happened to the horses, the assassins no longer had them by the time Jones decided it was possible to cross the river.[12]

13. The Hand of the Avenger

It was during those four days of hiding in the woods that Booth wrote most of his diary entries that have survived. The diary is actually a small pocket memorandum book. It was taken from him at the Garrett farm upon his capture. Not used as evidence in the trial of the conspirators, the memo book, known as Booth's diary, first came to the attention of the public through General Lafayette C. Baker in his memoirs, published in 1867.

In the diary Booth compared himself with Marcus Junius Brutus (c.78–42 B.C.), who was a member of the conspirators who killed Gaius Julius Caesar (100–44 B.C.), and to William Tell, who defied the Austrian imperial governor Gessler in fourteenth-century Switzerland. Booth drew out his comparison, calling Lincoln "a greater tyrant than they ever knew," and emphasized that he had no personal wrong to avenge but was motivated by his allegiance to the Southern cause. Booth also made an enigmatic reference to "the very little I left behind to clear my name," presumably his letters. How Booth could think that anything he might have said could possibly clear his name remains a mystery, for some of his fellow conspirators were hanged on evidence much weaker than that which could have been brought against Booth had he lived to stand trial. The rest of the diary consists of some self-pity and expressions of regret at shedding blood.

The most controversial thing about the diary is that there are forty-three sheets, a total of eighty-six pages, missing. It is obvious from looking at the stubs of the missing pages that most of them were cut out at the same time. This has led to speculation that Booth may have filled those missing pages with information about the conspiracy, perhaps naming others involved. The remaining stubs of many of the missing pages show traces of writing on them.

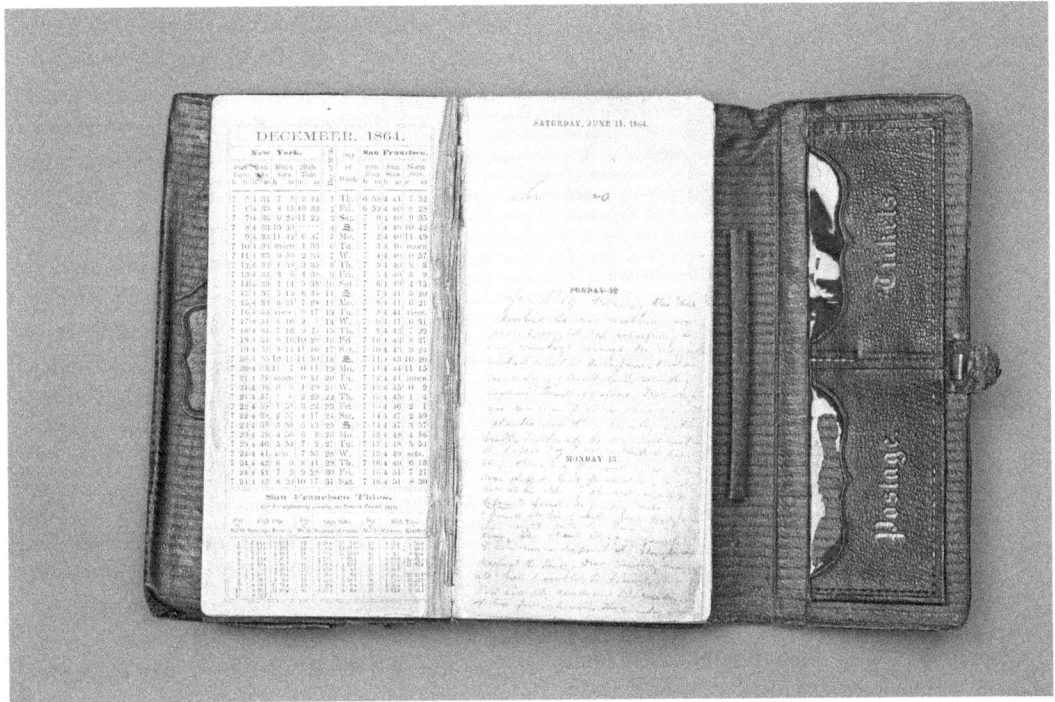

Booth used a small memo book as his diary. Many of the pages were removed, and there has been much speculation about what was, or may have been, written on them (Library of Congress).

An examination of the diary was made by the Federal Bureau of Investigation in 1977, using modern scientific methods such as ultraviolet reflectance, visible fluorescence with ultraviolet excitation, reflected infrared luminescence, and x-rays. The FBI reported that "no invisible writings, obliterations, alterations, or other unusual characteristics were found." In addition to the lighting tests, the handwriting in the diary was compared with two letters now in the National Archives known to have been written by Booth: his "To Whom It May Concern" letter and a letter to his mother. The FBI concluded that all of the writing in the diary was made by the person who wrote the letters.[13]

Booth's broken leg was swollen and inflamed, causing him much pain. There was nothing to do but wait and suffer from exposure, wondering all the while whether they might be discovered. Booth had told Jones that he did not intend to be taken alive, and Jones believed him.

Although there is some uncertainty whether it was Thursday, April 20, or Friday, April 21, Jones overheard a local man tell a group of soldiers that the men they sought had been seen in St. Mary's County, to the south, whereupon the soldiers took off in that direction. "'Now or never,' I thought, 'is my chance.'" Jones later wrote. Evidence suggests it was more likely to have been April 20 when Jones rode out to meet Booth and Herold, the evening darkness becoming more profound with fog. With Booth riding Jones' horse while Herold and Jones walked, cautiously watching to avoid being spotted, they made their way to Jones' house. Not wanting them to be seen by his family, Jones made Booth and Herold wait while he went inside. After eating the food Jones brought out to them, Booth and Herold were led to the river at Pope's Creek, near Dent's Meadow, where Jones had a small boat hidden. Carefully shielding the small candle with which he showed Booth the compass, Jones directed him toward Machodoc Creek on the Virginia shore. Booth steered from the stern while Herold stroked the oars. Jones refused Booth's offer of money for the help he had given, accepting only $18, the price he had paid for the boat. They shoved off into the river and were soon lost in the foggy darkness.[14]

Thomas A. Jones. Jones was a Confederate agent who helped maintain the "secret line" of communications across the Potomac River during the war. As Booth and Herold hid in the woods, Jones brought them food and news of their deed, then helped them cross the river. Though suspected of aiding the assassins, Jones escaped prosecution (Library of Congress).

Whether Booth misread the compass, or they were pulled off course by tides or river currents, or, as Booth wrote in his diary, they encountered a Union patrol boat, the fugitives did not make it where they had wanted to go, but found themselves upriver at Nanjemoy Creek, still on the Maryland side. They may have gotten lost, or they may have been trying to establish contact with the Confederate underground. Peregrine Davis (?–1876) owned property where

Booth and Herold had landed. Herold knew Davis, so he and Booth hid the boat and went to the nearby house of John J. Hughes (1825–1892), who was Davis' son-in-law. Hughes allowed them to stay in an outbuilding near his house and fed them. As the sun set that evening, April 22, Booth and Herold boarded their boat again and headed across the river. Jones may have told them to look for two Confederate agents, Thomas Henry Harbin and Joseph N. Baden (?–1874), who by this time were already on the Virginia side of the river. Whether or not they were looking for those two, Booth and Herold were following the Confederate "secret line" and making contact with many who were involved with the Confederate Secret Service.

Finally landing on the Virginia shore, Booth and Herold found themselves about a mile from the home of Mrs. Elizabeth Rousby Quesenberry (1826–1896). Although she claimed innocence, it is likely that Mrs. Quesenberry, who was related to a number of prominent aristocratic families, was waiting for the fugitives. She could have heard about them from Thomas Harbin, who was in the neighborhood at that very moment. Herold had walked to Mrs. Quesenberry's house while Booth waited at their landing point, Gambo Creek. Harbin brought food and directed Booth and Herold to the nearby home of William L. Bryant (1811–?), who would take them to the farm of a wealthy pro–Confederate, Dr. Richard Henry Stuart (1808–1889). Booth had heard of Dr. Stuart from Dr. Mudd. Dr. Stuart was living on his farm, called Cleydael, which was about eight miles inland from Booth and Herold's landing site. Bryant provided horses and took the pair to Cleydael, arriving after sundown on April 23.

Dr. Stuart later claimed to be most inhospitable. He either knew who they were or guessed, and with a house full of company, in addition to having had previous trouble with Union authorities over his Southern views, he said he wanted no part of these fugitives. He would not even treat Booth's broken leg, telling him that he was not a surgeon. Stuart did furnish the men with food, and told them to seek shelter for the night at the cabin of William Lucas (1820–?), a free black, who lived about a quarter of a mile from Stuart. Bryant took them to Lucas' cabin, then went home. Lucas did not want white men he did not know in his house. He told them he could not take them in because his wife was sick. Booth demanded they be allowed to stay the night, showing Lucas his knife. The Lucases moved out. Booth's anger and disappointment showed in the note he wrote to Dr. Stuart, sarcastically thanking him for the food and upbraiding him for his lack of hospitality. Using pages taken from his diary, Booth wrote two versions of this note, reducing the amount of money he paid the doctor from five dollars to two and a half. He kept the first note in his diary and gave the second one, along with the money, to Lucas, who brought it to Stuart.

Thomas H. Harbin. He was another Confederate agent who helped Booth, both before and after the assassination (courtesy of Surratt House Museum/MNCPPC).

The following morning, Booth and

Herold paid Lucas twenty dollars to take them as far as Port Conway, where there was a ferry across the Rappahannock River. Charley Lucas (c.1844–?), son of William, drove them in the Lucas' wagon, making the ten-mile trip in about two hours. It was now about eleven, and the ferry was on the opposite shore at Port Royal. Herold inquired of a local fisherman, William Rollins (1833–1901), about the ferry. When Rollins told them they would have to wait, Herold offered to pay Rollins to take them across. Rollins wanted to attend to his fishing business first. Booth and Herold would have to wait.[15]

While they were waiting, three men rode up. They introduced themselves as Confederate soldiers, First Lieutenant Mortimer Bainbridge Ruggles (1844–1902), Private Absalom Ruggles Bainbridge (1847–1902), and Private William Storke Jett (1847–1885). According to Ruggles, he and his companions were on their way home when they happened to encounter Booth and Herold. Herold at first gave them false names, but Booth admitted his true identity and confessed his crime. He also told them that there were rewards on his head totaling $150,000. Ruggles said that he and his comrades admired Booth's courage and that they did not want "blood money." They agreed to help the fugitives. Bainbridge, though not agreeing in every detail with Ruggles, told essentially the same story, expressing pity for Booth, who was by now in very poor condition from his injury and exposure.[16]

William Rollins got the ferryman, James Thornton, to bring the ferry across so that the assassins and their soldier friends could cross. The ferry was a simple flat boat operated by pushing it with a long pole. Upon arriving at Port Royal, Jett inquired of Sarah Peyton if she could put up Booth and Herold. At first she agreed, but changed her mind when considering the impropriety of it; her brother, Randolph Peyton, was not at home. Jett decided to try the home of Richard Henry Garrett (1806–1878), about three miles south of Port Royal. The Garrett family, pro–South but denying any knowledge of who their visitors were, agreed to let Booth and Herold stay with them. While Booth was resting at the Garrett house, Herold continued south with the three soldiers toward the town of Bowling Green. They stopped along the way at "The Trappe," a tavern which dated back to colonial times. The Carter family, owners and proprietors, were well known to the Confederate underground. With four young unmarried daughters, "The Trappe" was known for more than drinks. After their dalliance at "The Trappe," Ruggles and Jett rode on to Bowling Green and stayed at the Star Hotel, where Jett visited with the proprietor's daughter, Izora Gouldman (1847–1929). Bainbridge and Herold went out to the home of another of Mosby's veterans, Joseph B. Clarke, where they spent the night.[17]

The Garretts made their guest comfortable, allowing Booth to eat with the family and sleep in the bedroom of the Garretts' sons. He slept late the next morning, April 25, but the Garretts held breakfast for him. They said afterward that Booth told them he was a Confederate veteran named Boyd, and his broken leg was a wound he had received during the evacuation of Petersburg, Virginia. The oldest of the Garretts' sons, John Muscoe "Jack" Garrett (1840–1899), heard details of the assassination that morning from a neighbor. He discussed the subject at mid-day dinner, and "Mr. Boyd" showed much interest, although he said he thought that the reward for the assassin should be much higher. After the meal, "Boyd" asked for a map of Virginia, but had to settle for a large map with less detail, the only one his hosts had. He told Jack Garrett that he was looking for the way to Orange Courthouse, and beyond that to General Joseph Eggleston Johnston's Confederate army, and then to Mexico.

When Herold returned to the Garrett farm, Booth told one of the Garrett boys to go upstairs and get his pistols. Jack Garrett was becoming suspicious of the visitors. Around four o'clock Ruggles and Bainbridge came by and told Booth that federal cavalry had been reported crossing the Rappahannock ferry. Booth and Herold made for the nearby woods, Herold returning after a few minutes. He talked with Jack Garrett, asking if Garrett thought the report about the cavalry was true. While they were talking they saw cavalrymen ride by, heading south. Herold asked Garrett if he knew of any horses for sale, and Garrett replied that the opposing armies had taken all the available horses. Herold asked if he and Booth might hire a conveyance. Garrett told him there was a black man named Freeman who might be able to furnish one. Herold gave Garrett a U.S. ten-dollar note and asked him to arrange it. He went to Freeman's, but Freeman was not home. His wife told Garrett that the federal cavalry were looking for white men.

By this time the Garretts had grown uneasy about their visitors. They allowed the two men to share their supper and to sit out on the porch for some time, but refused to let them spend another night in the house. It was decided that they would sleep in the barn, a shed used for drying tobacco, which contained the stored furniture of friends and a quantity of hay. Booth and Herold went to the barn, bringing all their weapons with them. Although the Garrett boys had locked the barn door, they were so suspicious of the two men in the barn that Jack and his brother William H. Garrett (1845–1920) decided to sleep out in the corn cribs near the barn. William brought his pistol.[18]

About two in the morning of April 26, 1865, federal soldiers arrived at the Garrett farm. For days they had been chasing about the countryside and they were very tired. Now, however, it seemed the object of their search was finally at hand. The earnestness of the cavalrymen, especially of their leaders, was easily explained by the sensational news that was only now, over ten days later, reaching this part of Virginia — news that President Abraham Lincoln had been assassinated, and the soldiers were pursuing his killers. Information from those the soldiers questioned led them to the conclusion that they were on the right track. A combination of trickery, threats, and the use of photographs — possibly the first time authorities had had photos to show to witnesses — had brought forth information that the men they sought were not far ahead of them.

The soldiers were headed by three men, and some confusion has resulted ever since about just who really was in command. First Lieutenant Edward Paul Doherty (1840–1897), of the 16th New York Cavalry, was officially in command, but he had to compete with two Baker detectives: Luther Byron Baker (1830–1896) — a cousin of General Lafayette C. Baker, chief of the War Department detectives — and Everton Judson Conger (1834–1918). The confusion over who was in command arises from the fact that L. C. Baker was a commissioned officer of the army and L. B. Baker and Conger were part of his command. Doherty, however, had been detailed to Gen. Baker, so it would seem that whomever Baker designated would command the detachment.

The men who took their orders from all three officers were a haphazard collection of twenty-six members of the 16th New York Cavalry. Two were sergeants, Andrew Wendell (1838–1908) of Company E and Thomas H. "Boston" Corbett (1832–?) of Company L; Corbett was the senior of the two sergeants. Corporals included Michael Moore Hornsby (1836–1914) of Company H; Oliver Lonkey (1846–1911) of Company E, who was the senior corporal; Herman Neugarten (1833–?) of Company H; Michael Uniace (1830–?) of Company C; John Walz (1843–1904) of Company H; John Winter (1843–1922) of Company I; and Carl Zimmer (1835–1911) of Company C. The privates were David Baker (1844–1911) of Company H; William Byrne (1839–1901) of Company C; Frederick Dietz (or Deitz)

(1837–1904) of Company E; Godfrey Phillip Hoyt (1828–1905) of Company C; Martin Kelly (1830–1915) of Company C; Franklin McDaniels (1840–1914) of Company C; William McQuade (1830–?) of Company H; John William Millington (1843–1914) of Company H; John Myers (1827–1904) of Company H; Emory Parady (1844–1924) of Company H; Henry Putnam (1843–?) of Company C; John Ryen (1833–1911) of Company C; Lewis Savage (1844–1884) of Company A; Johan Adolph Singer (1839–?) of Company M; Abram Snay (1846–1928) of Company A; Carl John Anton Steinbrigge (1840–1910) of Company M; and Joseph Zisgen (1833–1914) of Company L.[19]

Upon arriving at the Garrett farm, Doherty detailed six of his men to take up positions behind the outbuildings. The rest of the men surrounded the house. When Richard Garrett answered the pounding on his door, he was harshly questioned. Each of the officers claimed credit for getting the location of the fugitives from the Garretts. "I [Doherty] seized him [Richard H. Garrett], and asked him where the men were who were there yesterday. He replied that they had gone to the woods when the cavalry passed the previous afternoon." "I [Conger] turned ... and said to one of the men, 'bring in a lariat rope here, and I will put that man [Garrett] up to the top of one of those locust trees.'" Baker, claiming to be on the porch before Conger, and not even mentioning Doherty, said that when he pointed his pistol at Garrett and demanded he tell where "the men who have been staying here" were, one of the sons of Garrett came forward and offered to show them. The stories of the three officers are in general agreement about everything except which one of them did the questioning.

Richard Baynham Garrett (1854–1922), one of the younger sons, confirmed the threat made to hang his father. His older brother Jack had been discovered sleeping out near the tobacco barn and was brought up to the house by Corporal Lonkey. Jack confirmed that the men were in the barn. Lonkey told the officers that he and the other soldiers had heard movement coming from the barn. Suspicious of "Mr. Boyd" and his companion, Mr. Garrett had asked his two older sons, Jack and William, both of whom were recently returned from Confederate service, to lock the visitors in the tobacco barn and stand guard on them. The brothers had been sleeping in a corn crib when the soldiers arrived.

The barn was surrounded. Baker and Conger were asserting themselves, freely ordering the soldiers about, and Doherty, resenting their usurpation of his command, stayed in the background from here on, according to Baker. Doherty's account has him exercising a commanding role throughout. Baker sent Jack Garrett into the barn to talk the fugitives into giving themselves up. They talked, but when Booth reached for his pistol and cursed Garrett ("Damn you! You have betrayed me!"), Garrett made a hasty exit. Conger then told Baker to order the men in the barn to surrender in five minutes or the barn would be burned.

Booth tried stalling for time. He called out to the soldiers, "Who are you? What do you want? Whom do you want?" Baker answered, "We want you, and we know who you are. Give up your arms and come out!" Booth asked for time to consider, and Baker granted him ten or fifteen minutes. While the conversation was going on, the tired and cold soldiers gathered firewood and built several fires to warm themselves. They could not see the fugitives inside the dark barn, in spite of the large spaces between the boards to let in air to dry tobacco, but now, standing by their fires, the soldiers were visible to Booth. Private Dietz later expressed his surprise that Booth did not shoot at the soldiers.

Again Booth asked who the soldiers were. "This is a hard case: it may be I am to be taken by my friends." He seemed to be hoping against hope that these might be Confederate soldiers surrounding the barn. Then Booth offered to come out if Baker would withdraw the men a hundred yards and form them in line. "I will come out and fight you," Booth said. When all such offers had been made and rejected, Booth replied, "Well, my brave boys, prepare a stretcher for me!" The soldiers were impressed with Booth's calm courage as he defied them.

Now Herold begged Booth to let him surrender. "You don't choose to give yourself up, let me go out and give myself up." Booth answered, "No, you shall not do it!" When Herold stepped toward the door Booth ordered him to stop, threatening to shoot him. Hearing Baker remind them that they had only five minutes to surrender, Herold told Booth, "I am going, I don't intend to be burnt alive." Seeing his friend's determination, Booth changed his mind and called to Baker, "There's a man in here [who] want[s] to come out." Baker shouted his terms: "Hand out your arms!" Herold answered, "I have none." Upon Baker's questioning, Booth answered, "The arms are mine, and I have got them." Conger urged Baker to accept Herold unarmed. The barn door was partially opened and Herold was told to show his hands. When he did, Baker pulled him out and turned him over to Private McQuade, who searched him. Private Ryen tied Herold to a tree and Private Millington guarded him.

One fugitive was now in custody. Corporal Herman Neugarten had already laid some combustible material against the side of the barn, ceasing this activity when threatened by Booth, who still had the advantage of seeing the soldiers without their seeing him. Col. Conger "went around to the corner of the barn, pulled some hay out, twisted up a little rope about six inches long, set fire to it, and stuck it back through on top of the hay [inside the barn].... It blazed very rapidly,—lit right up at once." Conger could hear Booth moving around inside, and the sound of something hitting the floor, which Conger assumed was Booth's crutch. Baker was looking in through the barn door, "and could see Booth distinctly." After trying to put out the fire without success, "he now turned, dropped one crutch, and with the aid of the other came toward the door. About the center of the barn he stopped, drew himself up to his full height and seemed to take in the entire situation.... He stood erect and defiant.... There was a carbine [in] one hand, a revolver in the other, a belt held another revolver and a bowie knife." Booth now began to limp toward the barn door, his weapons at the ready. As Conger ran toward the barn door he heard a single pistol shot.

Booth collapsed on the floor of the flaming barn. Accounts differ on what happened next. Jack Garrett said he ran in the barn and pulled Booth out before any of the soldiers took action. Both Baker and Conger said they entered the barn and examined Booth before carrying him out of the barn. They even had time for a short discussion of whether Booth had shot himself, with Conger proposing the idea and Baker denying it, saying, "I had my eye upon him every moment." Even Doherty, who disagreed with Baker and Conger on many things, said, "The soldiers and two detectives, who were there, went into the barn and carried out Booth." None of the three officers mentioned any of the Garretts helping to get Booth out of the burning barn.

Booth was taken out and laid on the ground. Conger, thinking him dead, turned and helped try to control the fire, but the barn, filled with dry hay and stored furniture, continued to burn. When some movement of Booth's eyes and mouth was noticed, water was brought and applied to his face. Baker later wrote that Booth was able to say only, "Tell mother, tell mother..." before losing consciousness. By now the fire was so hot that it was necessary to move Booth. He was taken over to the house and laid on a mattress and pillows, provided by the Garrett women. Booth, awakening, cried, "Oh, kill me! Kill me quick!" Baker replied,

"No, Booth, we do not want you to die; you were shot against orders." Again the assassin lost consciousness. Sergeant Andrew Wendell was sent back to Port Royal to bring in a doctor.[20]

Booth had been shot through the neck with a .44 caliber pistol. The man who claimed credit for the shooting was Sergeant Thomas H. "Boston" Corbett. Corbett had been watching Booth through the boards of the barn for several minutes. "He was taking aim with the carbine, but at whom I could not say. My mind was upon him attentively to see that he did no harm; and, when I became impressed that it was time, I shot him. I took steady aim on my arm, and shot him through a large crack in the barn."

Corbett, born in London, England, in 1832, came to America with his family in the late 1830s. He worked as a hatter in New York, Boston, and Richmond. Taking to drink when his wife and baby died in childbirth, he was reformed by the Salvation Army, and became a fervent Christian. Joining the Methodist Episcopal Church in 1857, he renamed himself, as he said

Boston Corbett. Sergeant Corbett took credit for firing the shot that killed Booth. He led an unhappy life and suffered mental problems. His ultimate fate remains unknown (Library of Congress).

the disciples were renamed, taking the new name "Boston," after the city where he was then living. He would hold up the production line among the hat-makers by stopping to pray whenever a co-worker swore. Tempted by prostitutes after a religious meeting, he was admitted to the Massachusetts General Hospital on July 16, 1858, after castrating himself in order, as he said, "to be holy." After several hospital visits, Corbett was discharged August 15, being described as "all healed."

Enlisting at the beginning of the Civil War, Corbett was taken prisoner for the first time at Harpers Ferry, Virginia, on September 15, 1862, and was exchanged on October 8. He enlisted in Company L of the 16th New York Cavalry on August 4, 1863. He was described as five feet, four inches tall, with a small, delicate build, brown hair and blue eyes. His religious convictions caused him to suffer the ridicule of his fellow soldiers, but he earned the respect of those who could admire his dignity and devotion to his beliefs under the most difficult of conditions. Taken prisoner again near Centreville, Virginia, on June 24, 1864, he spent five months in prison camps at Andersonville and Camp Miller, Georgia. After being exchanged, Corbett entered the Division One Hospital in Annapolis, Maryland, and from there went to Lincoln Hospital in Washington, DC.

After three weeks in the hospital, he received a thirty-day leave, returning to the 16th

New York Cavalry, then stationed at Vienna, Virginia. His promotion to sergeant had just come through. After searching their area for the assassins, some of the men were sent to Washington to be available there, Sergeant Corbett among them. He was one of the soldiers who marched in Lincoln's funeral procession in Washington on April 19, 1865.[21]

Baker tells us that as Booth revived somewhat as he lay on the Garretts' porch, he had more to say, with several people around him listening. Unable to clear his throat, he asked for help, Conger pressing as hard as he dared in a vain effort to aid Booth in coughing. Booth put out his tongue, but no blood was observed. The doctor now arrived. Dr. Charles Urquhart, Jr. (c.1794–1866), had been a doctor in the nearby town of Port Royal since 1821. Assisting the doctor was Miss Lucinda Keeling Boulware Holloway (1831–1909), a sister of Richard Garrett's wife, who was living with the Garretts. Dr. Urquhart soon determined that there was no hope. Booth was still talking. "Tell mother I died for my country. I did what I thought was best." Then he exclaimed, "my hands," and his hands were held up so he could see them. He looked at the hands he recognized as his own, now unable to move, as if they no longer were a part of him. "Useless," he muttered, "useless!" According to Baker, those were his last words. However, what if anything, Booth was able to say, considering his severe and painful neck wound, cannot now be known. As the sun rose he breathed his last.[22]

Conger took Booth's effects, including the diary, and left for Washington. Lt. Baker took charge of the remains, procured a wagon and a negro driver named Freeman, and set out for Belle Plain, where the steamer *John S. Ide* waited to take the body back to Washington. Baker later told how anxious he became when no other cavalrymen joined him. He sent a corporal back to urge Doherty to catch up with him, and he felt doubts about the old negro's knowledge of the back roads. They passed returning Confederate soldiers, some of whom inquired what Baker had sewn up in a blanket in the wagon. Baker encouraged them to believe it was the body of a dead Union soldier. At one point, the old wagon partially collapsed and the body slid forward. Freeman had to go under the wagon to repair the damage and dripping blood fell on his hand. This caused him to cry out in terror, "It will never wash off. It is de blood of a murderer."

Calming down, the man fixed his wagon and the two continued their journey. Finally arriving at the Potomac, Baker found the landing had been relocated farther down the river. Leaving Freeman with the body, Baker rode his exhausted horse around to the landing, where he found Doherty's men waiting. Taking a boat from the steamer, Baker led some of the men back upriver to the point where he had hidden the body. Freeman was there, and Baker paid him and sent him on his way.

Bringing the body back to the *John S. Ide*, Baker was at last able to get some rest as the steamer proceeded back to Washington. Lt. Baker was met by his cousin, General Lafayette C. Baker, and other officials of the War Department, including Surgeon General Joseph K. Barnes and General Thomas Thompson Eckert (1825–1910) of the telegraph office. Lt. Baker made a full report of the capture to Secretary of War Edwin McMasters Stanton.[23]

An autopsy was performed at the Navy Yard on the deck of the U.S.S. *Montauk*, at 2 P.M. on April 27. Those present for the autopsy were Surgeon General Barnes; Dr. Joseph Janvier Woodward (1833–1884) of the Army Medical Museum, who did the actual work of the autopsy; Judge Advocate General Joseph Holt (1807–1894); John A. Bingham (1815–1900); General Thomas T. Eckert; William George Moore (1829–1898) of the War Department; General L.C. Baker, and his assistants Luther Byron Baker and Everton Judson Conger; and photographers Alexander Gardiner (1821–1882) and his assistant Timothy N. O'Sullivan (c.1840–?). There were also several witnesses present to identify the remains and ensure that they were those of Booth: Dr. John Frederick May (1812–1891), who had operated on Booth a year before; Charles L. Dawson (?–1874), clerk at the National Hotel, where Booth had stayed; Booth's dentist, Dr. William M. Merrill; Seaton Munroe (?–1896), a lawyer whose brother was Captain Frank Munroe (1842–1877) of the Marine Corps (Seaton Munroe had known Booth socially); William Wallach Crowninshield, an acting master in the U.S. Navy; Charles M. Collins, also of the navy, who was the *Montauk*'s signal officer; Sergeant John M. Peddicord (?–1910), one of the Marine guards; and John Leonard Smith, one of Provost Marshal James L. McPhail's (1816–1874) detectives, who was also the brother-in-law of George Atzerodt. There were others on hand as well, and security seems to have been surprisingly poor, with a lady friend of one of L. C. Baker's detectives being permitted to cut a lock of Booth's hair, which Baker would not let her keep.[24]

The doctors determined that Booth died as the result of a pistol ball having passed through his neck, entering on the right and exiting on the other side, fracturing the fourth and fifth lumbar vertebrae, severing the spinal cord. General paralysis would have immediately resulted from such an injury. Cause of death was asphyxia. The third, fourth and fifth cervical vertebrae were removed during the autopsy and are now in the collection of the Armed Forces Institute of Pathology in Washington, DC.[25]

Identification of the remains has been a controversial aspect of the autopsy. Seaton Munroe stated, "I am confident that it is the dead body of J. Wilkes Booth." Charles Dawson noted that the initials "JWB" on the hand corresponded to marks he had seen on Booth's hand when he registered at the National Hotel. Dr. Merrill examined the teeth and recognized the two

Booth autopsy on board the U.S.S. *Montauk*. Booth's remains were examined and his identity established on the deck of the *Montauk* at the Washington Navy Yard (*Harper's Weekly*, May 13, 1865).

recent fillings, then called "plugs," as his work. But most controversial is the testimony of Dr. May, who later stated that he at first was unable to recognize the body as Booth's, and was convinced only when the corpse was placed in a sitting position. The scar from the operation May had performed on Booth was recognized by the doctor. Photographs of the corpse were taken, but they have never been made public, and no trace of them can now be found. Dr. Barnes noted in his report that "the leg and foot were encased in an appliance of splints and bandages," with "a fracture of the fibula 3 inches above the ankle joint." This corresponds to the injury treated by Dr. Samuel A. Mudd.

It is curious that better witnesses were not called upon to identify the remains. There were many acquaintances of Booth in Washington who knew him far better and had seen him more recently than most of the witnesses. A more positive identification at the autopsy probably would have gone a long way to eliminate rumors of Booth's survival and escape.[26]

The following day the two Bakers and an enlisted man picked up the body of Booth, which had already been autopsied, and took it out in a small boat into the Anacostia River. Crowds along the river bank followed them, eager to see where Booth's body would be sunk into the water. The Bakers, anxious that no one know precisely where the remains were to rest, kept on going, the swampy shore preventing the onlookers from following. They waited at Giesboro Point until it was thoroughly dark, then slowly returned to the Washington Arsenal. It had all been a trick to fool the crowds. Booth's body was actually buried beneath the floor of a room in the Arsenal. Soon the remains of the executed conspirators joined it in nearby graves.[27]

14. The Long Good-bye

> All along the road it has been affecting to see the people assembled not only at stations, but in front of farm houses, by the fences, and in fields beside the railway; to gaze at our passing funeral train — women often weeping and men standing respectfully uncovered.
> Robert C. Shenck

A vast national pageant, unprecedented in American history and still one of the best-remembered events of the nation's past, Lincoln's long homeward journey and multiple funerals were especially remarkable in that they had to be planned and organized on the spur of the moment. The work of making the arrangements was undoubtedly eased by the general unity brought about by shock and grief. Lincoln's friend, journalist Noah Brooks, described the scene in Washington on the morning of April 15, 1865. "Instantly flags were raised at half-mast all over the city, the bells tolled solemnly, and with incredible swiftness Washington went into deep universal mourning. All stores, government departments, and private offices were closed, and everywhere, on the most pretentious residences, and on the humblest hovels, were the black badges of grief."[1]

Secretary of War Edwin M. Stanton took personal charge of the funeral arrangements, as he did most of the affairs of the government. The first thing that had to be decided was where Lincoln was to be buried. His hometown of Springfield, Illinois, was not the obvious choice. New York City made a bid, quickly rejected. The unused tomb beneath the Capitol dome in Washington, which had been designed for George Washington, was proposed. But the desire to show the remains to the greatest number of people, together with a strong showing by the Illinois delegation, which included congressmen, the present governor, former governors and office holders on many levels, proved decisive. Lincoln's remains would be transported back along the route he had taken on his inaugural journey four years before. Funerals would be held in cities along the way, beginning with Washington. To head the military guard on the journey, Stanton chose Major General David Hunter, the same man who had accompanied Lincoln on his inaugural journey.[2]

Sands and Harvey (Washington undertakers), supplied the coffin, "covered with fine broadcloth, lined with fine white satin trimmed with best mounting, solid silver plate bullion fringe tassels, etc., heavy lead lining and walnut outside case." The commissioner of public buildings, Benjamin Brown French (1800–1870), was billed $1,500 for the coffin, a huge sum at that time. The coffin was further described by the *Springfield State Journal* of May 4, 1865, as

> probably the handsomest ever constructed in this country.... Lined with lead, and covered with black cloth, of the richest and most expensive quality, heavily fringed with silver,

with four silver medallions on each side in which are set the handles. The outside of the coffin is festooned with massive silver tacks, representing drapery, in each fold of which there is a silver star, and the outer edges are adorned with silver braid, with five tassels, five inches in length, each side having upon it four massive handles, and at the head and foot there are stars. Upon the top row there is a row of silver tacks, extending the entire length of both sides, about two inches from the edge. Upon the center is a silver plate, encircled by a shield, formed also of silver tacks, and the face lid and top are united with five silver stars. The inside of the face lid is raised with white satin, the corner piece being trimmed with black and white silk braid, festooned at each corner with four silver stars. The remainder of the inside of the coffin is lined with box-plaited satin, the pillow and lower surface being of fine white silk, and the whole being encircled with chenille as in fringe. The upper third of the coffin is lined with rich white satin."[3]

On Tuesday, April 18, the remains, having been embalmed the previous Saturday by Harry P. Cattell, who had performed the same service three years before on Lincoln's son Willie, were displayed in the East Room of the White House. 25,000 people passed by the lead-lined mahogany coffin, resting under a canopy seven feet high. The following day the first of many services was held. The new president, Andrew Johnson, was joined by all the Cabinet officers, except the severely wounded Seward. General Ulysses S. Grant headed the army officers, and Admiral David G. Farragut the navy. The president's two sons, Robert Todd Lincoln, and Thomas "Tad" Lincoln, were there, but not his widow, confining herself to her room upstairs, unable to control her grief. Many other dignitaries were present, including governors of states, foreign diplomatic representatives, clergymen and bureaucrats — in all, six hundred people.[4]

When the final prayer had been said, soldiers of the Veteran Reserve Corps carried the coffin out the north entrance and into the waiting hearse. The dignitaries followed and assumed their places for the procession to the Capitol. Among the hundreds of troops in the procession was the Marine Corps Band, which played a dirge composed for the occasion by Major General Bernard, the drums muffled. The pallbearers, members of Congress, were Senators Lafayette Sabine Foster (1806–1880), Edwin Dennison Morgan (1811–1883), Reverdy Johnson (1796–1876), Richard Yates, Sr. (1819–1873), Benjamin Franklin Wade, and John Conness (1821–1909), with House of Representatives members Henry Laurens Dawes (1816–1903), Alexander Hamilton Coffroth (1828–1906), Green Clay Smith (1826–1895), Schuyler Colfax (1823–1885), Henry Gaither Worthington (1828–1909), and Elihu Benjamin Washburne. Six gray horses drew the hearse, with another gray horse, empty boots in the stirrups, to symbolize the fallen

U.S. Grant. General Grant, commanding general of the army in 1865, participated in the funerals of Lincoln. He is shown here wearing a black ribbon on his left arm, indicating that the photograph was taken during the mourning period for the president (Library of Congress).

Funeral procession in Washington. This was the first of the multiple funeral parades and services conducted for Lincoln over the period of two weeks. Photographs showing the troops standing still were necessary because of the long exposure time required for photographs at the time (Library of Congress).

president. Delegations from most of the Union states were represented, as were clerks from the various government departments, and even a group of aged veterans of the War of 1812. Various ethnic and patriotic organizations, some hundreds of members strong, joined the solemn procession. Thousands of black soldiers marched in the funeral procession, but were relegated to the end of the long column. At 3:30 P.M. the casket was placed on the catafalque in the Capitol rotunda. The catafalque was designed by Benjamin B. French. The large paintings in the rotunda were covered, as were the statues, except for that of Washington, which was draped with a mourning sash.[5]

All day Thursday, April 20, from 6 A.M. to 9:30 P.M., the public passed through the Capitol rotunda, including many soldiers from camps and hospitals especially to see their fallen chief, until thirty thousand had passed, and still more thousands had to be turned away. Early the next morning, after a final viewing by high officers and Cabinet members, the casket was taken to the Baltimore and Ohio Railroad depot and loaded aboard a special railroad car.[6]

The coffin used for Lincoln's remains was elaborately decorated with silver fixtures and drapery. Flowers were placed around and on it at places of display (National Park Service).

The railroad car, "United States," that carried Lincoln's remains on the funeral journey was built at the U.S. Military Railroad Shops at the Orange and Alexandria railroad yard in Alexandria, Virginia, in 1864. The superintendent of car repair, Benjamin Patten Lamason, designed the car, dividing it into three compartments: a drawing room at one end, parlor at the other, with a state room in the middle. It featured upholstered walls, etched glass windows, sofas (which could be made into beds), a desk, chairs and a bookcase. Although it has been reported that the car was armored, that cannot now be confirmed. The car was originally fitted with sixteen wheels, though that may have been only for better balance. Because of the variety of gauges of track in use at the time, the wheels were made with a wider track than normal,

President Lincoln's railroad car. The *United States* had been specially built for the use of the president, but he never used it in life. It saw much hard service as a regular passenger coach over the following years (Library of Congress).

to run on tracks of different widths. This would make it slide back and forth when running, causing uncomfortable swaying and bumping. In spite of the government's having spent over $10,000 on the special car, Lincoln never used it in life, and neither did any other president.[7]

Sergeant Myron H. Lamson, a military railroad mechanic, was in charge of converting the *United States* for the funeral journey. A set of rollers was installed in one end on which to slide the coffin in and out, and the catafalque was installed in the car. The entire train was draped in black satin with silver fringe and tassels. The smaller coffin of the president's son Willie was carried back to Springfield aboard the same car as his father's.[8]

Since there were many different railroads, the train saw a change of engines several times during the trip. For the first leg of the journey, from Washington to Baltimore, the train cars were pulled by the engine *Edward H. Jones*, with another engine running ahead to ensure the track was clear.[9]

After two hours the train arrived at Baltimore's Camden Station and the Lincoln coffin was taken to the Merchant Exchange. Again, as at every other stop along the way, thousands of mourners filed by to view the remains.[10] In charge of the arrangements at Baltimore was Major General Lew Wallace, having just returned from negotiation with the warring factions in Mexico. Shortly after the Lincoln funeral, Wallace would be summoned to Washington to serve on the military commission for the trial of the assassination conspirators.[11]

The Northern Central Railroad took charge of the train for the run from Baltimore to Harrisburg, Pennsylvania. Along the way the train stopped at York, Pennsylvania, where a wreath was laid on the coffin.[12] The train's arrival in Harrisburg was saluted by twenty-one guns and tolling bells. The heavy rain that began falling just before the train pulled in made many think it was Heaven's own sorrow and wrath being expressed. The storm nearly spoiled the funeral procession, thoroughly soaking the mourners. The Hall of the House of Representatives at the state capitol was where the crowds viewed the remains on Saturday, April 22, the constant rain of the previous evening at least partially relenting.[13]

The casket was returned to the funeral car and the train left Harrisburg at 11 A.M. The Pennsylvania Railroad's engine number 331 was under the operation of John E. Miller. Thousands of mourners waited in towns along the route, even where the train did not stop, to see it go by. In Lancaster, Pennsylvania, former president James Buchanan, who had been so relieved to turn over the reins of the government to Lincoln four years before, now turned out to mourn his successor, in the company of Representative Thaddeus Stevens (1792–1868), one of the leading "Radical Republicans," who had opposed Lincoln's lenient reconstruction policy.

At 4:30 P.M. the funeral train arrived at Philadelphia's Broad Street Station. The Lincoln casket was taken by special hearse to Independence Hall, where Lincoln lay in state in the room in which America had been born nearly eighty-nine years before.[14] One hundred thousand marched in the funeral procession, with another three hundred thousand looking on. Lines had been forming to view the remains even before their arrival, and from 6 A.M. Sunday morning until 1 A.M. the next morning thousands filed through the historic building for this last look. People waited an average of four to five hours in lines that stretched up to five miles long to gain entrance. As at other stops, thousands had to be turned away when the appointed time came to close the coffin and return it to the train.[15]

Traveling by way of the Camden and Amboy Railroad, the train stopped at Trenton, New Jersey, then went on to Newark and Jersey City, where the funeral car crossed over to New York City on the ferry boat *New York*.[16]

Funeral procession in New York City. New York's parade was the largest of the many funeral parades along the route back to Springfield for burial (Library of Congress).

In New York it was reported that the huge crowds of that city's population were further swelled by thousands from neighboring cities and states. The casket was borne on a specially built car fourteen feet long by eight feet wide, and pulled by sixteen gray horses. All was draped in black cloth, set off with white and silver trim and flowers, topped by a high canopy and a miniature temple of liberty. Preceding the funeral car marched units of police and soldiers, with military bands spaced between. Commanding generals and colonels and their staff officers rode at the head of each unit. General John Adams Dix (1798–1879), who had commanded the New York area throughout the war, and was that day observing his sixty-seventh birthday, rode with his staff just in front of the funeral car. Following close behind the car was an even more aged general, Winfield Scott, who had been a national hero when Lincoln was still a small child. In another carriage rode Admiral Farragut and General Hunter.

The military portion of the procession was followed by legions of civilian groups and individuals, both New Yorkers and visitors, such as the Rev. Phineas Densmore Gurley (1816–1868), who had delivered an impressive prayer at Lincoln's bedside at the moment of his death. Governor Richard James Oglesby (1824–1899) of Illinois, Governor William Milo

Catafalque in New York City. Each city along the funeral route used a special hearse or conveyance, many built for the occasion. New York's was particularly elaborate and large (*Harper's Weekly*, May 6, 1865).

Stone (1827–1893) of Iowa, Senators James Warren Nye (1815–1876) of Nevada and Henry Bowen Anthony (1815–1884) of Rhode Island, and Representatives Elihu B. Washburne and John Franklin Farnsworth (1820–1897) of Illinois. Washburne, an old friend of Lincoln's, had been the first to greet him upon his arrival in Washington as president-elect. Among the other members of Congress in the procession was Senator Ira Harris (1802–1875) of New York, whose daughter Clara had been sitting in the theatre box only a few feet away from Lincoln when the fatal shot was fired. The long line of state and municipal officials was followed by diplomats representing more than forty nations. A detachment of the New York State Volunteers marched, bearing their flags torn by bullets, many of the men with an arm missing or other obvious injuries. On and on came the huge procession, political, military, civic, ethnic, fraternal, religious, and professional organizations, represented by hundreds, even thousands. The portion of the procession composed of citizens and groups from Brooklyn alone numbered over 10,000. Again, blacks had to take a place to the rear of the column, but many who stayed to see them march by remarked upon their dignity and obviously sincere grief. An oration by George Bancroft (1800–1891) highlighted the ceremonies.[17] The coffin rested in New York's City Hall as the people filed by, hour after hour. Mourners passed through at one hundred per minute, until more than one hundred fifty thousand had briefly glimpsed the remains. One hundred thousand had marched in the parade before nearly a million onlookers.[18]

Embalmers were called upon to attend to the remains, which by now were beginning to show the effects of time. Their work was considered successful. A photograph of the open casket was taken in New York but Secretary Stanton ordered the negative destroyed because Mrs. Lincoln had objected to "the shrunken and unnatural expression."[19] A single print survived, though it was not seen again for nearly ninety years.

Funeral decorations and displays in the Victorian era were more elaborate than would probably be seen today. Lincoln being president of the United States, with the additional circumstances of his death, brought forth a great outpouring of grief all across the nation. Public buildings were hung with great quantities of cloth or crepe, often wrapped around columns to create a spiral pattern. Large banners were hung from buildings, both public and private, with statements such as "The Nation Mourns," "The Greatest Man of Our Century," "Noblest Martyr to Freedom," "Rest In Peace Noble Soul." Black armbands or a length of black ribbon tied around one sleeve can be seen in photographs of prominent men of the time, indicating the photo was made during the mourning period. The funeral train was decorated with black cloth and a photo of the deceased placed on the engine. At every stop along the route of the train, black draped many buildings, and elaborate arches were constructed with messages of grief on them. Each city had a hearse to transport the coffin from the train to the place of viewing, with both hearse and viewing area swathed in black. Soldiers in full uniform stood guard around the coffin, both on the train and at each stop.[20]

On Tuesday, April 25, the funeral train resumed its journey. The Hudson River Railroad

Removal of coffin from New York City Hall. Several strong men were required to carry the heavy coffin whenever it had to be brought into a public building or placed on a special viewing stand (*Harper's Weekly*, May 13, 1865).

sent the engine *Constitution* over the track ahead of the funeral train, with George W. Wrightson at the controls of the engine *Union*. By late that evening the train reached Albany, where the casket was taken to the state capitol.[21] Congressman Robert Cumming Schenck (1809–1890) of Ohio, who made the journey even though he had been a critic of Lincoln, observed, "All along the road it has been affecting to see the people assembled not only at stations, but in front of farm houses, by the fences, and in fields beside the railway; to gaze at our passing funeral train — women often weeping and men standing respectfully uncovered."[22] The New York Central's engine *Dean Richmond* drew the train across New York State to Buffalo.

The multi-funerals had by now been going on for a week, but there was no lessening of interest. Even in the smaller cities the crowds numbered in the tens of thousands. Former president Millard Fillmore participated in the ceremonies at Buffalo, and even Canadians crossed over to witness the solemn spectacle. The journey resumed by way of Erie, Pennsylvania, to Cleveland, Ohio, with the Cleveland, Painsville and Ashtabula Railroad using the same engine that had pulled Lincoln's train on his inaugural journey, the "William Case," with John Benjamine as engineer. Special trains carried people to Cleveland to see the spectacle. Thirty-six guns were fired as the funeral train arrived at Cleveland's Euclid Street Station. The crowds were solemn and respectful, but police had their hands full arresting pick-pockets.[23] Schenck, commenting on his desire to leave the train, wrote, "It seems my duty to continue through for there had been a shameful falling off of the Congressional delegation."[24]

News of the extravagances of each city now roused the remaining cities to seek to outdo what had gone before. If they could not match the numbers of the eastern cities, they sought to make up for it with intensified fervor.[25] The Cleveland, Columbus and Cincinnati Railroad's engine *Nashville* drew the funeral train to Columbus, engineered by George West. Throughout most of Saturday, April 29, eight thousand people per hour passed by the open casket as it lay in the Ohio State Capitol. Outside, the huge crowd heard the oration given by Job Stevenson. Bells tolled, guns boomed, bands played the solemn music appropriate for the occasion. At six o'clock the coffin was closed and loaded back aboard the train, which departed from Columbus at eight P.M. The Columbus and Indianapolis Central Railroad, with engineer James Gourley, brought the train into Indianapolis, Indiana, at 7 A.M. on Sunday, April 30. The crowd that watched the procession to the state capitol numbered fifty thousand, the largest in the city's history at that time. Even the rain, which began falling about the time the train arrived, could not break up the solemn crowds. Governor Oliver Hazzard Perry Throck Morton (1823–1877) and General Joseph Hooker (1814–1879) rode at the head of the column, followed by six white horses drawing the hearse, decorated lavishly, as at other stops on the journey. Long lines of soldiers stood along the entire route from the train depot to the capitol.[26]

The cities along the route of the funeral train were not the only ones observing Lincoln's passing. On Thursday, April 20, San Francisco, California, saw a procession of 15,000 mourners, three miles long. Services were observed all over California and Nevada, and many other places that had never seen Lincoln in person.[27]

After traveling over the Lafayette and Indianapolis Railroad to Lafayette, Indiana, the train was transferred to the Louisville, New Albany and Chicago Railroad, whose engine, the *Persian*, was operated by A. Rupert for the journey to Michigan City, Indiana. The train stopped under an elaborately decorated canopy and people were permitted to pass through

Cook County Courthouse, Chicago. Crowds of people can be seen entering or exiting the courthouse for viewing the remains. Thousands passed rapidly by the casket at each city along the route. The building is decorated with mourning bands of black and white (Library of Congress).

the train car. So many people were anxious to view the remains that they pressed dangerously upon one another, several being knocked down and trampled upon. Soldiers had to threaten to stop allowing people aboard to restore order. As at every other stop, thousands were turned away. Engineer Frank Valkenberg, in the engine *Ranger*, took the train on from Michigan City to Chicago. A great arch, whose center span rose twenty-seven feet above ground, was the focus of attention as the coffin was taken off the train and loaded into the ceremonial hearse for the procession along Michigan Avenue, Lake Street and Clark Street to the courthouse, where the remains lay in state to be viewed as one hundred twenty five thousand people passed through.[28]

When it had belatedly been decided that Lincoln's resting place would be Springfield, there was a flurry of activity building arches along the rail route and setting up facilities for the ceremonies. At first it was proposed that a tomb be erected on the Mather Place, where the new state capitol would later be built. When Mrs. Lincoln objected to this and insisted upon Oak Ridge Cemetery, a temporary vault became the focus of attention.

Springfield had grown considerably since Lincoln left four years before. Its fifteen thousand people could stroll broad streets paved with planks, though mud was still a problem, and people were fined for letting their hogs run loose. Sixty-three saloons were operating,

Old State Capitol, Springfield. Lincoln's remains were displayed in the chamber of the House of Representatives, in this building which he knew so well. The Old State Capitol still stands, restored as it was in Lincoln's time (Library of Congress).

and horse-drawn streetcars passed along gas-lit streets. The city was strained to the limit, having to deal with one hundred fifty thousand visitors.[29]

In Springfield, Lincoln's former home was hung with both black and white drapery, and the Old State Capitol was likewise elaborately hung with black and white around the windows, along the eaves of the roof, and all over the dome. The building that had housed Lincoln's law office had heavily draped windows and balcony railing. An arch made of cuttings from evergreen trees had been formed at the gateway to Oak Ridge Cemetery, Lincoln's last resting place. Many parlors contained glass-domed displays, often with a cross or picture of Lincoln. Lapel badges were available, made of cloth or metal, or both, often with a picture. Ads for these and other types of decorations appeared in newspapers for weeks after the assassination. There was, no doubt, a certain amount of cashing in on the mourners' desire to display their bereavement, but the grief was genuine, and persisted long after the funerals were concluded.[30]

The Chicago, Alton and St. Louis Railroad ran the last engine to pull the Lincoln funeral train, engineered by James Colting in engine number 58. At every town along the tracks between Chicago and Springfield, whether or not the train was scheduled to stop, thousands waited at the stations or along the tracks. The train arrived, late by almost an hour, just before nine o'clock on the morning of Wednesday, May 3. Edmund Beall, a young veteran who had helped drape the Lincoln house and had worked on setting up the benches at the tomb, was on the platform when the train pulled in. "It was almost impossible to keep the crowd back. A splendid hearse was waiting and after the body was placed in the hearse, the American flag was placed over the casket.... Pickpockets were very numerous. I remember General Joe Hooker spying one, as the pickpocket was robbing one of the spectators, and he gave the thief a kick that sent him not less than ten to fifteen feet." The great hearse was the same one that had carried the remains of Senator Thomas Hart Benton (1782–1858). After passing through town to the statehouse, the casket was displayed in the Hall of the House of Representatives. By ten o'clock the first of the mourners entered and filed past the coffin. All the rest of the day and through the night people climbed the stairs and took their last look.

At ten the next morning the casket was removed to the waiting hearse, as a choir of two hundred and fifty sang hymns, and the procession to the cemetery got under way. Local tinsmith Samuel S. Elder, whose shop was close to the statehouse, had sealed the lead-lined coffin just before it had been taken out for the last portion of its journey. Along with the generals and statesmen also rode "Old Bob," the horse that had carried Lincoln around the judicial circuit years before, now walking riderless. Principal speaker at the funeral service was Matthew Simpson (1811–1884), an Episcopal bishop and friend of Lincoln, whose eloquence at patriotic meetings throughout the war was legendary. The Reverend Albert Hale opened the service with a prayer, then a dirge composed by G. W. Root was sung, followed by a reading of Lincoln's Second Inaugural Address, by the Reverend A. C. Hubbard, then Bishop Simpson's address.[31]

The war had ended and the people had rejoiced, but the bitterness and blood of four hard years of fighting had not been publicly noted until Lincoln's funeral had provided the occasion. Not only had a great leader been lost, but a whole nation now mourned the hundreds of thousands of casualties of the war, and took note of the great ordeal through which the nation had passed. It would be said later that Stanton and others arranged the multiple funerals in order to fan the flames of hatred for the South, but report after report of the crowds and their behavior told the same story, a universal outpouring of mourning and genuine grief. Those who saw the great spectacle were astounded by the size of the crowds again and again. The feelings they reported were genuine, not managed or arranged.

Bishop Simpson closed his oration with a quote from his friend. "How joyful that [the flag] floated over parts of every state before Mr. Lincoln's career was ended! How singular that to the fact of the assassin's heel being caught in the folds of the flag we are probably indebted for his capture. The time will come when, in the beautiful words of him whose lips are now forever sealed, 'The mystic chords of memory, which stretch from every battlefield and from every patriot's grave, shall yield a sweeter music when touched by the angels of our better nature."[32]

15. Rest in Peace

> But where shall wisdom be found?
> And where is the place of understanding?
> Man knoweth not the price thereof;
> Neither is it found in the land of the living.
>
> Job 28: 12–13

After Lincoln's remains were brought to Springfield they were placed in a receiving vault at Oak Ridge Cemetery on May 4, 1865.[1] The National Lincoln Monument Association had been founded by a number of Lincoln's friends, and they had the remains moved to a temporary tomb about seventy-five yards from the receiving vault.[2] On December 21, 1865, when the removal took place, the coffin was opened to confirm the identity of the remains.[3]

The association initiated a competition for designs for a permanent monument to enclose the tomb. It wasn't until 1868 that this competition was finally organized and designs received. Thirty-one artists submitted a total of thirty-seven designs. They included sculptors Vinnie Ream (1847–1915) and Leonard Wells Volk (1828–1895), who had known Lincoln and had made casts of his face and hands from life. The winning design was by Larkin Goldsmith Mead, Jr. (1835–1910), of Brattleboro, Vermont.[4] Construction began September 9, 1869. With the completion of the catacomb crypt, the remains were moved from the temporary vault on September 19, 1871. It was found that the lead lining of the coffin was broken, requiring the transfer of the remains to another coffin lined with iron. Again the coffin was opened and the remains identified by the same individuals who had done so in 1865. When the white marble sarcophagus was ready to receive the coffin on October 9, 1874, the iron coffin was too large to fit, and a new one of red cedar lined with lead replaced it. The workmen doing the transfer again had to open the coffin, and they all agreed upon the identity. The monument was completed and dedicated on October 15, 1874. The cost of construction had been $173,000.[5]

In 1867 a Springfield, Illinois, lawyer suggested to two men that they might steal Abraham Lincoln's remains and hold them for ransom. They could break into the tomb and take the remains south, even as far as Mexico. The men the lawyer talked to refused to be involved in such a scheme, and nothing came of it. However, in 1876 a serious attempt was made by a gang of counterfeiters to steal the remains in an effort to obtain the release from prison of a skilled counterfeit bill engraver.[6]

Printed money, called "greenbacks," were widely circulated during the Civil War, beginning with the Legal Tender Act of February 25, 1862. After $450 million in paper had been issued, Congress attempted to discontinue their use on December 18, 1865, but their popularity with the public kept the greenbacks in circulation.[7] Benjamin F. Boyd was one of the

Receiving vault, Oak Ridge Cemetery. Lincoln's casket was placed in this vault until a permanent tomb could be constructed (photograph by author).

best engravers of his time. Unfortunately, he was also a counterfeiter. The counterfeiting business in the Midwest was dealt a serious setback on October 20, 1875, when Boyd was arrested by the U.S. Secret Service. James B. Kinealy (1832–?), officially a carpenter and livery stable operator, was actually a front man for counterfeiters. He and his associates in crime began to suffer with Boyd's arrest, and Kinealy had an idea to get Boyd released and back to work. He proposed to his counterfeiter friends that they break into the Lincoln tomb, steal the remains, and hide them in the Sangamon River. At the right moment, Kinealy would claim he had found the remains and claim the rewards, which he expected to be considerable. The gang was set to act on July 4, 1876, the eve of the nation's centennial, but one of their members bragged to a prostitute about the scheme. The woman passed on the information to the police. As word of their plot got out, the would-be grave robbers dispersed.[8]

Kinealy was unwilling to give up his scheme, so he recruited another gang to try again. Wanting to stay behind the scenes, Kinealy made a Chicago bartender named Terrence Mullen (1849–?) his chief operative. Mullen, 5' 6¾" tall, 176 pounds, and with a large handlebar moustache, was the proprietor of "The Hub," a saloon at 294 W. Madison Street in Chicago. Mullen's principal assistant was John Hughes, known as "Jack." For his particular expertise, Lewis C. Swegles (c.1850–?), who told Hughes he was a body snatcher who supplied medical schools, was also enlisted.[9]

Unknown to Mullen and Hughes, Swegles was a "roper" for the Secret Service. A roper was an undercover informant who would win the confidence of the criminals, join their organization, then report on their activities to the lawmen. Not officially a Treasury agent, Swegles would be paid for his services. The man to whom he reported was Patrick D. Tyrrell (1832–?), U.S. Secret Service chief for the Chicago area. A former Chicago police detective, Tyrrell was brought into the Secret Service by the former chief of Chicago police, Elmer E. Washburn (1834–1918), who had been Secret Service chief from 1874 to 1876.[10] When Swegles told Tyrrell about the grave robbing plot, Tyrrell reported it to his chief. At that time, the Secret Service was primarily involved in counterfeiting cases, not in protecting presidents, dead or alive. The new chief, James J. Brooks, told Tyrrell to contact the late president's son, Robert T. Lincoln, who lived in Chicago. Tyrrell met with Robert Lincoln on October 28, 1876. When Robert learned what the counterfeiters were planning, he asked Tyrrell to prevent it. Reporting this request to Chief Brooks, Tyrrell was authorized to proceed with the investigation.[11]

The key man in uncovering and defeating the plot was Swegles. Tyrrell sent Swegles back to continue to learn more and report it all to him. He also suggested to the Lincoln tomb caretakers that no guards be posted, in order to catch the thieves in the act. Robert Lincoln asked a Lincoln family friend, Leonard Swett, to assist him in handling all matters relating to the tomb robbery attempt.[12]

Swegles reported that in a meeting of the conspirators on November 2, Mullen had suggested they demand a ransom. They still wanted the release of Boyd, but they now believed that a great deal of money could be made as well. The figure of $200,000 was agreed upon. On November 6, Swegles told Tyrrell that the attempt to steal the body would occur the following night, November 7. The excitement of election day would help to distract the authorities. Also, Mullen wanted to act before the harsh winter weather arrived. Tyrrell now was hard pressed to be ready to foil the thieves. Unable to spare any additional Secret Service agents, he was able to recruit Elmer E. Washburn, his former boss. Robert Lincoln suggested the detectives get in touch with Allan Pinkerton, who had been instrumental in saving Lincoln's life in 1861. Pinkerton supplied two of his men to help Tyrrell and Washburn, John C. McGinn and George Hay.[13]

Election night, 1876, was a good choice for the grave robbers, for the presidential election campaign was extremely hard fought and close, an occasion of much excitement. When Tyrrell met Washburn on the evening of November 7, he found his former chief had obtained two more men, John McDonald and John English, both veterans of the Secret Service. English, now a *Chicago Tribune* reporter, was sworn to secrecy but was confident of getting a scoop for his paper. The detectives stationed themselves inside the tomb, in Memorial Hall. The labyrinthine design of the tomb ensured that the robbers would not know the detectives were there. It had been agreed that Swegles would get to them while Mullen and Hughes were breaking into the sarcophagus. While waiting, the detectives became anxious when no signal came from Swegles. Unknown to them, the robbers had encountered problems and delays breaking in. They pressed Swegles into service holding a lamp as they worked on the sarcophagus, making it impossible for Swegles to slip out and get word to the detectives. At last the moment came, but Swegles had to take a roundabout course, for Mullen and Hughes came outside with him.

Lincoln's tomb, Springfield. The permanent tomb in Oak Ridge Cemetery sits on top of a hill. The sculpture groups represent the various military services. The tomb has been rebuilt several times, and it was here that grave robbers attempted to steal the remains in 1876. Photograph of the reburial in 1901 (Library of Congress).

Finally receiving the signal from Swegles, Tyrrell and his men drew their guns and hurried outside. In making their way around the tomb to its opposite side, Hay accidentally discharged his pistol. The loud report warned Mullen and Hughes, who dropped everything and ran. Tyrrell, peering through the blackness, spotted a man and called to him to halt. Shots were exchanged. Finally, upon hearing Tyrrell's voice, the other man called out to him. Tyrrell and his men moved in, only to discover that Hay was the man Tyrrell had been firing upon. Fortunately, no one had been hit, but Mullen and Hughes had escaped.[14]

When news of the attempted tomb robbery got out there was a mixture of indignation, disbelief, and cynicism. Some saw political motives behind the crime, to sway voters one way or the other in a close election. The *Chicago Tribune* of November 8 called the crime "one of the most infamous outrages which the mind of man can conceive of," and further stated, "The scheme concocted by these men is certainly unparalleled in the history of crime and, now that there is evidence of minds so debased, it is certain that measures will be taken to guard the monument and prevent future attempts."[15]

Lincoln's coffin was secretly placed in one of the recesses in the walls on November 15, 1876. It had to be moved again on November 22, 1878, when the installation of statuary required changes in the recesses. On April 14, 1887, a new vault beneath the floor of the sarcophagus was completed. Lincoln's remains were again moved, and once again the coffin was opened and a positive identification made. The remains of Mary Todd Lincoln were placed beside those of her husband upon her death in 1882.

Unequal settling of the stone structure opened cracks that were worsened by the ravages of the elements. By 1899 the tomb needed to be rebuilt, and again the Lincoln remains had to be moved to a temporary vault. Robert Lincoln arranged with J. S. Culver, of the Culver Construction Co. of Springfield, to bury the remains inside a steel cage, which would then be immersed in concrete, presumably eliminating for all time the possibility of interference. Although Robert Lincoln did not want the Lincoln casket opened, it was thought by those present that an identification should be done before they would be permanently entombed in concrete. On September 26, 1901, the coffin was opened and the remains viewed for the fifth and final time. In spite of the passage of time, the viewers could easily recognize the remains as those of Abraham Lincoln.

Lincoln's casket was placed in a vault ten feet beneath the floor of the catacomb, sheathed by and made a part of a solid block of steel-reinforced concrete. The casket lies in an east-west orientation, with the head to the west. The monument had to be rebuilt again in 1930, being taken apart and entirely reconstructed. Work was finished in June 1931, with an expenditure of $175,000.[16]

16. Aftermath

> When I have seen by Time's fell hand defaced
> The rich-proud cost of outworn buried age;
> When sometime lofty towers I see down-razed,
> And brass eternal slave to mortal rage;
> When I have seen the hungry ocean gain
> Advantage on the kingdom of the shore,
> And the firm soil win of the watery main,
> Increasing store with loss and loss with store;
> When I have seen such interchange of state,
> Or state itself confounded to decay;
> Ruin hath taught me thus to ruminate,
> That time will come and take my love away.
>   This thought is as a death, which cannot choose
>   But weep to have that which it fears to lose.
> William Shakespeare, Sonnet 64

Following the assassination of Lincoln, official protection for the president of the United States was allowed to decline. No official full-time protective organization existed for decades. The United States Secret Service, the agency that today has primary responsibility for protecting the president and other leaders and their families, was occasionally given a protective assignment, but only on an unofficial basis. It was not until 1907 that Congress finally appropriated funds "for the protection of the person of the President of the United States," a duty that fell to the Secret Service because they were the only federal investigative and law enforcement agency other than the U.S. Marshals Service. The Secret Service's presidential protection function was considered a temporary one, subject to renewal, until 1951, when it was finally made a permanent duty.[1]

The people who had figured in the story of Lincoln's assassination lived out their lives usually quietly.

After Thomas A. Jones had managed to get Booth and Herold across the Potomac River, both he and Samuel Cox, Sr., were arrested. They had been questioned by the soldiers looking for Booth, and were suspected of involvement. Held at Bryantown, Maryland, they were joined by another suspect, Dr. Samuel A. Mudd. Oswald Swann had told the authorities that Cox had let the man with a broken leg into his house. Cox steadfastly denied it. He received support from a black servant, Mary Swann. Sharing a jail cell with Jones, Cox whispered to him, "What shall we do, Tom?" to which Jones replied, "Stick to what you have said and admit nothing else." The soldiers and their commander, Colonel Henry Horatio Wells (1823–1890), used every sort of threat and intimidation they could to get the men to confess. Cox finally admitted to Wells that two men had stopped at his house, but denied that he had known who they were. After two days, Cox was taken to Washington and locked in Carroll Prison. Jones followed him after another week. Although no longer in the same cell together, Jones and Cox managed to meet in the exercise yard. Cox told Jones that he was being held in solitary confinement and that his spirits were low. Soon, though, the rigorous questioning relaxed. The government chose not to try to make a case against either Cox or Jones. After six weeks Jones was released, and Cox followed him to freedom about a week later.

After his release, Cox returned to his life at his farm, Rich Hill. He continued to advocate the building of a railroad, hoping to profit from encouraging the establishment of a settlement in Charles County, called Cox's Station. There Cox built a hotel and store, and several houses. Laying out one-acre plots, he had a few takers. Cox also served four years as president of the County Board of School Commissioners. Samuel Cox, Sr., died January 7, 1880.[2]

Lieutenant Edward P. Doherty's share of the reward money was $5,250. Attempting to claim a share of rewards offered by the cities of Washington and Baltimore, Doherty went to court. The U.S. District Court for DC ruled that the city of Washington had had no authority to offer a reward. His appeal to the U.S. Supreme Court was fruitless. A new administration in Baltimore repudiated the reward offered by that city, and Doherty did not pursue the matter.

Appointed a second lieutenant of the Fifth Regular Cavalry in July 1866, Doherty became inspector general of the Department of Georgia, under the command of Major General George Gordon Meade. He was promoted to first lieutenant in March 1867. From March 1868 to November 1869, Doherty served in Kansas and Nebraska. Promoted to captain, he took part in Indian fighting, becoming acquainted with William Frederick "Buffalo Bill" Cody (1846–1917), then serving as a scout for the army. Doherty served in Wyoming the following year. Tried by a military commission that charged him with being "morally unfit of character," Doherty was found guilty and dismissed from the army on December 27, 1870.

Doherty was married to Catherine J. Gautier on November 17, 1871. Her father, Charles Gautier, owned the restaurant in Washington where Booth had met with his fellow conspirators. Doherty's son, Charles J. G. Doherty (?–1939), was his only child.

For several years Doherty was a street contractor in New Orleans, Louisiana, returning to New York City in 1886. From 1888 until his death, he was New York City's inspector of street pavings. Active in veterans organizations, he was commander of post 436 of the Grand Army of the Republic, and belonged to the 71st Regiment Veterans and the Press Veterans. He twice served as grand marshal in Memorial Day observances.

Dohety kept in contact with Boston Corbett by letter, even suggesting that they appear together on the stage in a "panorama" of the capture of Booth. Corbett did not respond to that suggestion. "Buffalo Bill" Cody also kept in touch with Doherty, later writing to Mrs. Doherty to assure her that her husband had been wrongfully convicted at his court martial.

Edward P. Doherty died of heart disease at his home at 533 West 144th Street, New York City, on April 3, 1897. Services were held at the church of St. Charles Boromeo, with James Rowan O'Bierne (1838–1917), who had also chased Booth, serving as a pallbearer. Burial was at Arlington National Cemetery.[3]

Everton J. Conger told his version of the capture and death of Booth at the trial of the conspirators in 1865, at the trial of John Surratt in 1867, and at the impeachment investigation of President Andrew Johnson in 1867. He stuck to his story that he had commanded the soldiers who caught Booth, and Booth said nothing to implicate anyone else as he was dying, and that Booth's diary had not been tampered with after Conger took it from him.

Conger collected $15,000 of the reward money offered for Booth, the largest share paid to a single individual. He loaned $5,000 of it to a friend but was never repaid. The remainder of the money he used to build a house in Carmi, Illinois, where he had moved with his family in 1869. Returning to the practice of dentistry, he also studied law with his brother, Chauncey S. Conger, who was a circuit judge in Carmi. Everton Conger was admitted to the bar in 1871, and was elected police magistrate. In 1880, he was appointed a federal judge in Montana Territory. Another brother, Omar Dwight Conger (1818–1898), served in the U.S. Congress as a representative from Michigan from 1869 to 1881, and as United States senator from 1881 to 1887. Everton conger moved to Honolulu, Hawaii, in the early 1890s, where his brother-in-law, Joseph B. Poindexter, became a judge. The former colonel became friendly with the Hawaiian queen, Liliuokalani (1838–1917), the last Hawaiian monarch.

Early in 1915, the aged Colonel Conger visited his daughter in Long Beach, California. While he was in town, he was invited to attend a performance of the film *The Birth of a Nation* by the film's director, David Wark Griffith (1875–1948). Conger appeared on stage and addressed the audience about the capture of Booth.

Everton J. Conger died July 12, 1918, in Honolulu. Judge Poindexter accompanied the remains to Dillon, Montana, for burial.[4]

Initially, Boston Corbett returned to the hat-making business, working for Samuel Mason of Boston, one of his pre-war employers. He gave several interviews in the postwar years. By 1870 he was working in a hat factory near Philadelphia and living alone at 328 Pine Street, in Camden, New Jersey, in a "little forlorn-looking house," cooking for himself. He held religious services in this house, using a Windsor chair for a pulpit. By 1886 Corbett moved to Kansas, claiming a soldier's homestead near the town of Concordia. He lived alone, frightening off visitors. During this time Corbett exchanged letters with his former commanding officer, Edward Doherty.

In 1887 Corbett became third assistant doorkeeper of the Kansas legislature, but lost the job when, on February 15, 1887, he threatened the officers of the House with a pistol, and had to be subdued by the police. Adjudged insane, he was confined to the asylum in Topeka, where he continued to show signs of mental imbalance, including trying to attack an attendant with a knife. Escaping from the asylum on May 26, 1888, he fled to Neodesha, Kansas, where he may have visited an old friend, Richard Thatcher, who had been with him in Andersonville. Thatcher indicated Corbett was going to Mexico. That is the last we know of him for sure. Stories have been told of Corbett becoming a salesman based in Enid, Oklahoma. The claim of a man in Texas received much attention, but ultimately proved false. A man fitting Corbett's general description, calling himself "Tom Corbett from Boston," was reported killed in the great forest fire at Hinckley, Minnesota, in 1894. It could have been the real Boston Corbett, but no remains of "Tom Corbett of Boston" were ever found.[5]

Convicted and sentenced to life in prison at hard labor, Samuel Bland Arnold was imprisoned at Fort Jefferson at the southern end of the Florida Keys. His clerical experience got him a job at the provost marshal's office. Because his shackles made noise, which disturbed the officers, Arnold was allowed to be unshackled. He kept notes on everything he saw and heard, later describing many instances of brutal treatment by officers, not only of the prisoners, but also of the enlisted men doing guard duty. He expressed his belief that it was the intention of the government that the conspiracy prisoners should never leave Fort Jefferson alive. One of the conspirators, Michael O'Laughlen, died of yellow fever, as did a number of other prisoners and guards. Arnold, who recovered from the disease, assisted fellow prisoner Dr. Mudd in treating the sick.

Arnold passed up an offer for early release if he would implicate others in the conspiracy. As Congress was preparing to impeach President Andrew Johnson, they sent an officer, William H. Gleason (1829–1902), to interview the prisoners, all of whom stuck to their stories. On March 1, 1869, as he was about to leave office, President Johnson pardoned Arnold, stating, "It is apparent that the said Arnold rendered no active assistance whatsoever to the said Booth and his confederates."

Samuel Arnold spent his later years on his farm in Anne Arundel County, Maryland. He was a recluse who remained bitter over his experiences. The account he had been writing over the years was finally published in the Baltimore American in 1902. Developing consumption, Arnold died at his sister-in-law's home in Baltimore on September 21, 1906. He was buried at Greenmount Cemetery, where O'Laughlen and Booth are also interred.[6]

George Andrew Atzerodt dropped his knife in an F Street gutter, pawned his pistol at Matthews and Co. grocery store in Georgetown, getting ten dollars for it, and left Washington. As Atzerodt headed toward his cousin's house in Montgomery County, Maryland, his room at the Kirkwood House yielded clues for the authorities. A knife and pistol were found, along with a map of Virginia and a coat with a bank statement for "Mr. J. Wilkes Booth, in account with the Ontario Bank, Canada," in the pocket. Atzerodt did not leave these items behind; they had been planted by Booth and Herold in order to further incriminate him. The authorities were aided in their search for Atzerodt by his brother John, who was by this time a detective living in Baltimore and serving on the force of Baltimore Provost Marshal James L. McPhail. John gave a good description of his brother and told of occasions when George had been seen with John Surratt and Herold. He probably also suggested that George might be found at his cousin's house. Atzerodt stopped at the home of Hezekiah Metz, where he casually joined in the speculation about the assassination, then went on to the house of his cousin, Hartman Richter. Here he was arrested early on the morning of April 20, 1865. As the soldiers were unsure what each suspect knew, or whom was involved, they also arrested Richter. Both men were taken back to Washington and held aboard the monitor U.S.S. *Saugus* at the Navy Yard.

In trying to save himself, Atzerodt proved to be very cooperative. He made four confessions, adding more details and naming other conspirators. Stable manager John Fletcher, who had rented a horse to Atzerodt on April 14, quoted him as saying, "If this thing happens tonight, you will hear of a present." When Fletcher said he thought the horse might be unsuitable to take out that night, Atzerodt replied, "She is good upon the retreat." These statements must have carried a lot of weight with the military commission at the trial. Another witness, Marcus P. Norton, testified he saw Atzerodt meet with Booth and near enough to say they were talking about "Mr. Johnson." Atzerodt's lawyer, William Emile Doster, tried to use the defendant's bad qualities in his favor, establishing Atzerodt's cowardly nature to suggest he would not have had nerve enough to kill Johnson. Atzerodt, heavily chained and required to wear a large iron ball linked to his leg irons, often cowered and tried to conceal himself when he was referred to directly. In the end, Atzerodt was found guilty and sentenced to hang. His mother visited him the night before the execution, and the obvious distress of both mother and son made an impression upon the guards. He received one other visitor, an unknown woman, mistakenly presumed by reporters to be his sister. It was probably Mrs. Rose Wheeler, his Port Tobacco, Maryland, mistress. A minister, Dr. John George Butler (1826–1909), spent much time with Atzerodt, who seemed to benefit from the spiritual consolation.

Atzerodt died on the scaffold, next to Herold, Powell, and Mrs. Surratt, on July 7, 1865. Released to the family in 1869, Atzerodt's remains were first buried in Glenwood Cemetery, then moved to St. Paul's Cemetery, Druid Hill Park, in Baltimore, under the fictitious name Gottlieb Taubert.[7]

Standing trial with the other conspirators, Lewis Thornton Powell was one of four condemned to death. Unlike the others, Powell was stoical right to the end. Hanged on July 7, 1865, his final burial place remains unknown, although a skull discovered in the Smithsonian Institution in 1992 was identified as Powell's and buried beside the grave of Powell's mother in Geneva, Florida, on November 12, 1994.[8]

Together with Arnold, O'Laughlen, and Dr. Mudd, Edman Spangler was sent to the military prison, Fort Jefferson. Treatment of the prisoners there was harsh, though Spangler did not claim to have been singled out for discipline. Working at his carpentry, he made

Washington Arsenal yard with scaffold. This was the scene of the execution of four of those convicted of conspiring to kill the president. The scaffold can be seen on the right side, just inside the wall (Library of Congress).

Hanging. Four of the conspiracy suspects were executed on July 7, 1865, at the arsenal prison in Washington, DC. The four were, left to right, Mary Surratt, Lewis Powell, David Herold, and George Atzerodt. Initially buried at the arsenal, their remains were released to their families (Library of Congress).

wooden boxes and trinkets for the officers, who were impressed enough by his ability to treat him decently. The yellow fever epidemic claimed the life of one of the Lincoln conspiracy prisoners, O'Laughlen, but it also helped bring the three survivors closer together. Spangler became especially friendly with Dr. Mudd. When they were finally pardoned and released in 1869, Spangler had no one else to apply to but Mudd. He arrived at the Mudd farm, after two years of making his way north, and was welcomed as an old friend. With Ford's Theatre closed, Spangler was dependant on Mudd, who let him farm five acres. In exchange, Spangler did repair work for the Mudd family and their neighbors.

Not having bothered to build himself an adequate shelter, Spangler caught cold, ran a fever, and died on February 7, 1875. Dr. Mudd called his ailment "rheumatism of the heart." He was buried at the cemetery of St. Peter's Church in Bryantown, Maryland. His guilt, or lack of guilt, remains controversial to this day. Samuel Arnold suggested that Spangler knew of the abduction plot beforehand, but Atzerodt stated he believed Spangler to be innocent. Although Spangler stated that he was entirely innocent, his statement appears in a newspaper article that was obviously ghostwritten.[9]

At the trial of the conspirators, the case for Dr. Samuel Alexander Mudd soon began to look bad, and grew worse as the government prosecutors presented witnesses whose testimony, when viewed through the eyes of those looking for guilt, made the doctor seem not only to be lying but also deeply involved in the conspiracy. In considering their verdict, the military commission simply could not believe that Dr. Mudd did not recognize the man he treated at his home the night of the assassination. After having heard testimony such as Louis Weichmann's that Mudd knew Booth well, Mudd's denials and evasiveness seemed to justify the verdict of guilty. Voting on what punishment the doctor would receive, five of the commissioners favored death by hanging, with four voting for life imprisonment at hard labor. Because a two-thirds vote was required for the death sentence, Dr. Mudd's life was spared by a single vote.[10]

The prisoners were told of the guilty verdicts but not immediately informed of their punishment. The four who would not hang were left to wonder for hours and days. At first

Fort Jefferson. Four other conspiracy suspects were imprisoned at Fort Jefferson, located at the western end of the Florida Keys. Sentenced to life at hard labor were Samuel Arnold, Michael O'Laughlen, and Dr. Samuel Mudd. Sentenced to six years was Edman Spangler (courtesy of Surratt House Museum/MNCPPC).

it was planned to imprison Dr. Mudd and his three fellow prisoners in the penitentiary at Albany, New York. Two days before they were to be sent there the plan was changed. It was decreed that they be sent to Fort Jefferson instead. It probably was Secretary of War Edwin M. Stanton who suggested the change, perhaps fearing that an attempt might be made to liberate the prisoners.[11]

Dr. Mudd, with his medical background, was put to work in the prison hospital. Dr. Mudd and Arnold were not at first chained, since they worked indoors with the prison officers. Dr. Mudd's early letters from prison are full of suggestions, advice, and expressions of hope that his conviction might be overturned and he would soon be released. "I have had several opportunities to make my escape, but know, or believing, it would show guilt, I have resolved to remain peaceable and quiet, and allow the government the full exercise of its power, justice and clemency." The prisoners busied themselves doing craft work, making game boards, decorative boxes, even articles of furniture, all of which they sent to relatives and friends.[12]

In mid–September 1865, there was a change of the guard. The outgoing guards, with whom the prisoners had gotten along, were replaced by black soldiers of the 80th and 82nd U.S. Colored Infantry. Assuming he, as a Southern former slaveowner and Lincoln assassination conspirator, would be singled out for bad treatment, Dr. Mudd feared for his life. The idea of escape, which he had considered before, now became a plan of action. With the help of a crew member of one of the supply ships, Dr. Mudd hid himself aboard, under loose planks of a lower deck. Prison authorities realized he was missing before the ship sailed, however, and soon located the fugitive.

Now the harsh punishment Dr. Mudd had feared began. For the first time, he had to wear heavy chains, including an iron ball, and he was closely watched by guards. Removed from the prison hospital, he now had to do common labor in the yard in the blazing hot sun. His food was bad — as Arnold said, "putrid, unfit to eat!"[13]

With the failure of his escape attempt, Dr. Mudd turned his attention to the legal struggle to reverse his conviction. The legal battle continued, despite setbacks, until late 1868, when Judge Thomas Jefferson Boynton (1838–c.1870) of the District Court of the Southern District of Florida decided case no. 9,899, *Ex parte Mudd.* Boynton found that "the crime of murdering the President of the United States in time of civil war is triable by a military commission." Boynton also found that President Andrew Johnson's amnesty proclamation of 1868 did not apply to the assassination conspirators.[14]

Dr. Mudd grew bitter, and suspected his case was not being handled fairly by the government. When John H. Surratt was brought to trial in a civil court, the result was that the jury could not agree on his guilt and he was eventually set free. Dr. Mudd eagerly followed the trial in the newspapers, and hinted at his feelings in another letter to his wife. "For God's sake urge action on the part of those entrusted with the care of my case. [Jefferson] Davis has been set free, and Surratt, once regarded as his prime agent, seems now without a charge against him, and here am I, having suffered the tortures of the damned, ... without pity, sympathy, or consolation from an enlightened public."[15]

Conditions at Fort Jefferson grew rapidly worse. Discipline among the military guards was poor, with drunken officers looking the other way as non-coms beat and abused the privates, who passed along such treatment to the prisoners. By the beginning of September 1867, the feared epidemic of yellow fever was upon the island, striking down prisoners and guards alike. At first, Dr. Mudd expected the authorities to remove the prisoners from Fort Jefferson, but it was soon obvious that no one would leave. The post doctor died, and Dr.

Mudd served at the only medical man until a new doctor could arrive. On September 8, he wrote his cousin, "Nearly every man now on the island is infected with the disease. The hospitals are full, and the greatest consternation prevails."

Within days the population of Fort Jefferson was entirely in the grip of the epidemic. Dr. Mudd labored constantly to relieve the suffering of the stricken. Some of the other prisoners also volunteered, doing the disagreeable and dangerous duties so necessary to provide whatever hope there was. Supplies ran short, contact with the mainland having been halted, and scurvy cases began to be seen. Suffering patients could look beside their cots and see the coffins, ready and waiting, in which they would be buried. "The island which before was more like a place peopled by fiends..." wrote Arnold, "suddenly became calm, quiet and peaceful. Fear stood out in bold relief upon the face of every human soul."

Samuel Arnold fell ill with yellow fever, and Dr. Mudd isolated him and personally tended his fellow prisoner. Arnold was making a recovery when Michael O'Laughlen came down with the disease. Although at first it appeared O'Laughlen, too, would pull through, he began convulsing on September 21, and, despite the skills and efforts of Dr. Mudd, assisted by Spangler, their patient died a day and a half later.

Of three hundred who had caught the disease, the deaths were held down to forty, and prisoners and their guards alike credited Dr. Mudd with the saving of so many lives. After the worst seemed over, Dr. Mudd likewise became a casualty. Spangler and the recovering Arnold nursed the doctor according to Mudd's directions. As soon as Dr. Mudd was well enough to arise from his sickbed he resumed his duties tending the sick.

With the nightmare of the epidemic passed, efforts were renewed to have Dr. Mudd pardoned in recognition of his services. One of the guards wrote, "It is simple justice and gratitude to acknowledge the skilful and self sacrificing service he rendered." He went on to describe how Mudd, Arnold and Spangler went about their duties "without complaint, and with apparent cheerfulness; if the iron sometimes enter their souls, or the bitterness of their situation be felt, it is never exhibited."[16]

Near the end of 1867 the conspiracy prisoners were interviewed for the congressional committee investigating President Johnson. Arnold stated that the prisoners were told that if they would make sworn statements implicating others, they would be set free. Arnold insisted on writing his own statement, even though sick with dysentery. Spangler also made a statement, but Dr. Mudd did not. The prisoners were back in chains again, and Dr. Mudd learned that the petition sent by the garrison on his behalf had not been submitted to the authorities. Dr. Mudd believed that the petition had been destroyed by the fort commander.

Time dragged on. Months passed, finally a whole year and more after the epidemic, and Mudd and the others remained imprisoned. Receiving news that his mother had died, Dr. Mudd vented his grief and despair: "Can I forgive those who have so inhumanely and maliciously caused our separation, and deprived me of affording all the consolation in my power — a debt of love and gratitude I owe — to the kindest and most loving of mothers? May the chastisement of Heaven fall upon and crush them to a sense of their wrong."[17]

On February 13, 1869, President Johnson, about to leave office, issued a pardon for Dr. Mudd. Frances Mudd received the document personally from the president. Unable to catch the boat for Florida, having just missed its departure, she sent the papers to her brother in New Orleans, who got them to Fort Jefferson by March 8. Dr. Mudd arrived home on March 20, 1869, "frail, weak and sick, never again to be strong during the thirteen years he survived."

Catching a cold while visiting patients on New Year's Day in 1883, Dr. Mudd took to bed with a fever and died on the night of January 10, 1883, at the age of forty-nine years. He was buried in the cemetery of St. Mary's Church near Bryantown, Maryland.[18]

Over the years, efforts have been made to have Dr. Mudd's case reviewed. The Mudd family has spearheaded these efforts, especially Dr. Richard Dyer Mudd (1901–2002), who tirelessly crusaded on his grandfather's behalf for decades. In 1933 a bill was introduced in Congress to rename Fort Jefferson "Fort Mudd." The following year there was an effort to have the U.S. government compensate the Mudd family for Dr. Mudd's wrongful imprisonment. The first effort to set up a plaque in honor of Dr. Mudd failed in 1936, but that year saw the release of the film *The Prisoner of Shark Island*, which chronicled the story of Dr. Mudd. The visit of Dr. Richard Mudd and his family to Fort Jefferson in 1943 received considerable attention, and several more visits were made over the years. Throughout the period since the 1940s, the story of Dr. Mudd has been frequently told on radio, television and in motion pictures. President Dwight Eisenhower (1890–1969) signed a bill authorizing a plaque for Dr. Mudd, which was dedicated at Key West, Florida, on March 11, 1961. The home of Dr. Samuel Mudd was listed on the National Register of Historic Places in 1974. It has been skillfully restored and can now be visited by the public. The house was deeded to the Dr. Samuel A. Mudd Society, Inc., in 1983, and they now conduct tours and publish a newsletter.

The effort to overturn Dr. Mudd's conviction was spurred during the 1970s by the passage of resolutions to that effect by several of the states. In 1968, Dr. Richard Mudd submitted a formal petition to President Lyndon Johnson (1908–1973) to have the case reviewed. The matter was referred to the U.S. Army, which ruled against it. After Johnson left office, Dr. R. Mudd resubmitted his petition to succeeding presidents. In 1979, President Jimmy Carter (1924–) responded officially, stating, "Regrettably, I am advised that the findings of guilt and the sentence of the military commission that tried Dr. Mudd in 1865 are binding and conclusive judgments, and that there is no authority under law by which I, as President, could set aside his conviction." The letter went on to express the president's personal belief in the innocence of Dr. Mudd. A similar letter was sent by President Ronald Reagan (1911–2004).

In 1991 it was announced that the Army Board for Correction of Military Records would review Dr. Mudd's case. Although the ABCMR ruled in 1992 that Dr. Mudd had been tried by a court lacking proper jurisdiction and ought, therefore, to have his conviction set aside, the board was overruled by the acting assistant secretary of the army, William D. Clark. A change of administration and the appointment of new officials to review the appeal did not result in a different outcome. The Mudds brought suit against the army and finally won the long-sought vindication in 1998, but not an official clearing of the record of Dr. Mudd's conviction. The Mudd family has vowed to continue the fight.[19]

The strongest evidence against Mrs. Mary Elizabeth Surratt was the testimony of John M. Lloyd and Louid J. Weichmann. Controversy still surrounds their testimony and motives. The members of the military commission did not seem to have any real doubts about the guilt of Mary Surratt. She was convicted, and, together with Atzerodt, Herold, and Powell, sentenced to hang. However, several members of the commission recommended that her sentence be commuted to life. John P. Brophy (1842–1914) campaigned tirelessly on her behalf, first trying to discredit the testimony against her, then by seeking clemency. He took Powell's statement, that Mrs. Surratt was innocent, to the White House, but was denied permission to see the president. Mrs. Surratt's confessor and her daughter were likewise unable to see the president, his office being physically barred. Only Adele Cutts Douglas (1835–1899), widow of Stephen A. Douglas (1813–1861), was able to get to Johnson, but not to persuade him to spare Mrs. Surratt's life. Visiting her just before the execution, Brophy was told by Mrs. Surratt, "I die an innocent woman."

On July 7, 1865, Mary Surratt became the first woman ever executed by the federal government. Last-minute efforts to save her had come to nothing. A request to have a Christian burial service got nowhere, being referred to one official after another. Her remains were finally released to her family in 1869, and she was buried at Mount Olivet Cemetery in Washington, DC.[20]

Louis J. Weichmann. A boarder at the Surratt House, Weichmann was able to observe the comings and goings of the Booth conspirators. His testimony at the trial of the conspirators was very harmful, especially to Mrs. Surratt and Dr. Mudd. Still being debated is the question of whether Weichmann was only an observer or a participant in the conspiracy (Library of Congress).

John H. Surratt, Jr., was on his way to Canada when he heard of Lincoln's assassination. Contacts in the Confederate underground provided him with places to live and aid in escaping the Union detectives who were never very many steps behind. Crossing the Atlantic to Europe, he enlisted in the Papal Zouaves, the army of the pope. Discovered in Italy, he fled Italian and American authorities, finally being captured in Egypt. Standing trial for his life in 1867, the jury was unable to agree on a verdict, and Surratt eventually went free. After briefly trying his hand as a lecturer, he eventually settled into a quiet life as a clerk for a Baltimore steamship company. Retiring in 1915, he died on April 21, 1916.[21]

Fleeing southward after the fall of Richmond, Judah Philip Benjamin let his beard grow, kept his hat pulled down, and passed himself off as a Frenchman. After wandering through forests and swamps, and nearly losing his life as he risked stormy seas in an open boat, he reached the safety of the British West Indies, where he embarked for Britain by way of Havana, Cuba, finally reaching Southampton on August 30, 1865.[22]

Although now in his mid-fifties, Benjamin became a law student again, making a living by writing for newspapers. On June 6, 1866, only five months after his enrollment, Benjamin was admitted to the bar, and his legal career quickly prospered. In 1868 he published *Treatise on the Sale of Personal Property*, which became widely accepted in Britain as the standard work on the subject, in spite of its having been written by a foreigner. By 1869 he was practicing before Britain's highest courts and was having to turn away clients for lack of time. Although he had long been separated from his wife, he made regular trips to Paris to see her and his daughter, and was easily accepted in social circles in Britain and France. Seriously injured in a carriage accident in Paris in May 1880, his health declined, forcing his retirement from the law in 1883. He died in Paris on May 6, 1884, and was buried at Pere Lachaise Cemetery.[23]

The failure of the Confederate Canada mission to accomplish any of its major goals, together with the easy identification of its leaders, finally resulted in changes being made. Clement C. Clay had already gone home in December 1864, and Jacob Thompson received his orders from Secretary of State Benjamin on March 2, 1865. Although Lincoln was inclined to allow Thompson to escape, after the assassination Thompson and several others of the Canada mission were named as accomplices and rewards were put upon their heads. Thompson fled to Europe, where he remained until 1868. The rewards for Thompson and his associates were revoked on November 25, 1865, and no legal action was taken against most of them. Thompson lived in style at the Grand Hotel in Paris, and the some suspected that he had misappropriated Confederate funds from the Canada mission. When he returned home to Mississippi in 1868, Thompson, much of whose property had been ravaged by war, was still the owner of extensive real estate holdings. He denied having taken Confederate funds for his own use, and it appears that his legitimate personal wealth could account for his comfortable lifestyle.

Moving to Memphis, Tennessee, in 1870, Thompson became a successful businessman. In 1876, he was accused of being involved in the embezzlement of Interior Department funds during his tenure as secretary in the 1850s. This was clearly a political act as part of that year's close and controversial election. Thompson had been cleared of such charges at the time by a congressional committee. Jacob Thompson died March 24, 1885, in Memphis, and is buried at Elmwood Cemetery.[24]

George Nicholas Sanders had to become less conspicuous after an attempt to abduct him was made on August 5, 1865. He left Montreal on November 3, bound for Europe. Dividing his time between London and Paris, he was in the French capital during at least part of the existence of the Paris Commune in 1871. He returned to America in June 1872, where official charges against him and the other Confederate commissioners in Canada had long since been dropped. Horace Greeley was by then running against President Ulysses S. Grant, and Sanders' name surfaced in the Republican effort to discredit Greeley. Sanders publicly denied that he had any influence with Greeley, claiming that the Niagara Falls peace conference of 1864 had been "a proper attempt to bring about a peaceful end to a horrible war."

On the night of August 12, 1873, George N. Sanders suffered a heart attack and died in New York City. He was buried in Green Wood Cemetery.[25]

Thomas Nelson Conrad was given a pass by Lafayette C. Baker and allowed to go home. By this time the war was all but over, though organized resistance continued in some areas for several more weeks. Conrad was picked up by Union cavalrymen and, in spite of his pass, was held at Fredericksburg, and then sent by train toward Richmond. Escaping by jumping off the train near Ashland, Virginia, Conrad was obliged to remain in hiding for some time.

Returning to civilian life in the spring of 1866, Conrad opened the Upperville Academy in Fauquier County, Virginia. He married Emma S. Hall (?–1900) on October 4, 1866. They had seven children. From 1868 to 1871 he taught at the Rockville Academy in Montgomery County, Maryland, then became principal of the Preston and Olin Institute in Blacksburg,

Virginia. Conrad was instrumental in converting this small Methodist school into today's Virginia Polytechnic Institute. Beginning in 1873 he became editor of the *Montgomery Messenger* of Christiansburg, Virginia. A sub-professor of English at Blacksburg by 1877, and full professor in 1879, Conrad was president of the college from 1882 to 1886. Political changes forced Conrad out and in 1887 he became a faculty member at Maryland Agricultural College.

Telling stories of his spying days, though carefully censored, Conrad published A Confederate Spy in 1892, revised and republished as The Rebel Scout in 1904. Conrad was taken ill at the home of his daughter, Mrs. V. P. Beall, in Washington, DC, and died January 5, 1905. He was buried in Westview Cemetery in Blacksburg, Virginia.[26]

The young couple who shared the theatre box with the Lincolns on the fateful night, Henry Reed Rathbone and Clara Hamilton Harris, were married on July 11, 1867. They had three children. In February 1869, Henry was assigned to the 5th United States Infantry, with the rank of major. At his request, he was discharged from the army on December 31, 1870. Living on inherited wealth and making their home in Washington, DC, the Rathbones waited while family and friends attempted to secure Henry a diplomatic post. His mental condition deteriorated throughout the 1870s, and he would become jealous when other men paid attention to Clara. He also resented her attention to their children.

The Rathbones were living abroad by the 1880s, when Henry was appointed consul general in Hanover, Germany. By this time, Henry's mind would become overwhelmed as he contemplated Lincoln's assassination, blaming himself for failing to stop Booth and save the president's life. It was said that he threatened his wife more than once when in such moods. On December 23, 1883, Henry suffered another attack of madness, and went after his children. Clara rushed to defend them, and Henry shot her three times, then stabbed himself five times. Clara died immediately, but Henry regained his physical health, although his mind never recovered. German doctors examining him reported that he was insane and unaware of what he had done, inventing a story that an intruder had attacked him and his family. Convicted of murder, Henry was confined to the Hildesheim Asylum for the Criminal Insane. Refusing to socialize with asylum inmates, Henry was housed in a church residence near the asylum. The children were sent to live with Clara's brother, William Hamilton Harris, and his family. Henry Reed Rathbone died on August 14, 1911. He and Clara were both buried in Hanover, but the location of their graves is today unknown.[27]

Clara H. Harris. Stepsister and fiancée of Rathbone, Clara was happy to join the Lincolns for a night at the theatre, only to become witness to a tragedy and the victim of another tragedy later (courtesy of Surratt House Museum/MNCPPC).

Louis J. Weichmann, according to theatre owner John T. Ford, "considered his safety and Mrs. Surratt's conviction were consequent results and were inseparably connected." At another point, Weichmann told his interrogators prior to the trial, "You confused and terrified me so much yesterday that I was almost unable to say anything." John P. Brophy, a friend of both Weichmann and Mrs. Surratt, said Weichmann told him that his testimony was given under duress, and had he not been intimidated, he would have described her in a more favorable way.

After testifying at both the 1865 trial of the conspirators and the 1867 trial of John Surratt, Weichmann was appointed to a clerical position at the Philadelphia Custom House. He resigned this job in 1886 because of a change of political party, which put pressure on him from those who had been offended by Weichmann's trial testimony. Moving to Anderson, Indiana, he established the Anderson Business School. General Lewis Wallace, who knew Weichmann from the trial of the conspirators, helped Weichmann get a position as stenographer-typist for the Republican State Committee of Indiana. In the 1890s Weichmann wrote a lengthy history of the assassination, which was not published until three-quarters of a century later. He adamantly stuck to his claim of innocence. As he lay dying on the evening of June 5, 1902, Weichmann stated with his last breath that he had told the truth. His critics always questioned his honesty and motives almost as relentlessly as had the government investigators and trial lawyers.[28]

The Petersen House, across the street from Ford's Theatre, and its little back bedroom had suddenly, and briefly, been made the center of the nation's interest, as Abraham Lincoln lay dying. The simple room, decorated with a small table, the walnut four-poster bed (now in the collection of the Chicago Historical Society), and a few pleasant engravings on the walls, forever became one of the shrines of American history. Julius Ulke, one of the Petersen House boarders, lugged his camera down and set it up in the death chamber to record the scene for posterity. Ulke centered his photo upon a grimly eloquent relic, a pillow stained with blood. Later, William Tilton Clark (1842–1888), the soldier whose room had been taken over that night in his absence, assisted artists for the illustrated papers in their drawings, as did other Petersen House boarders. Photographs could not be published in those days, so Ulke's vivid photo of the scene was laid aside and forgotten, not to emerge for ninety-six years.

William A. Petersen (1816–1871) and his family continued to own and live in the house, and their heirs sold it on November 25, 1878, to Louis Schade (1829–1903), for $4,500. Schade was the editor of the *Washington Sentinel*, the newspaper being published in the front room of the basement. Schade's children used the Lincoln death chamber as a playroom. Alterations in the house included the addition of rooms in the back, next to the stairway, in the basement and first floor.

Beginning in 1880, Congress discussed the idea of a marker for the house, and one was installed in 1883. The Schade family, already experiencing constant inquiries from curiosity seekers, must have felt as if they were caretakers, rather than owners, of a piece of history. The house was leased to the Memorial Association of the District of Columbia in 1893, which opened a museum there on October 17 of that year. Osborn Hamiline Ingham Oldroyd (1842–1930) lived in the house from 1893 until 1930, serving as custodian of the museum on the first floor, where he exhibited items from his extensive Lincoln collection. The U.S. government purchased the house in 1896, for $30,000. Oldroyd and his wife were allowed to continue to live in the Petersen House as custodians, with the government eventually purchasing Oldroyd's collection.

In 1924 a bronze plaque replaced the original marble marker. Furniture from the Lincoln home in Springfield, Illinois, was installed in the house in 1932, including horsehair sofas and a rocking chair, candlesticks and vases. The room where Lincoln died was furnished with replicas of the original pieces, which had scattered after the assassination. A further $40,000 was spent, beginning in December 1958, to repair and restore the house under the National Park Service's "Mission 66" program. The rooms that had been added after the assassination were removed. The house was reopened to the public on July 4. 1959. Another restoration became necessary by 1978, when water damage was discovered. Much old paint and plaster was replaced, with care taken to duplicate materials originally used. New wallpaper was specially made, based upon the Ulke photograph and an original sample. Gas lighting fixtures made in 1850 were obtained, and replaced the less authentic previous ones. The new restoration was completed in 1980. The house stands today, looking much as it must have on that night in 1865, an object of curiosity, wonder and reverence.[29]

The trial of the men accused of trying to steal Lincoln's remains opened May 28, 1877, in Springfield, Illinois. Charles H. Reed headed the prosecution, and William "Billy" O'Brien defended Mullen and Hughes. The charges were attempting to steal Lincoln's remains and his casket, which was the property of the Lincoln Monument Association. The jury returned with a guilty verdict on May 31, 1877. The two defendants were sentenced to one year's imprisonment.

Mullen returned to saloon keeping after his prison term. He was again arrested in 1880 for passing counterfeit bills, but became an informer for the Secret Service to avoid prosecution. His information led to the arrest of "Big Jim" Kinealy, the originator of the plot, who went to prison for counterfeiting. Swegles, the undercover operator who had exposed the conspirators, disappeared from history shortly after the trial in which he had been a key witness. Tyrrell continued his detective profession, married his son's widow and moved to Kansas, where he lost his home to taxes in 1899. Separating from his wife, he returned to Chicago. Washburn went into banking, then engineering, working on several prominent public works projects.[30]

Of the many books that have been written about the death of Abraham Lincoln, several of the most provocative were by Otto Eisenschiml, whose bold—some would say reckless—theories have been a center of controversy since their first appearance. Paul Herman Buck (1899–1978), reviewing *Why Was Lincoln Murdered?*, stated, "This work is so sincere in purpose, so honest in scholarship, and so completely documented that it commands the utmost respect from the most meticulous student of history." But William Hanchett (1922–), in his *The Lincoln Murder Conspiracies*, bluntly stated that Eisenschiml "has shaped the facts to fit his theory, rather than his theory to fit the facts. His assertion that Stanton aspired to become the nation's postwar leader is pure fiction."

Otto Eisenschiml was born in Vienna, Austria, on June 16, 1880. His father, who had lived in America, advised Otto to go there to seek his fortune. By 1901, Eisenschiml's skill as a chemist led to a job with Carnegie Steel Corporation in Pittsburgh, Pennsylvania, where he worked until 1904. He was chief chemist of the American Linseed Co., of Chicago, from 1904 to 1907, and manager of their South Chicago plant from 1907 to 1912. He became president of the Scientific Oil Compounding Company in 1912, working on the development of paints, fungicides, and the window envelope. By the 1920s, he had become wealthy enough to devote himself to American history, a subject that had fascinated him since childhood. A frequent lecturer since 1903, he was also one of the founders of the Civil War Round Table of Chicago.

His father's service in the American Civil War attracted Eisenschiml to that period, and he began to specialize in the Lincoln assassination. *Why Was Lincoln Murdered?*, published in 1937, was a featured selection of the Book-of-the-Month Club, and had a tremendous impact. Eisenschiml asserted that the way events had unfolded suggested a conspiracy involving high officials of the Union government, led by Secretary of War Edwin M. Stanton. This idea was, and continues to be, very controversial, overshadowing the author's other ideas. Since the 1980s, Eisenschiml's theories have lost much of their power. Hanchett and others have pointed out weaknesses in Eisenschiml's research and especially in his conclusions. However, even Eisenschiml's most severe critics have to admit that he stimulated the interest of many later researchers and authors.

Eisenschiml's later books on the assassination were *In the Shadow of Lincoln's Death* (1940), *The Case of A.L.—Aged 56* (1943), *As Luck Would Have It* (1948), and *O.E.—Historian Without an Armchair* (1963). In addition, he wrote many articles and letters commenting on his own work and its reception, as well as upon the work of other authors. The lack of acceptance by professional historians made Eisenschiml bitter, and he often wrote critical commentary about historians and their methods. Otto Eisenschiml died on December 7, 1963. His ashes were scattered at Shiloh, Tennessee.[31]

Dr. Charles A. Leale was discharged from the army on January 20, 1866. Traveling to Europe, Leale studied the treatment of Asiatic cholera before returning home to New York City and the practice of medicine. He married Rebecca Medwin Copcutt (?–1923) on September 3, 1867, and they had six children. Leale was in charge of children's class at Northwestern Dispensary from 1866 to 1871; spent two years as physician at Central Dispensary; was president of the Bellevue Hospital Medical College Alumni Association in 1875; president of the New York County Medical Association from 1885 to 1886; president of St. John's Guild, 1891–1892; president of the New York Society for the Relief of Widows and Orphans of Medical Men from 1895 to 1896; and a companion, 1st class, of the Military Order of the Loyal Legion. His long silence about the role he had played on the night of the assassination was finally broken in 1909, when he gave a lecture and then published his story. Retiring in 1928, Dr. Charles A. Leale died June 13, 1932. He was buried at Oakland Cemetery in Yonkers, New York.[32]

With the Civil War over, the government sold off unneeded equipment, including the railroad car "United States." Lincoln's friend Ward Hill Lamon bought the car in 1866 for $6,850. Lamon was acting for Thomas Clark Durant (1820–1885), director of the Union Pacific Railroad, who wanted the car for his personal use. The Union Pacific sold the car to the Colorado Central Railroad in 1874 for $3,000. The car was remodeled as an ordinary coach and saw much hard service. By the early 1890s the car returned to the Union Pacific, which refurbished it and displayed it at the Trans-Mississippi Centennial Exhibition in Omaha in 1898. In 1904 the car was purchased by Franklin Snow of Peoria, Illinois, for $2,000, who exhibited it at the St. Louis World's Fair that year. Experiencing financial problems, Snow sold the car to Minneapolis entrepreneur Thomas Lowry (1843–1909). Lowry displayed the car in Columbia Heights, in northern Minneapolis. A grass fire nearby got out of control on March 18, 1911, burning about ten blocks, including the Lincoln funeral car, which had been stored in a shed. Souvenir hunters took many pieces of the wreckage.[33]

Abraham Lincoln received far more protection than any president before him, but he faced a greater danger than any of his predecessors. As we have observed, his contemporaries did not know or appreciate what sort of a man they had in their midst, and few would have imagined that he would be revered in times to come beyond any other American leader. In our wonderment and regret that Lincoln's life could not be saved, we must remember that thousands of his countrymen died in the huge war, and some feel that the final sacrifice of Lincoln's life provided the capstone, not only of that great conflict, but also on a whole era of American history. Lincoln's survival through his presidency is the miracle within the miracle of his very existence.

Appendix 1: Weapons of the Assassination Conspirators

The weapon used by John Wilkes Booth to kill Abraham Lincoln was a small pocket pistol. Exact dimensions of the pistol were $5^{27}/_{32}$ inches long, barrel $1^{15}/_{16}$ inches long, hammer to muzzle $2\frac{1}{4}$ inches, lock plate $2\frac{3}{4}$ inches long, and one inch from the top of the stock to the trigger guard. It fired a large ball of .44 caliber ($^{44}/_{100}$ of an inch in diameter). The ball that killed Lincoln was made of Britannia metal, an alloy of 93 percent tin, 5 percent antimony, and 2 percent copper, being somewhat harder than lead. Britannia metal had been in use since the 1760s as a base metal for making candlesticks, pots, urns, and a variety of other household objects. It tends to be white or silver in its natural color. The inside of the barrel was rifled — that is, spiral grooves had been cut inside of the barrel to cause the ball to rotate after firing. This rotation was intended to give the ball greater stability in flight. When fired, the ball traveled about five hundred feet per second. The pistol was muzzle-loaded; about ten grains of gunpowder was poured up the barrel, then the ball was pushed into the powder, greased paper or cloth enveloping the ball to hold it in place until firing. The hammer was cocked by hand, and released by pulling the trigger. It struck a metal cap, producing a spark that ignited the powder and fired the ball. Booth's pistol was made of iron with decorative silver mountings. The tarnished silver would take on a yellowish appearance, leading many accounts to erroneously describe it as brass.[1]

This type of pistol was designed by Henry Deringer (1786–1868) of Philadelphia, and made its debut in the 1830s. Its small size made it easy to conceal and thus the derringer became popular for protection. Derringers were manufactured by Colt, Remington, and other manufacturers, but Booth's pistol has the name "DERINGER" and "PHILADELA" stamped on the

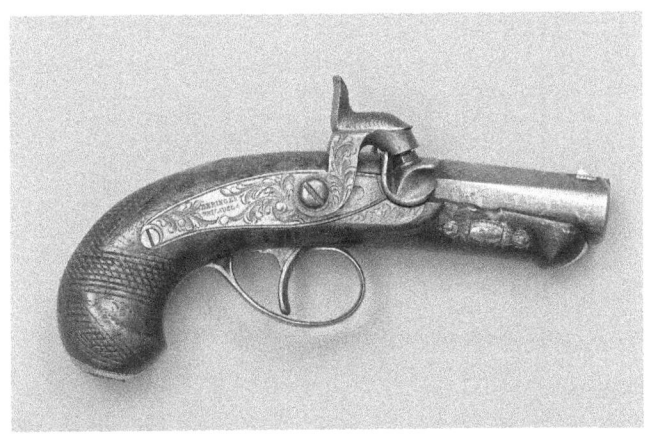

Booth's derringer. This small pocket pistol was the weapon that killed Abraham Lincoln (Library of Congress).

mountings. The more common spelling, "derringer," results from imitations and variations of Deringer's design, which he never patented.[2] Booth dropped the pistol in the theatre box, where it was found a few hours later. Turned over to the War Department's judge advocate, it became an exhibit at the Lincoln Museum at Ford's Theatre in 1939, and remains so today.

Booth's other weapon at the theatre was a large bowie knife with a blade 7¼ inches long. He used this knife to stab Colonel Henry R. Rathbone, and to slash at orchestra leader William Withers, Jr. He still had it with him when he was captured. This knife is also in the collection of the Lincoln Museum at Ford's Theatre.

When captured, Booth had a Spencer carbine, which fired a .50 caliber, 414-grain bullet, using a 45-grain black powder charge. This was one of the two carbines that had previously been hidden at the Surratt Tavern. He also carried two Colt .44 caliber army revolvers, model 1860, firing 207-grain bullets with a 28-grain black powder charge. He must have left these pistols with his horse, as he did not have them in the theatre.

The pistol carried by Lewis Powell when he attacked William H. Seward was a Whitney navy revolver, .36 caliber. When he attempted to shoot Frederick Seward the pistol misfired, so Powell used it as a club, beating the younger Seward and breaking the pistol's ramrod beneath the barrel. Powell also carried a large bowie knife, rather more elaborately decorated than Booth's. The silver pommel had an alligator on it, suggesting this may have been Powell's own knife, carried when he served in a Florida regiment, and not a knife given to him by Booth. Powell dropped his pistol at the Seward house, where it was found and used as evidence at the trial. It is now in the collection of the Lincoln Museum at Ford's Theatre. Powell dropped the knife outside in the street; it was found the next morning. Though used as evidence at the trial, the knife was claimed by Dr. John Wilson, an army doctor who assisted at the Seward house, and it remained in his family until sold in 1960 to Dr. John K. Lattimer, a New York surgeon and Lincoln collector. Some dispute that the Lattimer knife is the same one carried by Powell. At least one other knife had been displayed as the Powell knife.

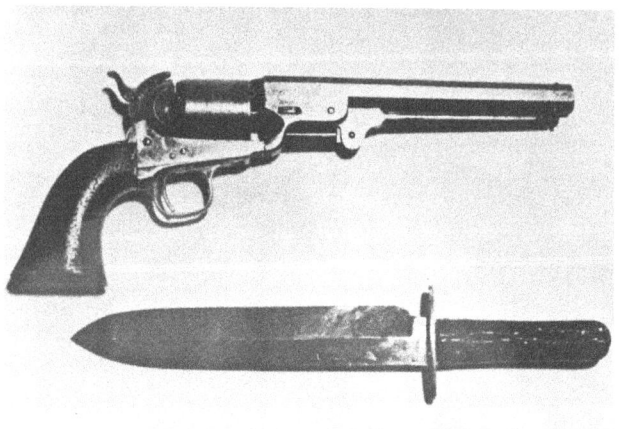

Booth's pistol and knife. The pistol was one of two revolvers Booth had with him upon his capture; the knife was used to stab Rathbone and slash at Withers, the orchestra leader (courtesy of Surratt House Museum/MNCPPC).

Booth purchased arms and equipment to be used by the conspirators late in 1864. Samuel Arnold described them as "2 carbines, 3 pairs Revolvers, 3 knives and two pairs of Hand cuffs." He later described the carbines as "Spencer Rifles." These weapons were shifted around, Booth giving them to Arnold, Arnold to Michael O'Laughlen, and O'Laughlen giving them to friends for safekeeping. Whether these are the same pistols and knives exhibited at the trial or others is unknown.

Louis J. Weichmann described seeing Powell and John Surratt "seated on a bed surrounded by brand-new spurs, bowie knives, and revolvers." Weichmann enumerated them as "eight brand-new spurs, two revolvers, and two bowie knives." This incident he dated March 15, 1865. These could have been some of the same weapons referred to by Arnold, since Weichmann twice calls them "brand-new." Two carbines were hidden at the Surratt Tavern, to be called for later by Booth and David E. Herold. These are the "shooting irons" that John M. Lloyd testified Mrs. Mary Surratt told him on the afternoon of April 14 to have ready by that evening. We do not know if they were the same ones mentioned by Arnold.[3]

George Atzerodt was seen in possession of a pistol and a knife. The pistol was another army .44 Colt, which he sold after the assassination. He threw away the knife. These weapons were exhibited at the trial.

The conspirators were well equipped with weapons, though the exact number and nature of those weapons cannot now be determined.

Appendix 2: Presidential Succession

Booth's conspiracy was to have included the assassinations of other leaders in addition to President Lincoln. Conspirator George A. Atzerodt was assigned to shoot Vice President Andrew Johnson, and Lewis Powell carried out a vicious attack upon Secretary of State William H. Seward. Many assumed at the time, and one still sees it related today, that this was a conspiracy to leave the United States leaderless.

In the charges and specifications against the accused fellow conspirators of Booth at their trial, it was stated that their intention was "to deprive the Army and Navy of the United States of a constitutional Commander-in-Chief ... and to prevent a lawful election of President and Vice President."[1] Under the law then in effect, "whenever the offices of President and Vice President shall both become vacant, the Secretary of State shall forthwith cause a notification thereof to be made to the executives of every state ... specifying that electors of the President of the United States shall be appointed or chosen in the several states within thirty-four days preceding the first Wednesday in December then next ensuing."[2] Thus, according to this interpretation, although the secretary of state was not then in the line of succession to become president, the law specified that he must notify the states to call a special election. If the secretary of state was dead or incapable of performing his duties, the states could not be notified and the United States would be, after a time, without a constitutionally appointed leader.[3]

Booth met newspaperman John Francis Coyle (c.1822–c.1909) on the afternoon of April 14, 1865, and questioned him about the presidential order of succession. Coyle told Booth that Vice President Johnson would succeed to the presidency if Lincoln were "removed." He may have mentioned Secretary Seward as a member of the order of succession. If he did, he gave Booth erroneous information.[4] Whether Booth mistakenly believed Seward was in the order of succession, or the assassin was aware of the secretary's duty to call a special election, he had a motive to kill Seward either way.

Why was Seward included among the victims of Booth's assassination plot? In the meeting of the conspirators at Gautier's Restaurant on March 15, 1865, no mention of Seward was made. At that time, the plan was to capture Lincoln, take him to Richmond, and hold him as a hostage to be exchanged for Confederate prisoners of war in Union camps.[5] If the plan was to cripple the Union government, capturing the president would have been far more effective than killing him, for at that time there was no provision for a situation where the president was alive but unable to carry out the duties of his office. The vice president, and the others in the order of succession, could not have assumed the presidential office unless the president was dead or had resigned. Whether the language of the Succession Act of 1792 could have been stretched to cover such a situation as having a president who was alive but was being held prisoner can only be speculated upon.[6] No such situation had, or ever has, faced the United States. A specific constitutional provision for presidential inability to perform the duties of the office, and providing for the removal, temporarily or permanently, of the president, did not exist until 1967.

If Booth had wanted to cause chaos by leaving the Union leaderless, he failed to include two other officials specified in the Succession Act. Under the law of 1792, if the presidential and vice presidential offices should both fall vacant at the same time, those next in line to "act as president" would have been the president pro-tempore of the U.S. Senate, followed by the speaker of the House of Representatives. On April 14, 1865, the Senate president pro-tempore was Senator Lafayette Sabine Foster, R-CT, and the House speaker was Representative Schuyler Colfax, R-IN. No attempts upon the lives of either of these men were made. Thus, if both Lincoln and Johnson had been killed, Foster would have been president, and the United States would not have been without a lawful leader even for an instant. Although the Constitution as originally written was vague on the question of whether Foster would have been president or "acting president," it is unlikely anyone would have challenged his assumption of the office. Twice before 1865 presidents had died in office, in 1841 and 1850. Both times the vice president had claimed the presidency, with little objection. Andrew Johnson was acknowledged to be president as soon as Lincoln was pronounced dead. A short time elapsed before he took the presidential oath, but when he took the oath, he did so as president. The tradition had already been established that the death or removal from office of the president made the vice president the president at that instant. Taking the oath is required of a president, but the oath taking is not what makes a person president.

To suggest that if Foster had become president the Radical Republicans would have rendered him ineffective, and, had Seward been dead, Foster might

Lafayette S. Foster. Had Booth's plan been carried out, including the assassination of Vice President Andrew Johnson, Foster would have become president. A senator from Connecticut, Foster was Senate president pro-tempore (Library of Congress).

Schuyler Colfax. Speaker of the U.S. House of Representatives, Colfax was next in line to succeed to the presidency after Foster. Colfax represented a district in Indiana (Library of Congress).

have been unable to have a new secretary of state confirmed in time to meet the deadline for calling a special election, as required by the 1792 Succession Act, is speculation at best. As a new president, Foster would no doubt have had some good will, and the Radical Republicans would have had to think twice about deliberately provoking a constitutional crisis. Foster could have nominated someone friendly to the radicals, such as Senator Charles Sumner, R-MA, who would not have been likely to be opposed.

But would there have been such a crisis at all? The 1792 act specified that the calling of a special election for president is the duty of the secretary of state, but it does not say that whoever is acting in that capacity in the official secretary of state's absence or incapacity could not have performed this duty. Just as there is always a president from moment to moment, so also is there someone to direct the duties of the State Department, and the other offices of the government. The whole machinery of the government cannot come to a halt because a particular person is unavailable. At the time of the assassination, the secretary of state was home in bed, recovering from serious injuries sustained in an accident, and unable to tend to his duties. But those duties were being carried out nonetheless. Assistant Secretary of State Frederick William Seward, son of Secretary William Seward, was acting secretary during his father's convalescence. That very day, April 14, Frederick Seward had attended a Cabinet meeting at the White House. No one challenged his right to be there in place of his father. State Department documents were issued bearing Frederick Seward's name, with the title "Acting Secretary."

But Frederick Seward was also seriously injured that night as he fought his father's would-be assassin. For some time it was feared that Frederick Seward would not recover. Had both Sewards died, the business of the State Department would have gone on. To quote from an official State Department history:

> Under the law creating the Department the Chief Clerk assumed charge of it, whenever there was an interregnum in the office of the Secretary of State, until the President designated someone to fill the office, but in 1853 an assistant Secretary of State was provided for by law, with power to act as Secretary during the latter's absence or during an interregnum.[7]

On April 14, 1865, the chief clerk of the State Department was William Hunter (1805–1886). He had served as a State Department clerk since 1829. Twice he had served as ad interim secretary: March 3–6, 1853, and December 13–16, 1860.[8] The business of the State Department could have been, and was, carried on by this very experienced man. State Department documents issued during the time when both Sewards were recovering bear the name of William Hunter, with the title "Acting Secretary."

John Wilkes Booth, an ardent supporter of the South and an apologist for slavery, had ample reason for wanting to kill William Seward. One of the first abolitionists to hold high office, one of those who had exercised near-dictatorial power early in the war, one whose skill as a statesman had helped prevent foreign intervention, which the South had hoped for and counted upon — all of these reasons and more marked Seward as a victim. The complicated laws of presidential succession, little known or understood by most Americans then as now. Would seem to be the least likely reason to strike at Seward. There is only the word of newspaperman Coyle that Booth asked about the order of succession, and then only on the very day of the assassination. Coyle waited more than thirty years to reveal that conversation. It might have happened as Coyle said, but the evidence is thin. Whether or not Booth understood the succession laws, whether he struck at Seward out of personal hatred or as part of a scheme to cripple the republic, the life of America paused only to mourn, and its heart never skipped a beat.

Since 1865, the laws of presidential succession have been changed three times, in 1886, 1947 and 1967. Today the Cabinet members are in the line of succession, after the speaker of the House and the president pro-tempore of the Senate, and in the order in which their departments were created. The modern secretary of defense takes the place of the former cabinet-level secretaries of war and navy.[9]

Notes

Chapter 1: National Crisis

1. Joseph Nathan Kane, *Facts About the Presidents* (New York: H.W. Wilson, 1993), pp. 93–94; Isaac N. Arnold, *The Life of Abraham Lincoln* (Lincoln: University of Nebraska Press, 1994), pp. 13–20; David Herbert Donald, *Lincoln* (London: Jonathan Cape, 1995), pp. 21–28.
2. I. N. Arnold, pp. 20–26; Walter B. Stevens, *A Reporter's Lincoln* (Lincoln: University of Nebraska Press, 1998), pp. 3–7; Donald, pp. 28–32, 34–35.
3. I. N. Arnold, pp. 33–41; Kane, p. 98; Donald, pp. 40–53.
4. I. N. Arnold, pp. 42–43; Stevens, p. 9; Donald, pp. 55–58; Joshua Wolf Shenk, *Lincoln's Melancholy* (Boston: Mariner Books, 2005), pp. 4–5.
5. I. N. Arnold, pp. 51–53, 57–59; Donald, pp. 60–64, 74–80.
6. Jean H. Baker, *Mary Todd Lincoln—A Biography* (New York: W.W. Norton, 1987), pp. 4–9; Kane, p. 94; I. N. Arnold, pp. 68–72.
7. William H. Herndon, *Life of Lincoln* (New York: Da Capo, 1983), pp. 182, 343–46, 349–51; J. H. Baker, pp. 141–43, 196, 227–28; Donald, pp. 160–61.
8. Kane, p. 94; J. H. Baker, pp. 119–25.
9. I. N. Arnold, pp. 82–83.
10. I. N. Arnold, pp. 76–80; Donald, pp. 119–41.
11. I. N. Arnold, pp. 112–23, 139–52.
12. Kane, pp. 94–95; Donald, pp. 230–56.
13. Lincoln to Isaac M. Schermerhorn, September 12, 1864, in Abraham Lincoln, *Speeches and Writings, 1859–1865* (New York: Literary Classics of the United States, 1989), pp. 630–31; I. N. Arnold, p. 178.

Chapter 2: President Elect

1. George S. Bryan, *The Great American Myth* (New York: Carrick & Evans, 1940), pp. 14–18.
2. U.S. Congress, *Biographical Directory of the U.S. Congress* (Washington, DC: Government Printing Office, 1989), p. 2084.
3. Alvy L. King, *Louis T. Wigfall, Southern Fire-eater* (Baton Rouge: Louisiana State University Press, 1970), pp. 105–6; Ward Hill Lamon, *Recollections of Abraham Lincoln* (Lincoln: University of Nebraska Press, 1994), pp. 264–65.
4. Charles P. Stone, "Washington on the Eve of the War," *Century Magazine* 26, no. 3 (July 1883): pp. 458–66.
5. L. E. Chittenden, *Recollections of President Lincoln and His Administration* (New York: Harper & Brothers, 1891), p. 39;
6. Edward D. Townsend, *Anecdotes of the Civil War* (New York: D. Appleton, 1884), pp. 22–25.
7. *Cincinnati Commercial*, February 27, 1861.
8. Elihu B. Washburne to Abraham Lincoln, February 3, 1861, Abraham Lincoln Papers, Vol. 32, Library of Congress.
9. Col. E. V. Sumner to J. G. Nicolay, January 7, 1861, John G. Nicolay Papers, Library of Congress.
10. Congressman John A. Gurley to Lincoln, December 31, 1860, Abraham Lincoln Papers, Vol. 24.
11. William H. Seward to Abraham Lincoln, December 28, 1860, Abraham Lincoln Papers, Vol. 24.
12. J. Medhill to Abraham Lincoln, December 31, 1860, Abraham Lincoln Papers, Vol. 24.
13. C. Carroll Hollis, "Lincoln Rejects a Bodyguard," *The Nation* 198 (February 17, 1964), pp. 173–74.
14. Stone, pp. 458–66.
15. Abraham Lincoln Papers, Vol. 22.

16. Abraham Lincoln Papers, Vol. 23.
17. Exhibit caption at Ford's Theatre Museum, 2000.
18. John Mason Potter, *13 Desperate Days* (New York: Ivan Obolensky, 1965), pp. xiiii, 23–25, 28, 32, 43, 57; "Mr. Lincoln's Progress," *Baltimore American*, February 19, 1861; "Attempt to Throw the Presidential Train from the Track," *Lafayette* (IN) *Journal*, February 18, 1861.
19. Bryan, pp. 21–22, 24; *Baltimore Sun*, February 27, 1861; *New York World*, February 19, 1861; *New York Evening Post*, February 23, 1861; *New York Tribune*, February 11, 1861.
20. Harold Holzer, ed., *Dear Mr. Lincoln* (Reading, MA: Addison-Wesley, 1993), pp. 43–44.
21. Donald, pp. 261–71.
22. Norma B. Cuthbert, ed., *Lincoln and the Baltimore Plot 1861* (San Marino, CA: Huntington Library, 1949), pp. 125–26.
23. *Lincoln Obsequies Scrapbook*, Library of Congress, microfilm frames 49–50.
24. Cuthbert, pp. 19–20; Isaac N. Arnold, "The Baltimore Plot to Assassinate Abraham Lincoln," *Harper's Monthly Magazine* 37, no. 217 (June 1868): pp. 123–28; James Grant Wilson and John Fiske, eds., *Appleton's Cyclopedia of American Biography* (New York: D. Appleton, 1887), p. 492.
25. *Lincoln Obsequies Scrapbook*, frame 50.
26. Allan Pinkerton, "Allan Pinkerton's Unpublished Letter," *The American Magazine* 75, no. 4 (February 1913), pp. 17–22.
27. Cuthbert, p. 117; "Highly Important From Albany," *New York Herald*, February 27, 1861, p. 5; "Who Saved Mr. Lincoln's Life in 1861?" *New York Times*, October 31, 1867, p. 2.
28. "Who Saved Mr. Lincoln's Life in 1861?"
29. Potter, *13 Desperate Days*, pp. 110–14, 132–40.
30. William A. Tidwell, with James O. Hall and David W. Gaddy, *Come Retribution* (Jackson: University Press of Mississippi, 1988), p. 232; "Scene at the Depot," *Baltimore American*, February 25, 1861; "Movements of the President Elect," *Baltimore Sun*, February 25, 1861, p. 1; Potter, *13 Desperate Days*, pp. 185–6.
31. Donald, pp. 278–79.
32. "Mr. Lincoln's Sudden Appearance in Washington," *Cincinnati Commercial*, February 25, 1861.

Chapter 3: Inauguration —1861

1. Stone, pp. 458–66.
2. Stephen B. Oates, *With Malice Toward None* (New York: Harper & Row, 1977), pp. 212–13.
3. Kenneth G. Alfers, *Law and Order in the Capital City: A History of the Washington Police, 1800–1886* (Washington, DC: George Washington University, 1976), pp. 23–24.
4. Stone, pp. 458–66.
5. I. N. Arnold, pp. 188–92; Horace Greeley, *Recollections of a Busy Life* (New York: J. B. Ford, 1868), p. 404.
6. Stone, pp. 458–66.
7. Elizabeth Todd Grimsley, "Six Months in the White House," *Journal of the Illinois State Historical Society* 19, no. 3–4 (October 1926–January 1927): pp. 43–73.
8. Chittenden, pp. 48, 115–16.
9. Bryan, pp. 56–57.

Chapter 4: Protecting President Lincoln

1. Abraham Lincoln Papers, Vol. 53.
2. *New York World*, February 17, 1869; *Washington National Intelligencer*, February 19, 1869.
3. Deborah Carbaugh, "Mr. Lincoln's Security," *Surratt Courier* 25, no. 8 (August 2000): pp. 4–7.
4. Holzer, pp. 334–49; Matthew Pinsker, *Lincoln's Sanctuary* (New York: Oxford University Press, 2003), p. 2.
5. Potter, pp. 66–68; Bryan, pp. 60–61; *Philadelphia Press*, April 27, 1865; *New York World*, April 24, 1861.
6. Carbaugh, pp. 4–7; Robert W. McBride, *Lincoln's Body Guard* (Indianapolis: Indiana Historical Society Publications, 1911), p. 34; John G. Nicolay Papers, Library of Congress.
7. *Historical Statistics of the United States, Colonial Times to 1970*, Bicentennial Edition, Part 1 (Washington, DC: U.S. Bureau of the Census, 1975), p. 26.
8. Bryan, p. 4; Richard M. Lee, *Mr. Lincoln's City* (McLean, VA: EPM Publications, 1981), pp. 12–13.
9. George A. Townsend, *The Life, Crime, and Capture of John Wilkes Booth* (New York: Dick and Fitzgerald, 1865), pp. 57–58.
10. David Rankin Barbee Papers, Box 5, folder 249, Georgetown University, Washington, DC; Abraham Lincoln Papers, Vol. 86, no. 18238.
11. Stanley Kimmel, *Mr. Lincoln's Washington* (New York: Coward-McCann, 1957), pp. 48–49, 66–67.

12. Benjamin Franklin Wade Papers, Vol. 10, Library of Congress.
13. *Providence Press*, August 26, 1861.
14. *London Times*, reprinted in *Freeman's Journal*, May 21, 1864.
15. *Columbus* (OH) *Crisis*, May 4, 1864.
16. Editorial in *Detroit Advertiser & Tribune*, May 25, 1865.
17. *Freeman's Journal*, May 9, 1863.
18. *London Herald*, November 12, 1864.
19. Philip H. Melanson, with Peter F. Stevens, *The Secret Service* (New York: Carroll & Graff, 2002), pp. 24–35.
20. Noah Brooks, *Washington in Lincoln's Time* (New York: Rinehart, 1958), pp. 43–44; Noah Brooks, "Personal Recollections of Abraham Lincoln," *Harper's New Monthly Magazine* 31, no. 182 (July 1865): pp. 222–30; *Richmond Times*, April 23, 1865; John G. Nicolay and John Hay, *Abraham Lincoln: A History* (New York: Century, 1890), Vol. 10, p. 287; Leonard Swett, "The Conspiracies of the Rebellion," *North American Review* 144 (February 1887): pp. 179–89; Carl Sandburg, *Abraham Lincoln—The War Years* (New York: Harcourt, Brace, 1939), Vol. 4, p. 243; Herbert Mitgang, ed., *Lincoln as They Saw Him* (New York: Rinehart, 1956), pp. 406–7, 417.
21. Frederick Hatch, "The Only Man Lincoln Feared," *Lincoln Herald* 101, no. 1 (Spring 1999): pp. 13–16.
22. James Speed, *Opinion on the Constitutional Power of the Military to Try and Execute the Assassins of the President* (Washington, DC: Government Printing Office, 1865), p. 3.
23. "Attempts Upon Lincoln's Life," *Cincinnati Enquirer*, August 15, 1885.
24. George Ashman, "Recollections of a Peculiar Service," *Magazine of History* 3, no. 4 (April 1906): pp. 247–53.
25. Frederick Hatch, "Lincoln Under Fire," *Journal of the Lincoln Assassination* 19, no. 1 (April 2005): pp. 2–7.
26. McBride, pp. 27–28; Earl Schenck Miers, *Lincoln Day by Day* (Dayton, OH: Morningside House, 1991), Part II, p. 239; Pinsker, p. 6. *Walt Whitman—Complete Poetry and Collected Prose* (New York: Literary Classics of the United States, 1982), pp. 732–33.
27. Oates, p. 401.
28. Otto Eisenschiml and E. B. Long, *As Luck Would Have It* (New York: Bobbs-Merrill, 1948), pp. 223–39; Michael W. Kauffman, "John Wilkes Booth and the Murder of Abraham Lincoln," *Blue & Gray Magazine* 7, no. 4 (April 1990): p. 9.
29. D. Mark Katz, "Booth's First Attempt," *Surratt Courier* 11, no. 6 (June 1986): pp. 1, 7–10.
30. Philip Van Doren Stern, *An End to Valor* (Boston: Houghton Mifflin, 1958), p. 16.
31. Dorothy Meserve Kunhardt and Philip B. Kunhardt, Jr., *Twenty Days* (New York: Harper & Row, 1965), pp. 34–35.
32. John S. Barnes, "With Lincoln from Washington to Richmond in 1865," *Appleton's Magazine* 9, nos. 5 and 6 (May/June 1907): pp. 515–24, 742–51; William H. Crook, *Through Five Administrations* (New York: Harper & Brothers, 1910), pp. 38–59; Robert Lincoln O'Brien, letter to David Rankin Barbee regarding W. H. Crook, January 4, 1951, D. R. Barbee Papers; *New York Tribune*, May 31, 1865; *New York Times*, September 14, 1862. Doris Kearns Goodwin, *Team of Rivals* (New York: Simon and Schuster, 2005), p. 718.
33. David Homer Bates, *Lincoln in the Telegraph Office* (New York: Century, 1907), p. 364.
34. *Cleveland Plain Dealer*, May 10, 1865; *New York Tribune*, July 11, 1864; War Department, Judge Advocate General Files, National Archives; Michael Burlingame and John R. Turner Ettlinger, eds., *Inside Lincoln's White House: The Complete Civil War Diary of John Hay* (Carbondale: Southern Illinois University Press, 1997), pp. 195–96.

Chapter 5: Presidential Health

1. Milton H. Shutes, *Lincoln and the Doctors* (New York: Pioneer, 1933), pp. 6, 65–67, 78, 85, 87, 88, 102.
2. J. H. Baker, pp. 205–11, 218–20: Elizabeth Keckley, *Behind the Scenes, Or, Thirty Years a Slave and Four Years in the White House* (New York: G. W. Carlton, 1868), pp. 102–5; Shenk, pp. 177–78.
3. J. H. Baker, pp. 222–25; "Serious Accident to Mrs. Lincoln," *Washington Evening Star*, July 2, 1863, p. 2. Havlik, Robert J., "Lincoln's Washington Carriages Revisited," *Lincoln Herald*, 112, no, 3 (Fall, 2010): pp. 155–80.
4. Kunhardt, pp. 59, 66–68.
5. Harriet F. Durham, "Lincoln's Sons and the Marfan Syndrome," *Lincoln Herald* 79, no. 2 (Summer 1977): pp. 67–71.
6. "Lincoln's Syndrome," *Newsweek* 59, no. 24 (June 11, 1962): p. 95.
7. "Abe's Malady," *Time* 111, no. 21 (May 22, 1978): p. 83.
8. Durham, pp. 67–71.
9. Caroline Decker, "Hopes Raised in Battle Against Rare Marfan Syndrome," *Los Angeles Times*, July 23, 1990.

10. Thomas H. Maugh II, "Gene Discovery Raises Hope For Marfan Syndrome Test," *Los Angeles Times*, July 25, 1991.
11. Martin D. Tullai, "Did Lincoln Suffer From Marfan Syndrome?" *Baltimore Sun*, April 5, 1987.
12. Sandburg, Vol. 4, p. 172.
13. Larry Thompson, "Experts Discourage Test of Lincoln Genes," *Washington Post*, April 16, 1992.
14. Brooks, "Personal Recollections."
15. Archer H. Shaw, *The Lincoln Encyclopedia* (New York: Macmillan, 1950), p. 87.
16. Shutes, p. 6.
17. Stefan Lorant, *Lincoln—A Picture Story of His Life* (New York: Bonanza Books, 1976), pp. 118–19.
18. Lloyd Lewis, *Myths After Lincoln* (New York: Grosset & Dunlap, 1941), p. 292.
19. Sandburg, Vol. 4, p. 182.
20. Marquis de Chambrun, "Personal Recollections of Mr. Lincoln," *Scribner's Magazine* 13, no. 1 (January 1893): pp. 26–38.
21. Sandburg, Vol. 4, pp. 242–43.
22. Lamon, pp. 114–18.
23. Gideon Welles, *Diary of Gideon Welles*, ed. Howard K. Beale (New York: W.W. Norton, 1960), pp. 282–83.
24. Crook, pp. 65–68.
25. These well-known photographs are often reproduced, as in Lorant, pp. 198 and 259.
26. Shutes, pp. 65–69. The double-image vision is mentioned by this source and the deviation of one eye is offered as an explanation.
27. *Philadelphia Sunday Dispatch*, December 6, 1863.
28. *New York Sunday Mercury*, February 23, 1862.
29. *Washington Daily Times*, March 23, 1865.
30. *Washington Evening Star*, March 18, 1865.
31. *Washington National Republican*, March 16, 1865.
32. "President Lincoln's Health," *Washington Evening Star*, March 17, 1865.
33. *Chicago Tribune*, March 22, 1865.
34. David Brown, "Lincoln May Be 1st Recorded Case of Rare Disease," *Washington Post*, November 26, 2007, p. A-8.
35. Mark E. Neely, Jr., *The Abraham Lincoln Encyclopedia* (New York: McGraw-Hill, 1982), pp. 237–38; Kane, p. 344.

Chapter 6: Reelection

1. Abraham Lincoln, "Response to Serenade, Washington, D.C., October 19, 1864," in Lincoln, *Speeches and Writings*, p. 635.
2. Shaw, pp. 10, 366–67.
3. Carolyn Goldinger, ed., *Presidential Elections Since 1789* (Washington, DC: Congressional Quarterly, 1987), pp. 103, 172.
4. Michael F. Holt, *Political Parties and American Political Development from the Age of Jackson to the Age of Lincoln* (Baton Rouge: Louisiana State University Press, 1992), pp. 334–38.
5. Harold M. Dudley, "The Election of 1864," *Mississippi Valley Historical Review* 18, no. 4 (March 1932): pp. 500–518.
6. Kane, pp. 57, 72, 80–81, 85, 91.
7. Dudley, pp. 500–518; William Frank Zornow, *Lincoln and the Party Divided* (Norman: University of Oklahoma Press, 1954), pp. 28, 33, 46, 48, 54, 75–76, 86.
8. William Frank Zornow, "Lincoln's Influence in the Election of 1864," *Lincoln Herald* 51, no. 2 (June 1949), pp. 22–32.
9. Dudley, pp. 500–518; William Frank Zornow, "Campaign Issues and Popular Mandates in 1864," *Mid-America* 35, no. 4 (October 1953): pp. 195–216; Zornow, *Lincoln and the Party Divided*, pp. 6–22, 119, 138–39; John C. Waugh, *Reelecting Lincoln* (New York: Crown, 1997), pp. 276–94.
10. Louis Taylor Merrill, "General Benjamin F. Butler in the Presidential Campaign of 1864," *Mississippi Valley Historical Review* 33, no. 4 (March 1947): pp. 537–70; William Frank Zornow, "The Union Party Convention at Baltimore in 1864," *Maryland Historical Magazine* 45, no. 3 (September 1950): pp. 176–200.
11. T. Harry Williams, "Voters in Blue: The Citizen Soldiers of the Civil War," *Mississippi Valley Historical Review* 31, no. 2 (September 1944): pp. 187–204; Zornow, *Lincoln and the Party Divided*, pp. 5–22, 33, 119–20.
12. William B. Hesseltine, *Lincoln's Plan of Reconstruction* (Gloucester, MA: Peter Smith, 1963), pp. 39, 64, 71–72, 121–33.
13. Zornow, *Lincoln and the Party Divided*, pp. 198–201.

14. Larry E. Nelson, *Bullets, Ballots, and Rhetoric* (University: University of Alabama Press, 1980), pp. 1, 14, 62, 87–89, 107–8.
15. Zornow, "Campaign Issues and Popular Mandates in 1864"; Zornow, *Lincoln and the Party Divided*, pp. 119–20.
16. Dudley, pp. 500–518; Goldinger, pp. 102, 173; John Rhodehamel and Louise Taper, eds., *"Right or Wrong, God Judge Me": The Writings of John Wilkes Booth* (Urbana: University of Illinois Press, 1997), p. 124; Waugh, pp. 295–97; Zornow, *Lincoln and the Party Divided*, pp. 142, 216.

Chapter 7: Confederate Secret Service

1. William A. Tidwell, *April '65—Confederate Covert Action in the American Civil War* (Kent, OH: Kent State University Press, 1995), pp. 31–56.
2. Eli N. Evans, *Judah P. Benjamin: The Jewish Confederate* (New York: The Free Press, 1988), pp. 3–48, 115–36.
3. Ibid., pp. 257–58.
4. Dumas Malone, ed., *Dictionary of American Biography* (New York: Charles Scribner's Sons, 1964), Vol. 9, pt. 2, pp. 459–60.
5. Tidwell, p. 107.
6. Jacob Thompson to Judah P. Benjamin, February 13, 1865, in *The War of the Rebellion: A Compilation of the Official Records of the Union and Confederate Armies* (Washington, DC: Government Printing Office, 1899), Series I, Vol. 43, Part II, pp. 930–36.
7. Tidwell, Hall, and Gaddy, p. 6; James D. Horan, *Confederate Agent* (New York: Crown, 1954), pp. 81–88, 298.
8. *War of the Rebellion*, Series I, Vol. 43, Part II, pp. 930–36.
9. Malone, Vol. 8, pt. 2, pp. 334–35.
10. Tidwell, Hall, and Gaddy, p. 192; Horan, pp. 108–9, 166–75.
11. Tidwell, Hall, and Gaddy, pp. 329–31, 333–34.
12. Ibid., pp. 19–22, 72–73, 237, 264, 275, 281–88, 292, 307–18, 409, 461.
13. Louis J. Weichmann, *A True History of the Assassination of Abraham Lincoln and of the Conspiracy of 1865*, ed. Floyd E. Risvold (New York: Alfred A. Knopf, 1975), pp. 47, 57, 60–61, 254; Tidwell, *April '65*, pp. 135, 144–45, 236–37.
14. Thomas A. Jones, *J. Wilkes Booth* (Chicago: Laird & Lee 1893), pp. 39–43.
15. "The Confederate Plan to Abduct President Lincoln," *Surratt Society News* 6, no. 3 (March 1981): pp. 3–6.
16. Tidwell, Hall, and Gaddy, p. 332.
17. Nancy D. Baird, "The Yellow Fever Plot," *Civil War Times Illustrated* 13, no. 7 (November 1974): pp. 16–23; Benn Pitman, *The Assassination of President Lincoln and the Trial of the Conspirators* (Cincinnati: Moore, Wilstach & Baldwin, 1865), pp. 54–57.
18. Tidwell, Hall, and Gaddy, pp. 27–28, 418–21.
19. John H. Surratt, Jr., quoted in Weichmann, pp. 432–33.

Chapter 8: John Wilkes Booth

1. Stanley Kimmel, *The Mad Booths of Maryland* (Indianapolis: Bobbs-Merrill, 1940), pp. 32–58; Asia Booth Clarke, *The Unlocked Book* (New York: G.P. Putnam's Sons, 1938), p. 41.
2. Kauffman, "John Wilkes Booth and the Murder of Abraham Lincoln."
3. Clarke, pp. 43–46.
4. Bryan, pp. 79–83.
5. Gordon Samples, *Lust for Fame: The Stage Career of John Wilkes Booth* (Jefferson, NC: McFarland, 1982), pp. 12–24; Kauffman, "John Wilkes Booth and the Murder of Abraham Lincoln," pp. 8–25, 46–62
6. Samples, pp. 52–56.
7. Kauffman, "John Wilkes Booth and the Murder of Abraham Lincoln," pp. 8–25, 46–62; Bryan, pp. 86–87.
8. Samples, pp. 65, 230–31. Nora Titone, *My Thoughts Be Bloody* (New York: Free Press, 2010), pp. 266–67.
9. Bryan, pp. 88, 276–78. Titone, p. 227.
10. Samples, pp. 217–21; Joseph George, Jr., "The Night John Wilkes Booth Played Before Abraham Lincoln," *Lincoln Herald* 59, no. 2 (Summer 1957): pp. 11–15.
11. Charlotte M. Martin, "The Stage Reminiscences of Mrs. Gilbert," *Scribner's Magazine* 29, no. 2 (February 1901): pp. 167–84.
12. Clara Morris, "Some Recollections of John Wilkes Booth," *McClure's Magazine* 16, no. 4 (February 1901): pp. 299–304.

13. Campbell MacCulloch, "This Man Saw Lincoln Shot," *Good Housekeeping* 84, no. 2 (February 1927): pp. 20–21, 112, 115–16, 121–22.
14. James M. McPherson, *Battle Cry of Freedom* (New York: Oxford University Press, 1988), pp. 6–41, 237–38, 281, 304, 593, 762; Rhodehamel and Taper, pp. 124–27.
15. Tidwell, Hall, and Gaddy, pp. 259, 273, 328–32.
16. Samples, pp. 223–24; Kauffman, "John Wilkes Booth and the Murder of Abraham Lincoln," pp. 8–25, 46–62; Frederick Hatch, "Lincoln, Booth, and the Bard," *Journal of the Lincoln Assassination* 17, no. 2 (August 2003): pp. 22–27.
17. John H. Surratt, Jr., "Rockville Lecture," in Weichmann, p. 431.
18. Samuel Bland Arnold, *Memoirs of a Lincoln Conspirator*, ed. Michael W. Kauffman (Bowie, MD: Heritage Books, 1995), p. 42.
19. *War of the Rebellion*, Series II, Vol. 8, pp. 883–85; Pitman, p. xv; Patricia L. Faust, ed., *Historical Times Illustrated Encyclopedia of the Civil War* (New York: HarperCollins, 1991), p. 120.
20. Samuel B. Arnold, statement made at Baltimore, Maryland, April 18, 1865, National Archives and Records Service, M-619, reel 458, frames 0305–0312.
21. Michael W. Kauffman, *American Brutus* (New York: Random House, 2004), pp. 184–86.
22. Weichmann, p. 110; D. H. L. Gleason, deposition, April 18, 1865, War Department Records, Judge Advocate General's files.

Chapter 9: Conspiracy

1. Nettie Mudd, ed., *The Life of Dr. Samuel A. Mudd* (La Plata, MD: Dick Wildes Printing, 1983), p. 355.
2. National Archives, War Department Records, File S, R.B.P. 554, JAO; Theodore Roscoe, *Web of Conspiracy* (Englewood Cliffs, NJ: Prentice-Hall, 1959), pp. 58–60.
3. S. B. Arnold, pp. 22–24.
4. Ibid., pp. 148–50.
5. Ben Perley Poore, *The Conspiracy Trial for the Murder of the President* (Boston: J. E. Tilton, 1865), Vol. I, pp. 419–21.
6. S. B. Arnold, pp. 150–51.
7. Hans Falckner, "On the Family and Homeland of Georg Andreas Atzerodt," unpublished paper prepared for James O. Hall, 1967, J. O. Hall Papers, Surratt Society, Clinton, Maryland.
8. Kauffman, "John Wilkes Booth and the Murder of Abraham Lincoln."
9. Tidwell, Hall, and Gaddy, p. 337.
10. S. B. Arnold, pp. 25–27.
11. Investigation and Trial Papers Relating to the Assassination of Abraham Lincoln, Microcopy M-599, Reel 4, Frames 0442–0485, National Archives.
12. Michael W. Kauffman, "David Edgar Herold, the Forgotten Conspirator," *Surratt Society News* 6, no. 11 (November 1981).
13. S. B. Arnold, pp. 25–27; Poore, Vol. I, pp. 115–16; Kauffman, "John Wilkes Booth and the Murder of Abraham Lincoln."
14. Bryan, p. 144.
15. Ibid., p. 107; M-599, Reel 2, Frames 986–87, 1038–40; Reel 3, Frames 611–17; Reel 4, Frames 197–98; Reel 6, Frames 86–89.
16. S. B. Arnold, pp. 24, 42–43, 147.
17. Ibid., pp. 148–49.
18. Poore, Vol. I, pp. 149–65.
19. Betty J. Ownsbey, *Alias "Paine": Lewis Thornton Powell, the Mystery Man of the Lincoln Conspiracy* (Jefferson, NC: McFarland, 1993), pp. 1–33.
20. Tidwell, Hall, and Gaddy, pp. 339–40; M-599, Reel 1, Frame 39; Reel 3, Frames 535–44; Reel 7, Frames 445–51.
21. Samuel Carter, III, *The Riddle of Dr. Mudd* (New York: G.P. Putnam's Sons, 1974), pp. 18, 27–36.
22. Carter, pp. 74–77; M-599, Reel 5, Frames 212–25.
23. Weichmann, pp. 32–35.
24. Bryan, pp. 104, 140, 207.
25. Poore, Vol. II, pp. 32–33, 461; M-599, Reel 6, Frames 359–62.
26. James O. Hall, *The Surratt Family and John Wilkes Booth* (Clinton, MD: Surratt Society, n.d. [1976]), pp. 1–6; Alfred Isacsson, "An Update on Mary Surratt and Her Offspring, Anna and Isaac," *Surratt Courier* 11, no. 5 (May 1986): p. 1.
27. Weichmann, p. 14.
28. Alan Axelrod, *The War Between the Spies* (New York: Atlantic Monthly, 1992), pp. 87–88; Hall, *Surratt*

Family and John Wilkes Booth, p. 9; Alfred Isacsson, "John Surratt and the Lincoln Assassination Plot," *Maryland Historical Magazine* 52, no. 4 (December 1957): p. 317; "John Surratt," *Philadelphia Times*, October 4, 1885.

29. Hall, *Surratt Family and John Wilkes Booth*, p. 12.
30. Weichmann, p. 431; Isacsson, "John Surratt and the Lincoln Assassination Plot," p. 319–21;Samuel B. Arnold and George A. Atzerodt, "The Lincoln Assassination," *New York Times*, January 19, 1869, p. 8.
31. Hall, *Surratt Family* and John Wilkes Booth, pp. 13–15.
32. Weichmann, pp. 98–100.
33. James O. Hall, "Letter," *Journal of the Lincoln Assassination* 9, no. 1 (April 1995): p. 18; Weichmann, pp. 432–33; Hall, *Surratt Family* and John Wilkes Booth, pp. 17–18. Isacsson, "John Surratt and the Lincoln Assassination Plot," pp. 322–33.
34. Isacsson, "John Surratt and the Lincoln Assassination Plot," pp. 323–27; Alexandra Lee Levin, "Confederate General Edwin Lee Was a Credit to His Famous Name," *America's Civil War* 5, no. 1 (May 1992): pp. 14, 68–74; Robert H. Moore, "Break Out!" *Civil War Times Illustrated* 30, no. 5 (November/December 1991): pp. 26, 52–61; Weichmann, pp. 437–38.
35. Hall, *Surratt Family and John Wilkes Booth*, pp. 1–11.
36. Tidwell, Hall, and Gaddy, pp. 91, 213.
37. Guy W. Moore, *The Case of Mrs. Surratt* (Norman: University of Oklahoma Press, 1954), p. 5.
38. M-599, Reel 6, Frames 0233–0257.
39. Poore, Vol. 1, pp. 75–76, 115–18.

Chapter 10: A Night of Horrors

1. Henry J. Raymond, *The Life and Public Services of Abraham Lincoln* (New York: Derby and Miller, 1865), p. 779.
2. George J. Olszewski, *Restoration of Ford's Theatre* (Washington, DC: United States Department of the Interior, National Park Service, 1963), pp. 43–45.
3. Kauffman, *American Brutus*, p. 40.
4. Olszewski, pp. 56–61; Charles A. Leale, "Lincoln's Last Hours," *Harper's Weekly* 53, no. 2721 (February 13, 1909): pp. 7–10, 27.
5. Bryan, pp. 181–82; Kauffman, *American Brutus*, pp. 72–73; Poore, Vol. II, pp. 70–71; Vol. I, pp. 190–203.
6. Joseph Nathan Kane, Janet Podell, and Steven Anzovin, *Facts About the States* (New York: W.H. Wilson, 1987), p. 468; Benjamin F. Shearer and Barbara S. Shearer, *State Names, Seals, Flags, and Symbols* (New York: Greenwood, 1987), pp. 30, 59.
7. Kauffman, *American Brutus*, pp. 7–9.
8. Michael Maione and James O. Hall, "Why Seward? The Attack on the Night of April 14, 1865," *Lincoln Herald* 100, no. 1 (Spring 1998): pp. 29–34; Helen Palmes Moss, "Lincoln and Wilkes Booth as Seen on the Day of the Assassination," *Century Magazine* 77, no. 6 (April 1909): pp. 950–53.
9. Poore, Vol. I, pp. 471–75.
10. Frederick W. Seward, *Reminiscences of a War-time Statesman and Diplomat, 1830–1915* (New York: G.P. Putnam's Sons, 1916), p. 259.
11. Patricia Carley Johnson, ed., "I Have Supped Full on Horrors," *American Heritage* 10, no. 6 (October 1959): pp. 60–65, 96–101.
12. F. W. Seward, p. 259; Poore, Vol. I, pp. 471–75; Johnson, pp. 60–65, 96–101.
13. Poore, Vol. I, pp. 479–80; Vol. II, pp. 3–5.
14. Poore, Vol. II, pp. 5–9.
15. Johnson, op. cit.
16. Poore, Vol. II, pp. 5–9.
17. Maxwell Whiteman, ed., *While Lincoln Lay Dying* (Philadelphia: Union League of Philadelphia, 1968), testimony of Alfred Cloughley.
18. Johnson, pp. 60–65, 96–101.
19. T.'S. Verdi, "The Assassination of the Sewards," *The Republic* 1 (July 1873): pp. 289–97.
20. Johnson, pp. 60–65, 96–101.
21. John K. Lattimer, *Kennedy and Lincoln* (New York: Harcourt Brace Jovanovich, 1980), p. 102.
22. Whiteman, Ferguson statement, p. 2.
23. Charles Sabin Taft, "Abraham Lincoln's Last Hours," *Century Magazine* 45, no. 4 (February 1893): pp. 634–36.
24. Whiteman, Hawk statement, first page.
25. Jas. S. Knox, "A Son Writes of the Supreme Tragedy," *The Saturday Review* 39, no. 6 (February 11, 1956): p. 11.
26. J. E. Buckingham, Sr., *Reminiscences and Souvenirs of the Assassination of Abraham Lincoln* (Washington, DC: Press of Rufus Darby, 1894), pp. 13–15.

27. Seaton Munroe, "Recollections of Lincoln's Assassination," *North American Review* 162, no. 473 (April 1896): pp. 424–34.
28. Roeliff Brinkerhoff, "Tragedy of an Age: An Eyewitness Account of Lincoln's Assassination," ed. A. M. Markowitz, *Journal of the Illinois State Historical Society* 66, no. 2 (Summer 1973): pp. 205–11.
29. Salmon P. Chase, *Inside Lincoln's Cabinet—The Civil War Diaries of Salmon P. Chase*, ed. David Donald (New York: Longmans, Green, 1954), pp. 266–67.
30. Chambrun, pp. 26–38.
31. Weichmann, p. 180.
32. Gay Wilson Allen, *The Solitary Singer* (Chicago: University of Chicago Press, 1985), pp. 332–33.
33. Martin Abbott, "Southern Reaction to Lincoln's Assassination," *Abraham Lincoln Quarterly* 7, no. 3 (September 1952): pp. 111–27.
34. Thomas Goodrich, *The Darkest Dawn* (Bloomington: Indiana University Press, 2005), p. 136.
35. Ibid., p. 138.

Chapter 11: Cause of Death

1. Leale, pp. 7–10, 27.
2. Shutes, pp. 112–16.
3. Leale, pp. 7–10, 27.
4. Charles S. Taft, "Last Hours of Abraham Lincoln," *Medical and Surgical Reporter* 12, Philadelphia (April 22, 1865): pp. 452–54; Leale, pp. 7–10, 27.
5. Shutes, pp. 116–18; Lattimer, pp. 34–40; Taft, pp. 452–54.
6. Joseph K. Barnes, ed., "Another Case of Alleged Fracture by Contre-coup ..." *Medical and Surgical History of the War of the Rebellion, Surgical History*, Part I, Vol. II (Washington, DC: Government Printing Office, 1870), pp. 305–6; Hans L. Trefousse, *Andrew Johnson—A Biography* (New York: W.W. Norton, 1989), p. 195.

Chapter 12: The Missing Guard

1. Washington Metropolitan Police Department, Precinct Records, 7th Precinct, National Archives, RG 351, entry 51. Notes from files of James O. Hall.
2. Lamon, pp. 274–75.
3. Washington Metropolitan Police Records, copy in files of J. O. Hall.
4. Justin G. Turner and Linda Levitt Turner, *Mary Todd Lincoln: Her Life and Letters* (New York: Alfred A. Knopf, 1972), p. 211.
5. Lamon, pp. 274–75.
6. Thomas F. Pendel, *Thirty-Six Years in the White House* (Washington, DC: Neale, 1902), pp. 39–40.
7. Crook, pp. 72–74.
8. M-599, Reel 4, Frames 0083–0084.
9. James O. Hall, notes on statement of Burke, files of J. O. Hall.
10. *New York Tribune*, April 17, 1865, p. 1, c. 2; Washington Metropolitan Police Records, copy in files of J. O. Hall.
11. Helen A. Du Barry, "Eyewitness Account of Lincoln's Assassination," *Journal of the Illinois State Historical Society* 39, no. 3 (September 1946): pp. 366–70.
12. Alfers, pp. 13, 15.
13. J. O. Hall, notes on Pendel from records of Washington Metropolitan Police Department and White House, files of J. O. Hall.
14. J. S. Barnes, pp. 515–24, 742–51.
15. O'Brien, O'Brien, letter to David Rankin Barbee regarding W. H. Crook, D. R. Barbee Papers.
16. James O. Hall, "A Noted Author Explains the Mystery of Lincoln's Guard," *Maryland Independent*, July 26, 1978.
17. Washington Metropolitan Police Records, copy in J. O. Hall papers; *New York Tribune*, June 11, 1863.
18. Otto Eisenschiml, *Why Was Lincoln Murdered?* (Boston: Little, Brown, 1937), pp. 12–16.
19. Ver Lynn Sprague, "Mary Lincoln—Accessory to Murder," *Lincoln Herald* 81, no. 4 (Winter 1979): pp. 238–42.
20. Hall, "A Noted Author Explains the Mystery of Lincoln's Guard."
21. Washington Metropolitan Police Records, notes in files of J. O. Hall.
22. George W. McElfresh, "Guarding Mr. Lincoln," *Ohio Soldier*, April 28, 1888.
23. Olszewski, p. 43.
24. Rhodehamel and Taper, p. 154.
25. Poore, Vol. I, pp. 195–98.

26. Frank Ford, letter to G. J. Olszewski, in Olszewski, p. 124; Poore, Vol. I, pp. 409–10.
27. Poore, Vol. I, p. 194.
28. *Washington National Republican*, June 8, 1865.
29. Major Henry R. Rathbone, affidavit, April 17, 1865, National Archives, War Department Records, File "R," R.B., JAO, p. 74.
30. Crook, pp. 72–74.
31. Gary R. Planck, *The Lincoln Assassination's Forgotten Investigator: A.C. Richards* (Harrogate, TN: Lincoln Memorial University Press, 1993), p. 12.
32. Poore, Vol. I.
33. Washington Metropolitan Police Records, "Police Blotter," notes in J. O. Hall Papers.
34. Department of the Metropolitan Police, Washington City, May 1, 1865, *Charge and Specifications against Patrolman John F. Parker*. Copy in J. O. Hall Papers.
35. Washington Metropolitan Police Records, Station House—Precinct Books, National Archives, RG 351, entry 51. Copy in J. O. Hall Papers.
36. Planck, p. 30.
37. Keckley, pp. 193–95.
38. Washington Metropolitan Police Records, National Archives, notes in J. O. Hall Papers.
39. J. O. Hall Papers, notes, John F. Parker file; Hall, "A Noted Author Explains the Mystery of Lincoln's Guard."
40. Claude Keiper, letter to David R. Barbee, April 23, 1943, D. R. Barbee Papers.
41. Certificate of Death, No. 72718, Permit no. 72754, Vital Records Section, Department of Human Resources, Government of the District of Columbia; *Washington Post*, June 29, 1890.

Chapter 13: The Hand of the Avenger

1. Roscoe, p. 131; James O. Hall, *John Wilkes Booth's Escape Route* (Clinton, MD: Surratt Society, 2000), pp. 1–4.
2. Poore, Vol. I, pp. 251–5; M-599, Reel 5, Frames 414–21.
3. Hall, *John Wilkes Booth's Escape Route*, pp. 4–5.
4. Michael W. Kauffman, "The Revenge of Old Glory: History vs. Myth in the Lincoln Assassination," *Lincoln Herald* 104, no. 4 (Winter 2002): pp. 141–50.
5. Poore, Vol. I, pp. 115–20.
6. James O. Hall, "John M. Lloyd—'Star Witness,'" *Surratt Society News* 2, no. 3 (March 1977): pp. 3–4.
7. Carter, pp. 121–28.
8. M-599, Reel 5, Frames 226–39.
9. Hall, *John Wilkes Booth's Escape Route*, p. 10; Kevin McManus, "They Call the Swamp Zekiah," *Washington Post*, May 10, 1996.
10. M-599, Reel 4, Frames 442–85; Reel 6, Frames 227–29.
11. Roscoe, p. 211.
12. Jones, pp. 66–82; Hall, *John Wilkes Booth's Escape Route*, p. 10; Frederick Hatch, "They Shot Horses, Didn't They? Booth and Herold in the Woods," *Journal of the Lincoln Assassination* 21, no. 3 (December 2007): pp. 42–46.
13. William Hanchett, "Booth's Diary," *Journal of the Illinois State Historical Society* 72, no. 1 (February 1979): pp. 39–56; Federal Bureau of Investigation, U.S. Department of Justice, "Report of the FBI Laboratory, Examination of John Wilkes Booth's Diary," 95–216208, Washington, DC, October 3, 1977; FBI memorandum from Robert T. Kelly to Mr. Kelleher, August 3, 1977, describing techniques used in examination of the diary.
14. Jones, pp. 90–110.
15. Hall, *John Wilkes Booth's Escape Route*, pp. 11–12; Michael W. Kauffman, "Booth's Escape Route—Lincoln Assassin on the Run," *Blue & Gray Magazine* 7, no. 5 (June 1990): pp. 8–22, 38–61.
16. Hall, *John Wilkes Booth's Escape Route*, pp. 12–13; Kauffman, "Booth's Escape Route"; Tidwell, Hall, and Gaddy, pp. 461–63, 465–68.
17. Hall, *John Wilkes Booth's Escape Route*, pp. 13–15; Kauffman, "Booth's Escape Route"; Tidwell, Hall, and Gaddy, pp. 474–76.
18. John M. Garrett, "The Statement of John M. Garrett," *Surratt Courier* 20, no. 3 (March 1995): pp. 4–9.
19. Steven G. Miller, "Rollcall for the Garrett's Farm Patrol," *Surratt Courier* 19, no. 9 (September 1994): pp. 3–5.
20. L. B. Baker, "An Eyewitness Account of the Death and Burial of J. Wilkes Booth," *Journal of the Illinois State Historical Society* 39, no. 4 (December 1946), 425–45; "Captain Doherty's Story," *New York Times*, August 22, 1879, p. 3; M-599, Reel 4, Frames 0442–0485; Steven G. Miller, "A Trooper's Account of the Death of Booth," *Surratt Courier* 20, no. 5 (May 1995): pp. 5–9; Poore, Vol. I, pp. 312–26; Vol. II, pp. 92–94; *The War of the Rebellion*, Series I, Vol. 46, part 1, pp. 1317–18.

21. Byron Berkeley Johnson, *Abraham Lincoln and Boston Corbett* (Waltham, MA: Byron Berkeley Johnson, 1914), pp. 44–50; *New York Times*, May 2, 1865, p. 1.
22. L. B. Baker, pp. 425–45; John L. Howard, "The Cases of A.L. and J.W.B.: A Modern Case Presentation," lecture at Surratt Society Annual Conference, Clinton, Maryland, March 20, 2004.
23. L. B. Baker, pp. 425–45; Hall, *John Wilkes Booth's Escape Route*, p. 16; Kauffman, "Booth's Escape Route."
24. Bryan, pp. 273–81.
25. Joseph K. Barnes, "Report Upon the Examination of the Body of J. Wilkes Booth, the Assassin," National Archives, RG 94, TR 132; Lattimer, pp. 69–88.
26. Bryan, pp. 273–81; Barnes, "Report Upon the Examination of the Body of J. Wilkes Booth, the Assassin"; Lattimer, pp. 69–88.
27. Bryan, pp. 290–95.

Chapter 14: The Long Good-bye

1. Noah Brooks, "The Close of Lincoln's Career," *Century Magazine*, May 1895, p. 23.
2. Lewis, pp. 105–10.
3. Wayne C. Temple, "Tinsmith to the Late Mr. Lincoln: Samuel S. Elder," *Journal of the Illinois State Historical Society* 71, no. 3 (August 1978): pp. 176–84.
4. Ralph G. Newman, "In This Sad World of Ours, Sorrow Comes to All," *Journal of the Illinois State Historical Society* 58, no. 1 (Spring 1965): pp. 5–20.
5. *Washington Evening Star*, April 20, 1865, p. 1.
6. Newman, pp. 5–20.
7. Raymond Borchers, "President Lincoln's Car," *Lincoln Herald* 86, no. 4 (Winter 1984): pp. 212–16.
8. David K. Nelson, "A Rolling Memento," *Civil War Times Illustrated* 34, no. 1 (March/April 1995): pp. 54–59.
9. Newman, pp. 5–20.
10. Ibid.
11. Robert E. Morsberger and Katharine M. Morsberger, *Lew Wallace: Militant Romantic* (New York: McGraw-Hill, 1980), pp. 156–67.
12. "Piloting the Lincoln Funeral Train," *Lincoln Lore*, no. 895 (June 3, 1946); Newman, pp. 5–20.
13. *Harrisburg (PA) Patriot and Union*, April 21, 1865.
14. Newman, pp. 5–20; "Piloting the Lincoln Funeral Train."
15. *Philadelphia Inquirer*, April 24, 1865.
16. Newman, pp. 5–20; "Piloting the Lincoln Funeral Train."
17. *New York Tribune*, April 26, 1865, pp. 1 and 8.
18. David T. Valentine, *Obsequies of Abraham Lincoln in the City of New York* (New York: Edmund Jones, 1866), p. 128.
19. Lewis, p. 122.
20. Kunhardt and Kunhardt, pp. 96–109.
21. Newman, pp. 5–20; "Piloting the Lincoln Funeral Train."
22. Allan Peskin, "Putting the 'Baboon' to Rest: Observations of a Radical Republican on Lincoln's Funeral Train," *Lincoln Herald* 79, no. 1 (Spring 1977): pp. 26–28.
23. "Piloting the Lincoln Funeral Train"; Newman, pp. 5–20; *Buffalo Morning Express*, April 28, 1865; *Cleveland Leader*, April 29, 1865.
24. Peskin, pp. 26–28.
25. Lewis, p. 124.
26. "Piloting the Lincoln Funeral Train," *Columbus Gazette*, May 5, 1865; *Indianapolis Daily Sentinel*, May 1, 1865.
27. B. F. Morris, affidavit, in *Memorial Record of the Nation's Tribute to Abraham Lincoln* (Washington, DC: W.H. & O.H. Morrison, 1865), p. 142.
28. "Piloting the Lincoln Funeral Train"; *Chicago Times*, May 2, 1865; Newman, pp. 5–20.
29. James T. Hickey, "Springfield, May, 1865," *Journal of the Illinois State Historical Society* 58, no. 1 (Spring 1965): pp. 21–33.
30. Kunhardt and Kunhardt, pp. 96–109.
31. Edmund Beall, "Recollections of the Assassination and Funeral of Abraham Lincoln," *Journal of the Illinois State Historical Society* 5, no. 4 (January 1913): pp. 488–92; James T. Hickey, "Springfield, May, 1865," *Journal of the Illinois State Historical Society* 58, no. 1 (Spring 1965): pp. 21–33.
32. "Piloting the Lincoln Funeral Train"; Beall, pp. 488–92; Newman, pp. 5–20; W. W. Sweet, "Bishop Matthew Simpson and the Funeral of Abraham Lincoln," *Journal of the Illinois State Historical Society* 7, no. 1 (April 1914): pp. 62–71.

Chapter 15: Rest in Peace

1. J. H. Baker, pp. 250–52.
2. Thomas J. Craughwell, *Stealing Lincoln's Body* (Cambridge, MA: The Belknap Press of Harvard University Press, 2007), p. 20–29.
3. "Viewing Lincoln's Remains," *Lincoln Lore*, no. 1611 (May 1972).
4. William J. Hosking, "Lincoln's Tomb — Designs Submitted and Final Selection," *Journal of the Illinois State Historical Society* 50, no. 1 (Spring 1957): pp. 51–61.
5. Bess King, *The Tomb of Abraham Lincoln* (Springfield, IL: Lincoln Souvenir & Gift Shop, 1941).
6. Bonnie Stahlman Speer, *The Great Abraham Lincoln Hijack* (Norman, OK: Reliance, 1990), pp. 2–3.
7. Faust, p. 323.
8. John Carroll Power, *History of an Attempt to Steal the Body of Abraham Lincoln* (Springfield, IL: H. W. Rokker Printing and Publishing House, 1890), pp. 14–27.
9. Earl C. Kubicek, "The Lincoln Corpus Caper," *Lincoln Herald* 82, no. 3 (Fall 1980): p. 474.
10. Speer, pp. 29–36.
11. Walter S. Bowen and Harry Edward Neal, *The United States Secret Service* (Philadelphia: Chilton—Book Division, 1960), p. 28–29.
12. Craughwell, pp. 95–96.
13. Bowen and Neal, p. 29.
14. Speer, pp. 79, 83–91.
15. Ibid., pp. 95–96.
16. Ibid., pp. 168–74.

Chapter 16: Aftermath

1. Melanson and Stevens, pp. 24–33.
2. Jones, pp. 121–26.
3. Steven G. Miller, "More on Capt. Doherty," *Surratt Courier* 15, no. 9 (September 1990): pp. 5–7.
4. Steven G. Miller, letter to author, September 16, 1989, Frederick Hatch Papers; D. R. Barbee Papers, Box 3, folder 178.
5. "Boston Corbett Insane," *New York Times*, February 17, 1887, p. 1; B. B. Johnson, pp. 49–55; Earl C. Kubicek, "The Case of the Mad Hatter," *Lincoln Herald* 83, no. 3 (Fall 1981): pp. 708–19; Grace Stageberg Swenson, "Boston Corbett: A Final Chapter?" *Lincoln Herald* 86, no. 3 (Fall 1984): pp. 150–56.
6. S. B. Arnold, pp. 65–132, 164–73.
7. Kauffman, "John Wilkes Booth and the Murder of Abraham Lincoln," pp. 8–25, 46–62
8. Ownsbey, pp. 136–54.
9. Carter, pp. 341–44.
10. Roy Z. Chamlee, Jr., *Lincoln's Assassins* (Jefferson, NC: McFarland, 1990), pp. 439–40.
11. Lewis, p. 214.
12. Carter, p. 229; N. Mudd, p. 119; Edmund Spangler, "A Letter from Edman Spangler," *Journal of the Lincoln Assassination* 1, no. 2 (August 1987): p. 13.
13. Peggy Robbins, "Dr. Samuel A. Mudd's Attempt to Escape from Fort Jefferson," *Civil War Times Illustrated* 16, no. 10 (February 1978): pp. 10–16.
14. Thomas Bland Keys, "Were the Lincoln Conspirators Dealt Justice?" *Lincoln Herald* 80, no. 1 (Spring 1978): pp. 36–46; *Federal Cases Comprising Cases Argued and Determined in the Circuit and District Courts of the U.S.* (St. Paul, MN: West, 1895), 17 Fed. Cas., p. 954.
15. Mudd, pp. 219, 239.
16. S. B. Arnold, pp. 86–87, 110–18; Mudd, pp. 258–59; Carter, pp. 314–15; A. O'D., "Thirty Months at the Dry Tortugas," *The Galaxy* 7, no. 2 (February 1869): pp. 282–88.
17. S. B. Arnold, pp. 114–15; Mudd, pp. 296–300, 316.
18. Mudd, pp. 319–20; Carter, pp. 348–49.
19. Dr. Richard D. Mudd, "Publicity in the Dr. Samuel A. Mudd Case, 1975," unpublished manuscript. Copy in Frederick Hatch Papers; "The Dr. Samuel A. Mudd House," informational brochure, Dr. Samuel A. Mudd Society, no date; Dr. R. D. Mudd, "Petition to the President in the Case of Dr. Samuel A. Mudd, 1970," unpublished manuscript, copy in Frederick Hatch Papers; President Jimmy Carter, letter to Dr. Richard D. Mudd, July 24, 1979, Richard Dyer Mudd, MD, Papers; "Disappointed Dr. Mudd Vows to Fight On," *JAMA* 268, no. 10 (September 9, 1992): p. 1336; Army Board for Correction of Military Records, "Transcript of Hearing in the Matter of Samuel A. Mudd, Deceased." Index No. 101.01, Board Date: January 22, 1992, Docket Number: AC91—05511.
20. Frederick Hatch, "The Men Who Hanged Mary Surratt," *Journal of the Lincoln Assassination* 22 (2008): pp. 2–20.

21. Isacsson, "John Surratt and the Lincoln Assassination Plot," p. 317
22. Donald Lankiewicz, "Journey to Asylum," *Civil War Times Illustrated* 26, no. 8 (December 1987): pp. 16–21, 44–45.
23. Evans, pp. 372–403.
24. U.S. Congress, *Biographical Directory*, p. 1932; Malone, pp. 459–60.
25. Malone, pp. 334–35.
26. M. Clifford Harrison, "A Fighting Confederate Chaplain Spy," *Virginia Cavalcade* 12, no. 4 (Spring 1963): pp. 18–22; Virginia Polytechnic Institute, *Alumni Register*, Vol. 4, 1906.
27. "Major Rathbone and Miss Harris, Guests of the Lincolns in the Ford's Theatre Box," *Lincoln Lore*, no. 1602 (August 1971).
28. Hatch, "Men Who Hanged Mary Surratt," pp. 2–20
29. Stanley W. McClure, *The Lincoln Museum and the House Where Lincoln Died* (Washington, DC: National Park Service, 1949); "Petersen House Rehabilitated," *Journal of the Illinois State Historical Society* 52, no. 3 (Autumn 1953): p. 440.
30. Speer, pp. 163–84.
31. Paul H. Buck, "Review of *Why Was Lincoln Murdered?*" *Saturday Review of Literature* 15, no. 22 (March 27, 1937); William Hanchett, *The Lincoln Murder Conspiracies* (Urbana: University of Illinois Press, 1983), pp. 159–83; *Who Was Who In America* (Chicago: Marquis Who's Who, 1968).
32. "Dr. C.A. Leale Dies; Saw Lincoln Shot," *New York Times*, June 14, 1932, p. 21; Harry Read, "A Hand to Hold While Dying — Dr. Charles A. Leale at Lincoln's Bedside," *Lincoln Herald* 79, no. 1 (Spring 1977): pp. 21–26.
33. Borchers, pp. 212–16; D. K. Nelson, pp. 54–59; Wayne Wesolowski and Mary Cay Wesolowski, *The Lincoln Train Is Coming* (Waukesha, WI: Kalmbach, 1995), pp. 14–15.

Appendix 1: Weapons of the Assassination Conspirators

1. Lattimer, pp. 24, 37, 47–49.
2. Richard Akehurst, *Antique Weapons for Pleasure and Investment* (New York: Arco, 1969), p. 118. S. B. Arnold, pp. 23, 137; John Kokkonen, "The Deadly Weapon," *Surratt Society News* 3, no. 1 (January 1978): p. 4;
3. Weichmann, pp. 97–98.

Appendix 2: Presidential Succession

1. Pitman, p. 19.
2. U.S. Congress, "An Act Relative to the Election of a President and Vice President ... etc.," *U.S. Stat. 240*; Revised Stat, && 146, 147, 148, 149, 150; March 1, 1792.
3. Maione and Hall, pp. 29–34.
4. John F. Coyle, "Wilkes Booth's Note," *Washington Post*, April 17, 1898, p. 6.
5. S. B. Arnold, pp. 135, 148–49.
6. U.S. Congress, "An Act Relative to the Election of a President and Vice President ... etc."
7. U.S. Department of State, *The Department of State of the United States* (Washington, DC: Government Printing Office, 1898), p. 18.
8. *History and Functions of the Department of State* (Washington, DC: Government Printing Office, 1901), p. 117.
9. Constitution of the United States of America, Amendment 25

Bibliography

Books

Akehurst, Richard. *Antique Weapons for Pleasure and Investment.* New York: Arco, 1969.
Alfers, Kenneth G. *Law and Order in the Capital City: A History of the Washington Police; 1800–1886.* Washington, DC: George Washington University, 1976.
Allen, Gay Wilson. *The Solitary Singer.* Chicago: University of Chicago Press, 1985.
Arnold, Isaac N. *The Life of Abraham Lincoln.* Lincoln: University of Nebraska Press, 1994.
Arnold, Samuel Bland. *Memoirs of a Lincoln Conspirator.* Ed. Michael W. Kauffman. Bowie, MD: Heritage Books, 1995.
Axelrod, Alan. *The War Between the Spies.* New York: Atlantic Monthly, 1992.
Baker, Jean H. *Mary Todd Lincoln—A Biography.* New York: W.W. Norton, 1987.
Bates, David Homer. *Lincoln in the Telegraph Office.* New York: Century, 1907.
Bowen, Walter S., and Harry Edward Neal. *The United States Secret Service.* Philadelphia: Chilton—Book Division, 1960.
Brooks, Noah. *Washington in Lincoln's Time.* New York: Rinehart, 1958.
Bryan, George S. *The Great American Myth.* New York: Carrick & Evans, 1940.
Buckingham, J. E., Sr. *Reminiscences and Souvenirs of the Assassination of Abraham Lincoln.* Washington, DC: Press of Rufus Darby, 1894.
Burlingame, Michael, and John R. Ettlinger, John R. Turner, eds. *Inside Lincoln's White House: The Complete Civil War Diaries of John Hay.* Carbondale: Southern Illinois University Press, 1997.
Carter, Samuel, III. *The Riddle of Dr. Mudd.* New York: G.P. Putnam's Sons, 1974.
Chamlee, Roy Z., Jr. *Lincoln's Assassins.* Jefferson, NC: McFarland, 1990.
Chase, Salmon P. *Inside Lincoln's Cabinet—The Civil War Diaries of Salmon P. Chase.* Ed. David Donald. New York: Longmans, Green, 1954.
Chittenden, L. E. *Recollections of President Lincoln and His Administration.* New York: Harper & Brothers, 1891.
Clarke, Asia Booth. *The Unlocked Book.* New York: G.P. Putnam's Sons, 1938.
Craughwell, Thomas J. *Stealing Lincoln's Body.* Cambridge, MA: The Belknap Press of Harvard University Press, 2007.
Crook, William H. *Through Five Administrations.* New York: Harper & Brothers, 1910.
Cuthbert, Norma B., ed. *Lincoln and the Baltimore Plot 1861.* San Marino, CA: The Huntington Library, 1949.
Donald, David Herbert. *Lincoln.* London: Jonathan Cape, 1995.
Eisenschiml, Otto. *Why Was Lincoln Murdered?* Boston: Little, Brown, 1937.
_____, and E. B. Long. *As Luck Would Have It.* New York: Bobbs-Merrill, 1948.
Evans, Eli N. *Judah P. Benjamin: The Jewish Confederate.* New York: The Free Press, 1988.
Faust, Patricia L., ed. *Historical Times Illustrated Encyclopedia of the Civil War.* New York: HarperCollins, 1991.
Federal Cases Comprising Cases Argued and Determined in the Circuit and District Courts of the U.S. St. Paul, MN: West, 1895, 17 Fed. Cas.
Goldinger, Carolyn, ed. *Presidential Elections Since 1789.* Washington, DC: Congressional Quarterly, 1987.
Goodrich, Thomas. *The Darkest Dawn.* Bloomington: Indiana University Press, 2005.
Goodwin, Davis Kearns, *Team of Rivals.* New York: Simon and Schuster, 2005.
Greeley, Horace. *Recollections of a Busy Life.* New York: J. B. Ford, 1868.
Hall, James O. *John Wilkes Booth's Escape Route.* Clinton, MD: Surratt Society, 2000.

_____. *The Surratt Family and John Wilkes Booth*. Clinton, MD: Surratt Society, n.d. (1976).
Hanchett, William. *The Lincoln Murder Conspiracies*. Urbana: University of Illinois Press, 1983.
Herndon, William H. *Life of Lincoln*. New York: Da Capo, 1983.
Hesseltine, William B. *Lincoln's Plan of Reconstruction*. Gloucester, MA: Peter Smith, 1963.
Historical Statistics of the United States, Colonial Times to 1970, Bicentennial Edition, Part I. Washington, DC: U.S. Bureau of the Census, 1975.
History and Functions of the Department of State. Washington, DC: Government Printing Office, 1901.
Holt, Michael F. *Political Parties and American Political Development from the Age of Jackson to the Age of Lincoln*. Baton Rouge: Louisiana State University Press, 1992.
Holzer, Harold, ed. *Dear Mr. Lincoln*. Reading, MA: Addison-Wesley, 1993.
Horan, James D. *Confederate Agent*. New York: Crown, 1954.
Johnson, Byron Berkeley. *Abraham Lincoln and Boston Corbett*. Waltham, MA: Byron Berkeley Johnson, 1914.
Jones, Thomas A. *J. Wilkes Booth*. Chicago: Laird & Lee, 1893.
Kane, Joseph Nathan. *Facts About the Presidents*. New York: H.W. Wilson, 1993.
Kane, Joseph Nathan, Janet Podell, and Steven Anzovin. *Facts About the States*. New York: W.H. Wilson, 1987.
Kauffman, Michael W. *American Brutus*. New York: Random House, 2004.
Keckley, Elizabeth. *Behind the Scenes, Or, Thirty Years a Slave and Four Years in the White House*. New York: G.W. Carlton, 1868.
Kimmel, Stanley. *The Mad Booths of Maryland*. Indianapolis: Bobbs-Merrill, 1940.
_____. *Mr. Lincoln's Washington*. New York: Coward-McCann, 1957.
King, Alvy L. *Louis T. Wigfall, Southern Fire-eater*. Baton Rouge: Louisiana State University Press, 1970.
King, Bess. *The Tomb of Abraham Lincoln*. Springfield, IL: Lincoln Souvenir & Gift Shop, 1941.
Kunhardt, Dorothy Meserve, and Philip B. Kunhardt, Jr. *Twenty Days*. New York: Harper & Row, 1965.
Lamon, Ward Hill. *Recollections of Abraham Lincoln*. Lincoln: University of Nebraska Press, 1994.
Lattimer, John K. *Kennedy and Lincoln*. New York: Harcourt Brace Jovanovich, 1980.
Lee, Richard M. *Mr. Lincoln's City*. McLean, VA: EPM Publications, 1981.
Lewis, Lloyd. *Myths After Lincoln*. New York: Grosset & Dunlap, 1941.
Lorant, Stefan. *Lincoln—A Picture Story of His Life*. New York: Bonanza Books, 1976.
Lincoln, Abraham. *Speeches and Writings, 1859–1865*. New York: Literary Classics of the United States, 1989.
Malone, Dumas, ed. *Dictionary of American Biography*. New York: Charles Scribner's Sons, 1964.
McBride, Robert W. *Lincoln's Body Guard*. Indianapolis: Indiana Historical Society Publications, 1911.
McClure, Stanley W. *The Lincoln Museum and the House Where Lincoln Died*. Washington, DC: National Park Service, 1949.
McPherson, James M. *Battle Cry of Freedom*. New York: Oxford University Press, 1988.
Melanson, Philip H., with Peter F. Stevens. *The Secret Service*. New York: Carroll & Graff, 2002.
Memorial Record of the Nation's Tribute to Abraham Lincoln. Washington, DC: W.H. & O.H. Morrison, 1865.
Miers, Earl Schenck. *Lincoln Day by Day*. Dayton, OH: Morningside House, 1991.
Mitgang, Herbert, ed. *Lincoln as They Saw Him*. New York: Rinehart, 1956.
Moore, Guy W. *The Case of Mrs. Surratt*. Norman: University of Oklahoma Press, 1954.
Morsberger, Robert E., and Katherine M. Morsberger. *Lew Wallace: Militant Romantic*. New York: McGraw-Hill Book, 1980.
Mudd, Nettie, ed. *The Life of Dr. Samuel A. Mudd*. La Plata, MD: Dick Wildes Printing, 1983.
Neely, Mark E., Jr. *The Abraham Lincoln Encyclopedia*. New York: McGraw-Hill, 1982.
Nelson, Larry E. *Bullets, Ballots, and Rhetoric*. University: University of Alabama Press, 1980.
Nicolay, John G., and John Hay. *Abraham Lincoln: A History*. New York: Century, 1890.
Oates, Stephen B. *With Malice Toward None*. New York: Harper & Row, 1977.
Olszewski, George J. *Restoration of Ford's Theatre*. Washington, DC: United States Department of the Interior, National Park Service, 1963.
Ownsbey, Betty J. *Alias "Paine": Lewis Thornton Powell, the Mystery Man of the Lincoln Conspiracy*. Jefferson, NC: McFarland, 1993.
Pendel, Thomas F. *Thirty-Six Years in the White House*. Washington, DC: Neale, 1902.
Pinsker, Matthew. *Lincoln's Sanctuary*. New York: Oxford University Press, 2003.
Pitman, Benn, ed. *The Assassination of President Lincoln and the Trial of the Conspirators*. Cincinnati: Moore, Wilstach & Baldwin, 1865.
Planck, Gary R. *The Lincoln Assassination's Forgotten Investigator: A.C. Richards*. Harrogate, TN: Lincoln Memorial University Press, 1993.

Poore, Ben Perley. *The Conspiracy Trial for the Murder of the President.* Boston: J.E. Tilton, 1865.
Potter, John Mason. *Plots Against Presidents.* New York: Astor-Honor, 1968.
_____. *13 Desperate Days.* New York: Ivan Obolensky, 1965.
Power, John Carroll. *History of an Attempt to Steal the Body of Abraham Lincoln.* Springfield, IL: H.W. Rokker Printing and Publishing House, 1890.
Raymond, Henry J. *The Life and Public Services of Abraham Lincoln.* New York: Derby and Miller, 1865.
Rhodehamel, John, and Louise Taper, eds. *"Right or Wrong, God Judge Me": The Writings of John Wilkes Booth.* Urbana: University of Illinois Press, 1997.
Roscoe, Theodore. *Web of Conspiracy.* Englewood Cliffs, NJ: Prentice-Hall, 1959.
Samples, Gordon. *Lust for Fame: The Stage Career of John Wilkes Booth.* Jefferson, NC: McFarland, 1982.
Sandburg, Carl. *Abraham Lincoln—The War Years.* New York: Harcourt, Brace, 1939.
Seward, Frederick W. *Reminiscences of a War-time Statesman and Diplomat, 1830–1915.* New York: G.P. Putnam's Sons, 1916.
Shaw, Archer H. *The Lincoln Encyclopedia.* New York: Macmillan, 1950.
Shearer, Benjamin F., and Barbara S. Shearer. *State Names, Seals, Flags and Symbols.* New York: H.W. Wilson, 1987.
Shenk, Joshua Wolf. *Lincoln's Melancholy.* Boston: Mariner Books, 2005.
Shutes, Milton H. *Lincoln and the Doctors.* New York: Pioneer, 1933.
Speer, Bonnie Stahlman. *The Great Abraham Lincoln Hijack.* Norman, OK: Reliance, 1990.
Stern, Philip Van Doren. *An End to Valor.* Boston: Houghton Mifflin, 1958.
Stevens, Walter B. *A Reporter's Lincoln.* Lincoln: University of Nebraska Press, 1998.
Tidwell, William A. *April '65—Confederate Covert Action in the American Civil War.* Kent, OH: Kent State University Press, 1995.
Tidwell, William A., with James O. Hall and David W. Gaddy. *Come Retribution.* Jackson: University Press of Mississippi, 1988.
Titone, Nora. *My Thoughts Be Bloody.* New York: Free Press, 2010.
Townsend, Edward D. *Anecdotes of the Civil War.* New York: D. Appleton, 1884.
Townsend, George Alfred. *The Life, Crime, and Capture of John Wilkes Booth.* New York: Dick and Fitzgerald, 1865.
Trefousse, Hans L. *Andrew Johnson—A Biography.* New York: W.W. Norton, 1989.
Turner, Justin G., and Linda Levitt Turner. *Mary Todd Lincoln: Her Life and Letters.* New York: Alfred A. Knopf, 1972.
U.S. Congress. *Biographical Directory of the U.S. Congress.* Washington, DC: Government Printing Office, 1989.
U.S. Department of State. *The Department of State of the United States.* Washington, DC: Government Printing Office, 1898.
Valentine, David T. *Obsequies of Abraham Lincoln in the City of New York.* New York: Edmund Jones, 1866.
Virginia Polytechnic Institute. *Alumni Register,* Vol. 4, 1906.
Walt Whitman—Complete Poetry and Collected Prose. New York: Literary Classics of the United States, 1982.
War of the Rebellion: A Compilation of the Official Records of the Union and Confederate Armies. Washington, DC: Government Printing Office, 1899.
Waugh, John C. *Reelecting Lincoln.* New York: Crown, 1997.
Weichmann, Louis J. *A True History of the Assassination of Abraham Lincoln and of the Conspiracy of 1865.* Ed. Floyd E. Risvold. New York: Alfred A. Knopf, 1975.
Welles, Gideon. *Diary of Gideon Welles.* Ed. Howard K. Beale. New York: W.W. Norton, 1960.
Wesolowski, Wayne, and Mary Cay Wesolowski. *The Lincoln Train Is Coming* Waukesha, WI: Kalmbach, 1995.
Whiteman, Maxwell, ed. *While Lincoln Lay Dying.* Philadelphia: Union League of Philadelphia, 1968.
Who Was Who In America. Chicago: Marquis Who's Who, 1968.
Wilson, James Grant, and John Fiske, eds. *Appleton's Cyclopedia of American Biography.* New York: D. Appleton, 1887.
Zornow, William Frank. *Lincoln and the Party Divided.* Norman: University of Oklahoma Press, 1954.

Articles

Abbott, Martin. "Southern Reaction to Lincoln's Assassination." *Abraham Lincoln Quarterly* 7, no. 3 (September, 1952): pp. 111–27.
"Abe's Malady." *Time* 111, no. 21 (May 22, 1978): p. 83.

Arnold, Isaac N. "The Baltimore Plot to Assassinate Abraham Lincoln." *Harper's Monthly Magazine* 37, no. 217 (June 1868): pp. 123–28.
Ashman, George. "Recollections of a Peculiar Service." *Magazine of History* 3, no. 4 (April 1906): pp. 247–53.
Baird, Nancy D. "The Yellow Fever Plot." *Civil War Times Illustrated* 13, no. 7 (November 1974): pp. 16–23.
Baker, L. B. "An Eyewitness Account of the Death and Burial of J. Wilkes Booth." *Journal of the Illinois State Historical Society* 39, no. 4 (December 1946): pp. 425–45.
Barnes, John S. "With Lincoln from Washington to Richmond in 1865." *Appleton's Magazine* 9, nos. 5 and 6 (May/June 1907): pp. 515–24, 742–51.
Beall, Edmund. "Recollections of the Assassination and Funeral of Abraham Lincoln." *Journal of the Illinois State Historical Society* 5, no. 4 (January 1913): pp. 488–92.
Borchers, Raymond. "President Lincoln's Car." *Lincoln Herald* 86, no. 4 (Winter 1984): pp. 212–16.
Brinkerhoff, Roeliff. "Tragedy of an Age: An Eyewitness Account of Lincoln's Assassination" Ed. A. M. Markowitz. *Journal of the Illinois State Historical Society* 66, no. 2 (Summer 1973): pp. 205–11.
Brooks, Noah. "The Close of Lincoln's Career." *Century Magazine*, May 1895, p. 23.
_____. "Personal Recollections of Abraham Lincoln." *Harper's New Monthly Magazine* 31, no. 182 (July 1865): pp. 222–30.
Buck, Paul H. "Review of *Why Was Lincoln Murdered?*" *Saturday Review of Literature* 15, no. 22 (March 27, 1937).
Carbaugh, Deborah. "Mr. Lincoln's Security." *Surratt Courier* 25, no. 8 (August 2000): pp. 4–7.
Chambrun, Marquis de. "Personal Recollections of Mr. Lincoln." *Scribner's Magazine* 13, no. 1 (January 1893): pp. 26–38.
"Confederate Plan to Abduct President Lincoln." *Surratt Society News* 6, no. 3 (March 1981): pp. 3–6.
"Disappointed Dr. Mudd Vows to Fight On." *JAMA* 268, no. 10 (September 1992): p. 1336.
Du Barry, Helen A. "Eyewitness Account of Lincoln's Assassination." *Journal of the Illinois State Historical Society* 39, no. 3 (September 1946): pp. 366–70.
Dudley, Harold M. "The Election of 1864." *Mississippi Valley Historical Review* 18, no. 4 (March 1932): pp. 500–518.
Durham, Harriet F. "Lincoln's Sons and the Marfan Syndrome." *Lincoln Herald* 79, no. 2 (Summer 1977): pp. 67–71.
Garrett, John M. "The Statement of John M. Garrett." *Surratt Courier* 20, no. 3 (March 1995).
George, Joseph, Jr. "The Night John Wilkes Booth Played Before Abraham Lincoln." *Lincoln Herald* 59, no. 2 (Summer 1957): pp. 11–15.
Grimsley, Elizabeth Todd. "Six Months in the White House." *Journal of the Illinois State Historical Society* 19, no. 3–4 (October 1926–January 1927): pp. 43–73.
Hall, James O. "John M. Lloyd—'Star Witness'." *Surratt Society News* 2, no. 3 (March 1977): pp. 3–4.
_____. "Letter." *Journal of the Lincoln Assassination* 9, no. 1 (April 1995): p. 18.
Hanchett, William. "Booth's Diary." *Journal of the Illinois State Historical Society* 72, no. 1 (February 1979): pp. 39–56.
Harrison, M. Clifford. "A Fighting Confederate Chaplain Spy." *Virginia Cavalcade* 12, no. 4 (Spring 1963): pp. 18–22.
Hatch, Frederick. "Lincoln, Booth, and the Bard." *Journal of the Lincoln Assassination* 17, no. 2 (August 2003): pp. 22–7.
_____. "Lincoln Under Fire." *Journal of the Lincoln Assassination* 19, no. 1 (April 2005): pp. 2–7.
_____. "The Men Who Hanged Mary Surratt." *Journal of the Lincoln Assassination* 22 (2008): pp. 2–20.
_____. "The Only Man Lincoln Feared." *Lincoln Herald* 101, no. 1 (Spring 1999): pp. 13–16.
_____. "They Shot Horses, Didn't They? Booth and Herold in the Woods." *Journal of the Lincoln Assassination* 21, no. 3 (December 2007): pp. 42–46.
Havlik, Robert J. "Lincoln's Washington Carriages Revisited," *Lincoln Herald*, 112, no. 3 (Fall 2010), pp. 155–180.
Hickey, James T. "Springfield, May, 1865." *Journal of the Illinois State Historical Society* 58, no. 1 (Spring 1965): pp. 21–33.
Hollis, C. Carroll. "Lincoln Rejects a Bodyguard." *The Nation* 198 (February 17, 1964): pp. 173–74.
Hosking, William J. "Lincoln's Tomb—Designs Submitted and Final Selection." *Journal of the Illinois State Historical Society* 50, no. 1 (Spring 1957): pp. 51–61.
Isacsson, Alfred. "An Update on Mary Surratt and her Offspring, Anna and Isaac," *Surratt Courier*, Vol. 11, no. 5, May, 1986, p. 1.
_____. "John Surratt and the Lincoln Assassination Plot." *Maryland Historical Magazine* 52, no. 4 (December 1957): p. 317.

Johnson, Patricia Carley, ed. "I Have Supped Full on Horrors." *American Heritage* 10, no. 6 (October 1959): pp. 60–65, 96–101.
Katz, D. Mark. "Booth's First Attempt." *Surratt Courier* 11, no. 6 (June 1986): p. 1, 7–10.
Kauffman, Michael W. "Booth's Escape Route—Lincoln's Assassin on the Run." *Blue & Gray Magazine* 7, no. 5 (June 1990): pp. 8–22, 38–61.
———. "David Edgar Herold, the Forgotten Conspirator." *Surratt Society News* 6, no. 11 (November 1981).
———. "John Wilkes Booth and the Murder of Abraham Lincoln." *Blue & Gray Magazine* 7, no. 4 (April 1990): pp. 8–25, 46–62.
———. "The Revenge of Old Glory: History vs. Myth in the Lincoln Assassination." *Lincoln Herald* 104, no. 4 (Winter 2002): pp. 141–50.
Keys, Thomas Bland. "Were the Lincoln Conspirators Dealt Justice?" *Lincoln Herald* 80, no. 1 (Spring 1978): pp. 36–46.
Knox, Jas. S. "A Son Writes of the Supreme Tragedy." *The Saturday Review* 39, no. 6 (February 11, 1956): p. 11.
Kokkonen, John. "The Deadly Weapon." *Surratt Society News* 3, no. 1 (January 1978): p. 4.
Kubicek, Earl C. "The Case of the Mad Hatter." *Lincoln Herald* 83, no. 3 (Fall 1981): pp. 708–19.
———. "The Lincoln Corpus Caper." *Lincoln Herald* 82, no. 3 (Fall 1980): p. 474.
Lankiewicz, Donald. "Journey to Asylum." *Civil War Times Illustrated* 26, no. 8 (December 1987): pp. 16–21, 44–45.
Leale, Charles A. "Lincoln's Last Hours." *Harper's Weekly* 53, no. 2721 (February 13, 1909): pp. 7–10, 27.
Levin, Alexandra Lee. "Confederate General Edwin Lee Was a Credit to His Famous Name." *America's Civil War* 5, no. 1 (May 1992): pp. 14, 68–74.
"Lincoln's Syndrome." *Newsweek* 59, no. 24 (June 11, 1962): p. 95.
MacCulloch, Campbell. "This Man Saw Lincoln Shot." *Good Housekeeping* 84, no. 2 (February 1927): pp. 20–21, 112, 115–16, 121–22.
Maione, Michael, and James O. Hall. "Why Seward? The Attack on the Night of April 14, 1865." *Lincoln Herald* 100, no. 1 (Spring 1998): pp. 29–34.
"Major Rathbone and Miss Harris, Guests of the Lincolns in the Ford's Theatre Box." *Lincoln Lore*, no. 1602 (August 1971).
Martin, Charlotte M. "The Stage Reminiscences of Mrs. Gilbert." *Scribner's Magazine* 29, no. 2 (February 1901): pp. 167–84.
McElfresh, George W. "Guarding Mr. Lincoln." *Ohio Soldier*, April 28, 1888.
Merrill, Louis Taylor. "General Benjamin F. Butler in the Presidential Campaign of 1864." *Mississippi Valley Historical Review* 33, no. 4 (March 1947): pp. 537–70.
Miller, Steven G. "More on Capt. Doherty." *Surratt Courier* 15, no. 9 (September 1990): pp. 5–7.
———. "Rollcall for the Garrett's Farm Patrol." *Surratt Courier* 19, no. 9 (September 1994): pp. 3–5.
———, ed. "A Trooper's Account of the Death of Booth." *Surratt Courier* 20, no. 5 (May 1995): pp. 5–9.
Moore, Robert H. "Break Out!" *Civil War Times Illustrated* 30, no. 5 (November/December 1991): pp. 26, 52–61.
Morris, Clara. "Some Recollections of John Wilkes Booth." *McClure's Magazine* 16, no. 4 (February 1901): pp. 299–304.
Moss, Helen Palmes. "Lincoln and Wilkes Booth as Seen on the Day of the Assassination." *Century Magazine* 77, no. 6 (April 1909): pp. 950–53.
Munroe, Seaton. "Recollections of Lincoln's Assassination." *North American Review* 162, no. 473 (April 1896): pp. 424–34.
Nelson, David K. "A Rolling Memento." *Civil War Times Illustrated* 34, no. 1 (March/April 1995): pp. 54–59.
Newman, Ralph G. "In This Sad World of Ours, Sorrow Comes to All." *Journal of the Illinois State Historical Society* 58, no. 1 (Spring 1965): pp. 5–20.
O'D, A. "Thirty Months at the Dry Tortugas." *The Galaxy* 7, no. 2 (February 1869): pp. 282–88.
Peskin, Allan. "Putting the 'Baboon' to Rest: Observations of a Radical Republican on Lincoln's Funeral Train." *Lincoln Herald* 79, no. 1 (Spring 1977): pp. 26–28.
"Petersen House Rehabilitated." *Journal of the Illinois State Historical Society* 52, no. 3 (Autumn 1953): p. 440.
"Piloting the Lincoln Funeral Train." *Lincoln Lore*, no. 895 (June 3, 1946).
Pinkerton, Allan. "Allan Pinkerton's Unpublished Letter." *The American Magazine* 75, no. 4 (February 1913): pp. 17–22.
Read, Harry. "A Hand to Hold While Dying—Dr. Charles A. Leale at Lincoln's Bedside." *Lincoln Herald* 79, no. 1 (Spring 1977): pp. 21–26.

Robbins, Peggy. "Dr. Samuel A. Mudd's Attempt to Escape from Fort Jefferson." *Civil War Times Illustrated* 16, no. 10 (February 1978): pp. 10–16.
Spangler, Edman. "A Letter from Edman Spangler." *Journal of the Lincoln Assassination* 1, no. 2 (August 1987): p. 13.
Sprague, Ver Lynn. "Mary Lincoln — Accessory to Murder." *Lincoln Herald* 81, no. 4 (Winter 1979): pp. 238–42.
Stone, Charles P. "Washington on the Eve of the War." *Century Magazine* 26, no. 3 (July 1883): pp. 458–66.
Sweet, W. W. "Bishop Matthew Simpson and the Funeral of Abraham Lincoln." *Journal of the Illinois State Historical Society* 7, no. 1 (April 1914): pp. 62–71.
Swenson, Grace Stageberg. "Boston Corbett: A Final Chapter?" *Lincoln Herald* 86, no. 3 (Fall 1984): pp. 150–56.
Swett, Leonard. "The Conspiracies of the Rebellion." *North American Review* 144 (February 1887): pp. 179–89.
Taft, Charles Sabin. "Abraham Lincoln's Last Hours." *Century Magazine* 45, no. 4 (February 1893): pp. 634–36.
Temple, Wayne C. "Tinsmith to the Late Mr. Lincoln: Samuel S. Elder." *Journal of the Illinois State Historical Society* 71, no. 3 (August 1978): pp. 176–84.
Verdi, T. S. "The Assassination of the Sewards." *The Republic* 1 (July 1873) pp. 289–97.
"Viewing Lincoln's Remains." *Lincoln Lore*, no. 1611 (May 1972).
Williams, T. Harry. "Voters In Blue: The Citizen Soldiers of the Civil War." *Mississippi Valley Historical Review* 31, no. 2 (September 1944): pp. 187–204.
Zornow, William Frank. "Campaign Issues and Popular Mandates in 1864." *Mid-America* 35, no. 4 (October 1953): pp. 195–216.
_____. "Lincoln's Influence in the Election of 1864." *Lincoln Herald* 51, no. 2 (June 1949): pp. 22–32.
_____. "The Union Party Convention at Baltimore in 1864." *Maryland Historical Magazine* 45, no. 3 (September 1950): pp. 176–200.

Newspapers

Baltimore American
Baltimore Sun
Buffalo Morning Express
Chicago Times
Chicago Tribune
Cincinnati Commercial
Cincinnati Enquirer
Cleveland Leader
Cleveland Plain Dealer
Columbus (OH) *Crisis*
Columbus Gazette
Detroit Advertiser & Tribune
Freeman's Journal
Harrisburg (PA) *Patriot and Union*
Indianapolis Daily Sentinel
Lafayette (IN) *Journal*
London Herald
London Times
Los Angeles Times
Maryland Independent
New York Evening Post
New York Herald
New York Sunday Mercury
New York Times
New York Tribune
New York World
Philadelphia Inquirer
Philadelphia Press
Philadelphia Sunday Dispatch
Philadelphia Times

Providence Press
Richmond Times
Washington Daily Times
Washington Evening Star
Washington National Intelligencer
Washington National Republican
Washington Post

Collections

Abraham Lincoln Papers, Library of Congress, Washington, DC.
Army Board for Correction of Military Records, U.S. Department of the Army.
Benjamin Franklin Wade Papers, Library of Congress.
David Rankin Barbee Papers, Lauinger Library, Georgetown University, Washington, DC.
Federal Bureau of Investigation, U.S. Department of Justice.
Ford's Theatre National Historic Site, National Park Service, Department of the Interior.
Frederick Hatch Papers.
Government of the District of Columbia, Department of Human Resources.
Investigation and Trial Papers Relating to the Assassination of Abraham Lincoln, Microfilm M-599, National Archives.
James O. Hall Papers, J. O. Hall Research Center, Surratt Society, Clinton, Maryland.
John G. Nicolay Papers, Library of Congress.
Lincoln Obsequies Scrapbook, Library of Congress.
National Archives and Records Service, Microcopy M-619.
Richard Dyer Mudd, MD, Papers, Lauinger Library, Georgetown University.
War Department, Judge Advocate General Files, National Archives.
War Department Records File, National Archives.
Washington Metropolitan Police Department Files, National Archives.

Official Documents

Barnes, Joseph K., ed. "Another Case of Alleged Fracture by Contre-coup ..." *Medical and Surgical History of the War of the Rebellion, Surgical History*, Part I, Vol. 2 (Washington: Government Printing Office, 1870), pp. 305–6.
_____. "Report Upon the Examination of the Body of J. Wilkes Booth, the Assassin." National Archives, RG 94, TR 132.
Constitution of the United States of America.
Speed, James. *Opinion on the Constitutional Power of the Military to Try and Execute the Assassins of the President*. Washington, DC: Government Printing Office, 1865.
Taft, Charles S. "Last Hours of Abraham Lincoln." *Medical and Surgical Reporter* 12, Philadelphia (April 22, 1865): pp. 452–54.
U.S. Congress. "An Act Relative to the Election of a President and Vice President ... etc.," *U.S. Stat. 240*, Revised Stat, && 146, 147, 148, 149, 150; March 1, 1792.

Unpublished Works, Miscellaneous Sources

"The Doctor Samuel A. Mudd House." Informational brochure, Dr. Samuel A. Mudd Society, no date.
Falckner, Hans. "On the Family and Homeland of Georg Andreas Atzerodt." Unpublished paper prepared for James O. Hall, 1967. J. O. Hall Papers, Surratt Society, Clinton, Maryland.
Howard, John L. "The Cases of A.L. and J.W.B.: A Modern Case Presentation." lecture at Surratt Society Annual Conference, Clinton, Maryland, March 20, 2004.
Mudd, Richard Dyer, MD "Petition to the President in the Case of Dr. Samuel A. Mudd." 1970, unpublished manuscript, copy in Frederick Hatch Papers.
_____. "Publicity in the Dr. Samuel A. Mudd Case." Unpublished manuscript, copy in Frederick Hatch Papers.

Index

Alabama 9, 51
American (Know-Nothing) Party 70
Anderson, William M. 30
Anderson, IN 162
Anthony, Henry B. 138
Arch Street Theatre 70
Arkansas 51
Armory Square Hospital 103, 107
Army Board for Correction of Military Records 158
Army Medical Museum 107, 129
Arnold, Samuel Bland: Booth conspirator 74–76, 77–82; death 152; early years 70, 77–78; imprisonment 151–52; pardoned 152; "Sam" letter 76, 78–79; writes memoirs 152
Arnold, William S. 78
assassination of Lincoln 91–94
Atlanta, GA 56
Atzerodt, George Andrew: Booth conspirator 75, 79–80, 94, 152, 170; confessions of 68, 152; early years 79–80; execution 153; nicknames 80; tried 152
Atzerodt, Johann E. C. (John C.) 79, 152
Atzerodt, Johann H. 79
Atzerodt, Victore F. H. 79
Augur, Christopher Columbus 36, 118

Baden, Joseph N. 58, 123
Bainbridge, Absalom R. 65, 124
Baker, David 1125
Baker, Edward Dickinson 7, 43
Baker, Lafayette Charles 26, 64, 67, 76, 121, 125, 129, 160
Baker, Luthor Byron 125–27, 129
Un Ballo in Maschera (opera) 14
Baltimore, MD 15–17, 35, 67, 69, 77–78, 136, 150, 152
Baltimore Plot 15–18
Bancroft, George 138
Barbee, David Rankin 111, 117
Barnes, John S. 111

Barnes, Joseph K. 98, 104, 107–108, 129
Bates, David H. 40–41
Bates, Dr. 80
Bayard, James A. 25
Beall, Edmund 142–43
Beall, Mrs. V. P. 161
Beauregard, Pierre G. T. 61
Bedell, Grace 15
Bedient, John A. 37
Beecher, Henry Ward 52
Bel Air, MD 69, 85
Bell, John 9
Bell, William H. 95–98
Bellevue Hospital Medical College 103
Belmont, August 62–63
Benjamin, Judah P. 58–60, 62, 68, 87, 159–60
Benjamine, John 140
Benton, Thomas Hart 143
Bernard, Gen. 133
Berry, William F. 6
Bingham, John A. 129
The Birth of a Nation (film) 151
Black Hawk Indian War 6
Blackburn, Luke Pryor 67
Blair, Francis Preston, Sr. 30
Bliss, Doctor Willard 107
"bloody shirt" issue 56
Bolton, John T. 103
Booth, Edwin 69, 74
Booth, John Wilkes: acting career 70–74; Albany, NY, appearance 13–14, 71; appearance before Lincoln 72; appearance of 72; assassinates Lincoln 91–94; autopsy of 71, 129–30; bow-legged 70; broken ankle of 94; burial 131; capture at Garrett Farm 124–29; Confederate involvement 58, 63–64, 78; confession of crime 119, 124; death 127–29; diary 94, 121–22, 129, 151; early life 69; election of 1864 57; escape route 118–29; fellow conspirators 26, 65–66, 94; finances 65, 152;

government knowledge of plot 76, 78–79; at hanging of John Brown 71; identification of remains of 130–31; at inauguration (1865) 40; injuries 71, 94, 119, 122, 131; inquires about presidential succession 170; kidnapping plot 65, 73–77, 86, 170–71; at Lincoln's last speech 81; marks on hands 130; meeting at Gautier's Restaurant 78, 80–82, 170; mental health 72; Montreal visit 63; motives for assassination of Lincoln 70, 72–74, 121; motives for assassination of Seward 170–71; oil speculations 74, 78, 82; personality 69–70, 72; political views 73; preparations at theatre 91; "Sic semper Tyrannis!" 94; southern patriotism of 73; Surratt House visits 75, 86, 88; trunks belonging to 66; Tudor Hall 85; writings of 121–22
Booth, Joseph 69
Booth, Junius Brutus, Jr. 74
Booth, Junius Brutus, Sr. 69
Booth, Mary Ann Holmes 69, 72
Boston, MA 65, 67, 71, 151
Bowen, Col. 14
Bowling Green, VA 124
Boyd, Benjamin F. 144–45
Boynton, Thomas J. 156
Branson, Margaret 83
Branson, Mary 83
Brawner, James 80
Breckinridge, John Cabel 9
Bregazzi, Antonio 107
Brinkerhoff, Roeliff 100
Britannia metal 167
Brooks, James J. 146
Brooks, Noah 32, 132
Brophy, John P. 158–59, 162
Brown, John 71
Browning, Orville H. 107
Brutus, Marcus Junius 121
Bryant, William L. 123
Bryantown, MD 86, 120, 149

Buchanan, James 10, 19, 21–23, 49–50, 52, 60, 63, 136
Buck, Paul H. 163
Buckingham, John Edward 99, 110
Buffalo, NY 13, 140
Burke, Edward 29
Burke, Francis P. 91, 110, 115
Burnside, Ambrose E. 64
Burroughs, John 37
Burroughs, Joseph 93–94
Burtles, William 120
Butler, Benjamin F. 27, 52–54
Butler, Henry 119
Butler, John G. 153
Byrne, William 125
Byron, Lord (George Gordon) 48

Caesar, Gaius Julius 121
California 140
Camden, NJ 151
Cameron, Simon 9
Campbell Hospital 75
Canada 55, 58, 63–68, 87, 140
Canning, Matthew W. 71
capitol, U.S. 10, 12, 21, 28, 118, 132, 134
Carmi, IL 151
Carroll Prison 150
Carter, Jimmy 158
Castle Thunder 75
Cattell, Harry P. 133
Catton, Bruce 35
cavalry scouts, Confederate 58
Cawood, Charles H. 65
Chambrun, Marquis de 100
Charleston, SC 59, 71
Chase, Salmon Portland 9, 44, 52, 100
Chicago, IL 9, 53, 62, 71, 141, 145–47, 163
Chicago Historical Society 162
Chittenden, Lucius E. 37
City Point, VA 40
Civil War 5, 29–30, 34–37, 51–52, 54, 71–72
Clark, William T. 158, 162
Clarke, Asia Booth 65, 69
Clarke, John Sleeper 69
Clarke, Joseph B. 124
Clay, Cassius Marcellus 23
Clay, Clement C. 61, 63, 160
Cleary, William W. 61
Cleavland, Judge 41
Cleveland, OH 71, 140
Clinton, MD 89
Cloud, Daniel M. 65
Cloughley, Alfred 97
Cobb, Silas T. 118–19
Cody, William F., "Buffalo Bill" 150
Coffroth, Alexander H. 133
Colfax, Schuyler 17, 133, 171
Collins, Charles M. 130
Colting, James 142

Columbus, OH 140
Confederate operations in Canada 55, 58, 60–68, 159, 160
Confederate Secret Service 58–68, 123
Conger, Chauncey S. 151
Conger, Everton J. 125–29, 150–51
Conger, Omar D. 151
Conness, John 133
Conrad, Lavinia T. 64
Conrad, Nelson 64
Conrad, Thomas N. 64–65, 85, 160–61
contre-coup 108
Cooper Union 8
Copcutt, Rebecca M. 164
Corbett, Boston 125, 128–29, 150–51
counterfeiters 144–45
Cox, Samuel 120, 149–50
Coyle, John F. 170
Crane, Charles H. 105, 107
Crawford, C. V. A. 37
Cronin, John R. 109, 112
Crook, William H. 40, 48, 109–13, 116
Crowninschield, William W. 130
Culver, J. S. 148
Curtis, Edward G. 105, 107–108
Cushman, Charlotte 71

Davenport, E. L. 75
Davis, David 9
Davis, Henry Winter 52
Davis, Jefferson 8, 41, 59–68, 73, 75, 101, 156
Davis, Peregrine 122–23
Dawes, Henry L. 133
Dawson, Charles L. 130
Dean, Apollonia 86
Delaware 51, 56
Democratic Party 7, 9, 51, 53–56, 101
Deringer, Henry 167
Dietz, Frederick 125–26
Dix, Dorothea 15
Dix, John A. 137
Doherty, Charles J. G. 150
Doherty, Edward P. 125–27, 129, 150
Donn, Alphonso T. 29, 109, 112
Doster, William E. 37, 64, 152
Douglas, Adele Cutts 159
Douglas, Stephen Arnold 6, 8, 9, 22, 62, 63, 159
Doyle, George 119
DuBarry, Helen 110–11
Durant, Thomas C. 164
Durham, H. C. 41

Early, Bernard J. 82
Early, Jubal A. 34, 36, 56, 67
Eckert, Thomas T. 129
Edelin, Columbus 10

Edmondson, Gabriel 65
Edwards, Elizabeth 6
Egypt 159
Eisenhower, Dwight D. 158
Eisenschiml, Otto 112, 163–64
Elder, Samuel S. 143
elections: of 1860 8–9, 51; of 1862 51, 53; of 1864 39, 44, 51–57
Ellsworth, Elmer 12
Elmira, NY 87
English, John 146
Erie, PA 140
Everett, Edward 33
Ewing, Thomas, Jr. 31–32

Farnsworth, John F. 138
Farragut, David G. 56, 133, 137
Federal Bureau of Investigation 122
Felton, Samuel Morse 15–16
Ferguson, James P. 94, 99, 108
Ferguson, William J. 94
Ficklin, Benjamin F. 24
Fillmore, Millard 52, 101, 140
Fitzpartick, Honora 86
Fletcher, John 118, 152
Flint, Austin, Sr. 102
Florida 9, 51
Floyd, John B. 10, 20
Foote, Henry, S. 60
Forbes, Charles 29, 91, 110–11, 115
Ford, Charles M. 107
Ford, Frank 113
Ford, Henry Clay 113
Ford, John T. 85, 162
Ford's Theatre 72, 74, 85–86, 91–95, 113–15, 154, 168
Forrest, Edwin 71
Fort DeRussy 35–36
Fort Jefferson 77, 151–52, 155–58
Fort Pulaski 40
Fort Slocum 35–36
Fort Stevens 35–37
Fort Sumter 23, 61
Foster, Lafayette S. 133, 171
Fox, Gustavus V. 36
France 60, 62
Frankfurter, Felix 35
Frantz, David 107
Frederick, MD 34
Freeman, Edward 125, 129
Frémont, John C. 8, 52
French, Benjamin B. 44, 132, 134
Front Street Theatre 85

Gambo Creek, VA 123
Gardiner, Alexander 129
Gardiner, Polk 119
Garfield, James A. 31
Garibaldi, Giuseppe 62
Garrett, John M. 124–28
Garrett, Richard B. 126
Garrett, Richard H. 124, 126
Garrett, William H. 125
Gatch, Charles D. 105

Gautier, Catherine J. 150
Gautier, Charles 150
Gautier's Restaurant 78, 80–82, 150
Gayle, George W. 39–40
George III, King 94
Georgetown, DC 64, 152
Georgetown College 77, 80, 83
Georgia 9, 51
Germany 70
Gessler 121
Gilbert, Anne H. 72
Gittings, John S. 17
Gleason, Daniel H. L. 76
Gleason, William H. 152
Goodwin, Col. 41
Gordon, Abraham M. 45
Gouldman, Izora 124
Gourlay, James 140
Grand Army of the Republic 150
Grant, Julia 44
Grant, Ulysses S. 35, 40–41, 44, 100, 133, 160
Great Britain (United Kingdom) 60, 62
Greek fire 62
Greeley, Horace 12–14, 22, 26, 52, 63, 72, 160
Green, Anne 64
Green, Thomas 64
Greenhow, Rose O'Neal 58
Greenmount Cemetery 152
Griffith, David W. 151
Grigsby, Aaron 5
Gunning, Thomas B. 99
Gurley, John Addison 11
Gurley, Phineas D. 137
Gurowski, Adam 33

habeas corpus 30, 51–52, 55
"Hail to the Chief" 91
Hale, Albert 143
Hale, John P. 40
Hall, Emma S. 160
Hall, James C. 105
Hall, James O. 112
Halleck, Henry W. 27, 35
Halpine, Charles 27
Hamilton, Frank H. 103
Hamlin, Hannibal 9, 12, 31, 53
Hanchett, William 163–64
Hanscom, Simon P. 115
Hansell, Emerick W. 97–98
Harbin, Thomas H. 58, 80, 86, 123
Harney, Thomas F. 68
Harpers Ferry, VA 71
Harris, Clara H. 91–94, 110, 138, 161
Harris, Ira 138
Harris, William H. 161
Harrisburg, PA 16–17, 136
Harrison, William H. 49
Hawaii 151
Hawk, Harry 99

Hay, George 146–47
Hay, John M. 23, 27, 32, 35, 44, 63
Hazelton, Joseph 72
Hazzard, George W. 12
Headley, John W. 62
Hegel, Georg Friedrich 33
Helm, Benjamin H. 44
Helm, Emily Todd 44
Henderson, James B. 82
Henry, Anson G. 42
Henry, Lemuel H. 65
Herndon, William H. 6, 7, 47
Herold, Adam G. 80
Herold, David Edgar: Booth conspirator 26, 65, 75, 77–78, 80–81; on Booth's escape route 118–20, 122–27; early life 80; employment 80; execution 153; personality 80
Herzen, Alexander I. 62
Hines, Thomas H. 60, 61, 63
Hinkley, MN 151
Hite, P. R. D. 41
Holcomb, James P. 62, 63
Holiday Street Theatre 85
Holloway, Lucinda K. B. 129
Holmes, Oliver Wendell, Jr. 35–37
Holt, Joseph 10, 20, 129
Honolulu, HI 151
Hooker, Joseph 54, 140, 143
Hopkins, D. 117
Hornsby, Michael M. 125
house where Lincoln died *see* Petersen House
Howell, Augustus S. 86, 87
Hoyt, Godfrey P. 126
The Hub 145
Hubbard, A. C. 143
Hughes, John 145–47, 163
Hughes, John J. 123
Hunter, David 13, 34, 132, 137
Hunter, William 172
Hurdle, Thomas T. 109
Hyams, Godfrey J. 67

Illinois 5–9, 50–51, 61
immigration 70, 79
Independence Hall 136
Indiana 5, 13–14, 51, 61
Indianapolis, IN 140
Ireland 70
Irving, Henrietta 71
Italy 159

Jackson, Andrew 3, 12, 50, 52
Jefferson, Joseph 71
Jefferson, Thomas 87
Jett, William S. 65, 124
Johnson, Andrew: assassination attempt planned 94, 170; funeral of Lincoln 133; impeachment 151, 152; Lincoln autopsy not attended by 107; Mary Lincoln's mistrust of 44, 101; pardons issued by 40, 152, 157; threats against 39; unionist views of 54, 72, 101; vice president 54, 56, 170
Johnson, Bradley T. 66–67
Johnson, Lyndon B. 158
Johnson, Reverdy 133
Johnson's Island 62, 66
Johnston, Joseph E. 101, 124
Jones, Thomas A. 59, 66, 120, 149–50
Judd, Norman B. 9, 16
Julius Caesar (play) 70, 74, 94

Kaiser, Peter H. 37
Kane, George P. 15, 17, 66
Kansas 12, 151
Kauffman, Michael W. 119
Keckley, Elizabeth 43, 45, 117
Keene, Laura 71, 94
Kelly, James 29
Kelly, Martin 126
Kennedy, John A. 16–17
Kentucky 51, 56
Kerney, Martin J. 69
Keyes, Erasmus D. 11
Kinealy, James B. 145, 163
King, Albert F. A. 105
King, William R. 39–40
Kirkwood House Hotel 152
Knights of the Golden Circle 61, 65, 81
Know-Nothing Party *see* American Party
Knox, James S. 99
Kossuth, Lajos 62

Lamar 75
Lamason, Benjamin P. 135
Lamon, Ward Hill 12, 17, 25, 39, 48, 109–10, 164
Lamson, Myron H. 136
Lancaster, PA 136
Lane, Harriet 23
Lane, James H. 12, 23, 27, 32
Laski, Harold 35
Lattimer, John K. 46, 168
Law, George 62
Leale, Charles A. 102–107, 164
Leech, Margaret 35
Lee, Edwin Gray 87
Lee, Fitz 64
Lee, Robert E. 34, 64, 72
Lewis, William S. 109, 112
Lichau House 78
Liebermann, Charles H. 105
Liliuokalani 151
Lincoln, Abraham: accidents 44; American archetype 1, 5; assassination of 91–94; autopsy of 46, 107–108; Baltimore plot against 15–18; beard of 14, 15; birth of 5; books and reading, love of 5; burial of 144–48; cas-

ket opened 144, 147–48; cavalry escort 37–39, 65; children of 7–8; coffin of 132–33, 135; in Congress 7–8; controversial 30–31; death 105; debates Douglas 6, 8; depression, mental 6, 42–43; desire to save union 9, 28, 51, 55; dreams and visions of 31, 47–48; early life of 5; education 5; Emancipation Proclamation 51; fatalism of 24–28, 31–33, 47, 48, 109; fire at White House stables 39; Fort Stevens incident 35–37; funerals of 132–143; habeas corpus, suspension of 30, 51–52, 55; health 42–50; height of 50; honesty 6, 55; horse of 143; house in Springfield, IL 7, 142, 163; humor 6; inaugural journey 12–18; inauguration (1861) 12, 19–24; inauguration (1865) 40; kidnapping plots against 24, 64–66, 74–77; last public speech 81; legal career 6, 8; "long nine" 50; Marfan's Syndrome and 44–47; marriage 6; medical treatment 102–105; office 29; photo of, in casket 139; photo of death chamber 107; plot to steal remains of 144–47, 163; police guards 109–17; political career 6–9; president-elect 10–18; railroad car of 134–36, 164; reaction to assassination of 100–101; Richmond visit 111; threats against 10–18, 21, 25–32, 39, 41, 81; tomb of 144–48
Lincoln, Edward Baker 7, 45, 50
Lincoln, Mary Todd: assassination witness 91–94; brothers of 43–44; burial 148; children 7, 17, 43, 45; chooses grave site 141; concern for Lincoln's safety 39, 49; criticism of 43; early life 6; guard accused 117; health 43; marriage 6; parents 6; personality 6; requests Parker as guard 109, 112; spiritualism 43; unable to attend funeral 133; White House redecorating 44
Lincoln, Nancy 5
Lincoln, Nancy Hanks 5, 50
Lincoln, Robert Todd 7, 36, 43–44, 106, 133, 146, 148
Lincoln, Sarah Bush Johnston 5, 15
Lincoln, Thomas 5
Lincoln, Thomas, Jr. 5
Lincoln, Thomas, "Tad" 7, 39–40, 45–46, 50, 133
Lincoln, William Wallace, "Willie" 7, 39, 43, 45–46, 50, 133, 136

Lincoln Monument Association 163
Lloyd, John M. 86, 90, 119, 158
Logan, Stephen T. 7
Long Beach, CA 151
Longfellow, Henry W. 33
Lonkey, Oliver 125
Los Angeles, CA 101
Loughran, Daniel 82
Louisiana 9, 12, 51
Lovejoy, Owen 31
Lowell, James Russell 33
Lowry, Thomas 164
Lucas, Charley 124
Lucas, William 123–24

Machodoc Creek, VA 122
Mahorney, Mary E. 119
Mallory, Stephen 101
Marfan, Bernard J. 44
Marfan's Syndrome 44–47
Marine Corps, U.S. 133
Marshall Theatre 71
Marshals Service, U.S. 149
Martin, Patrick C. 66
Martin, Robert M. 62
Maryland 12, 15, 34, 51, 58, 66, 69–70, 73, 119, 150
Mason, Samuel 151
Masons 117
Maulsby, P. H. 82
Maus, Mary A. 111
May, John F. 105, 130, 131
Mazzini, Giuseppe 62
McBride, Robert W. 37–39
McClellan, George B. 44, 53–55
McCulloh 75
McDaniels, Franklin 126
McDonald, Cornelia 101
McDonald, John 146
McElfresh, George W. 109, 112–13
McGee, Patterson 39
McGinn, John C. 146
McGowan, Theodore 110, 115
McKinley, William 31
McLernand, John A. 27
McManus, Edward 23
McPhail, James L. 130, 152
McQuaid, William 126–27
Mead, Larkin G. Jr. 144
Meade, George G. 150
Medary, Sam 30
Medhill, J. 12
Memorial Association of DC 162
Menken, Adah I. 71
Merrill, William M. 130
Metz, Hezekiah 152
Mexican War 8, 11, 19
Mexico 124, 136, 144, 151
Michigan City, IN 140–41
Miller, John E. 136
Millington, John W. 126–27
Milton Academy 70
Minor, William J. 101

Mississippi 9, 12, 51
Missouri 51
Monocacy, Battle of 34
Munroe, Frank 130
Munroe, Seaton 99–100, 130
Murphy, Edward 82
Myers, John 126

Nanjemoy Creek, MD 122
Napoleon III, Louis 63
National Hotel 49, 73, 79, 82, 84, 130
National Lincoln Monument Association 144
National Park Service 163
National Theatre 71, 74
Navy Yard, Washington 80, 117, 129, 152
Navy Yard Bridge 118
Neal, William R. 107
Neale, Richard 89
Neugarten, Herman 125, 127
Nevada 140
New Jersey 51, 56
New Orleans, LA 5, 12, 59, 71
New Salem, IL 5–6
New York 51
New York City, NY 62, 71, 100, 132, 136–39, 150
Niagara Falls peace conference 63, 160
Nichols, John W. 34
Nicolay, John G. 11, 23
Norris, Basil 98
Norris, William 58–59
North Carolina 51
Norton, John J. 65
Norton, Marcus P. 152
Nothey, John 90
Notson, William M. 105, 107
Nye, James W. 138

Oak Ridge Cemetery 141, 144
oath, presidential 171
O'Beirne, James R. 150
O'Brien, Robert Lincoln 111
O'Brien, William 163
O'Bryon, James R. 91
Oglesby, Richard J. 137
Ohio 14, 51, 61
O'Laughlen, Michael: Booth conspirator 75, 78, 81–82; death 152–53, 157; early life 69, 81; imprisonment 152
O'Laughlen, T. William 69, 81
Old Capitol Prison 64
Old Northwest 61
Old Point Comfort, VA 79
Oldroyd, Osborn H.I. 162
O'Leary 29
Olin, Abram B. 113–14
Ontario Bank 63, 66, 152
O'Sullivan, Timothy 129
Our American Cousin 91

Parady, Emory 126
Parker, John F. 91, 109–117
Parker, John T. 112
Parker House Hotel 65
Parr, David P. 83
Parramore, J. S. 41
patronage, political 52
Patten, John H. 75
"Peanut John" or "Peanuts" see Burroughs, Joseph
Peddicord, John M. 130
Pendell, Thomas F. 29, 109–111, 113
Pendleton, George H. 53
Pennsylvania 51
Penrose, Charles B. 40
Petersburg, VA 35
Petersen, William A. 162
Petersen House 103, 162
Peyton, Randolph 124
Peyton, Sarah 124
Philadelphia, PA 67, 71, 136, 151
pick-pockets 140, 143
Pierce, Franklin 20, 52, 62, 101
Pierrepont, Edwards 41
Pinkerton, Allan 15–17, 23, 25–27, 146
Poindexter, Joseph B. 151
Poland 33
police, Washington 109–117, 119
Polk, James K. 8, 52
Port Royal, VA 124
Port Tobacco, MD 79
Porter, David D. 40
Potomac River 59, 74, 79–80, 122, 129
Powell, Lewis Thornton: attack on Seward 94–99, 168, 170; Booth conspirator 75, 77–78, 82–83, 86; confederate involvement 83; declared innocent by Mrs. Surratt 158–59; early life 82–83; execution 153
Prescott, William H. 33
Presidential Succession 41, 170–73
Preston, William B. 112
The Prisoner of Shark Island (film) 158
prisoner of war camps 62, 87, 128
Putnam, Henry 126

Queen, William 66, 84
Quesenberry, Elizabeth R. 123
quinine 73

railroads 12–17, 134–36, 139–43, 164
Rains, Gabriel 58
Ramseur, Stephen 34
Rappahannock River 58, 124–25
Rathbone, Henry R. 91–94, 103, 110, 113, 161, 168
Reagan, Ronald W. 158
Ream, Vinnie 144

"Rebel Rose" see Greenhow, Rose O.
Reed, Charles H. 163
Reid, Anna J. 62
Reith, William 107
Republican Party 8, 136
rewards 124, 150–51, 160
Richards, Almarin C. 111, 116
Richardson, John 107
Richmond, VA 40, 58, 71, 74, 87
Richter, Hartman 152
Ritterspaugh, Jacob 85
Robinson, George F. 95–98
Robinson, Stuart 67
Rollins, James S. 32
Rollins, William 58, 124
Root, G. W. 143
Ruge, Arnold 62
Ruggles, Mortimer B. 124
Rullman's Hotel 80
rumors of assassination 94, 100
Rupert, A. 140
Rutledge, Ann 6
Ryen, John 126–27

St. Albans, VT 62–63, 67
St. Lawrence Hall 63, 66, 87
St. Louis, MO 71
St. Martin, Natalie 59
St. Paul's Cemetery 153
Samuel A. Mudd Society 158
San Francisco, CA 101, 140
Sandburg, Carl 35
Sanders, George Nicholas: advocate of assassination 63, 67; attempt to abduct 160; background 62–63; death 160; flight to Europe 160; involvement in St. Albans raid 63; involvement with Booth 66; revolutionary activities 62–63
Sands and Harvey 132
Sangamon County, IL 6
Savage, Lewis 126
Schade, Louis 162
Schenck, Robert C. 132, 140
Schwartz, Harold 45
Scott, Mrs. 85
Scott, Thomas A. 28
Scott, Winfield 10–11, 14, 16, 19–20, 28, 137
secession 9–10, 12, 19, 54, 72, 101
secret line, Confederate 58, 119, 122
Secret Service, U.S. 145–47, 149, 163
Seddon, James A. 63–64
Seward, Anna W. 97
Seward, Augustus 96–98
Seward, Fanny 95–98
Seward, Frances A. 97–99
Seward, Frederick W. 16, 95–99, 168, 172
Seward, William Henry: advice to Lincoln 10–12, 53; assassination attempt upon 94–99, 168, 170; criticism of 30, 33; mistrust of 44; presidential candidate 9, 53; protective collar 99; secretary of state 170, 172; senator 9, 63; threats against 39, 41
Seymour, Horatio 53
Shakespeare, William 47, 74
Shelton, Joseph 112
Sheridan, Philip H. 56
Sherman, John 30
Sherman, William T. 40, 48, 56, 62, 101
"Sic semper Tyrannis!" 56, 62, 94, 101
Signal Bureau and Signal Corps, Confederate 58
Simpson, Matthew 143
Singer, John A. 126
Slater, Sarah A. 86–87
slavery 8–9, 33, 44, 51–52, 59–60, 72, 87, 172
Smith, Andrew C. 109
Smith, Green Clay 133
Smith, John L. 130
Smithsonian Institution 153
Smoot, Richard M. 80, 86
Snay, Abram 73
Snow, Franklin 164
soldier vote 53–55
Soldiers Home 37–38, 65, 75, 81
Sons of Liberty 32, 61
Sotos, John 50
South Carolina 9
Spangler, Edman: Booth conspirator 77, 84–85, 93; death 155; early life 85; friendship with Dr. Mudd 154–55; imprisonment 154; incriminating behavior 85; innocence or guilt of 84, 155
Speed, James 34
spiritualism 43
Spotswood Hotel 87
Sprague, Ver Lynn 112
Springfield, IL 6, 132, 141–43
staff, presidential 23, 27, 29
Stanton, Edwin McMasters: alarm at Confederate advance on Washington 35–36; funeral of Lincoln managed by 132, 143; imprisonment of conspirators 156; involvement in Lincoln murder plot 163–64; involvement in 1864 election 55; and Lincoln's safety 31, 36, 75–76; photo of Lincoln in casket 139; rumors of assassination of 100; visits wounded Seward 99
Star Hotel 124
Star Saloon 91
State Department, Confederate 58
State Department, U.S. 33, 170, 172
Steinbrigge, Carl J. A. 126

Stephens, Alexander H. 72
Stevens, Isaac I. 35
Stevens, Thaddeus 136
Stevenson, Job 140
Stingler & Siege 67
Stone, Charles P. 10, 12, 20–22
Stone, Robert K. 49, 104, 107–108
Stone, William M. 137–38
Stowe, Harriet Beecher 47
Strategy Bureau, Confederate 58
Stuart, James E. B. 64
Stuart, John Todd 6
Stuart, Richard H. 123
Submarine Battery Service, Confederate 58
Sumner, Charles 33, 44, 106, 172
Sumner, Edwin Vose 11
Supreme Court, U.S. 52
Surratt, Elizabeth S. "Anna" 89–90
Surratt, Isaac D. 85, 89–90
Surratt, John H., Jr.: Booth conspirator 66, 74–77, 80, 83–87, 152; Confederate involvement 65–68, 85–87; death 159; description 85; early life 85; escape 87, 159; hides weapons at tavern 119, 168–69; later life 159; tried 41, 77, 151, 156, 159, 162
Surratt, John H., Sr. 85, 89–90
Surratt, Mary E.: Booth conspirator 77, 80, 86, 88, 90; burial 159; Confederate involvement 86–87, 90; early life 87–88; execution 153, 159; house in Washington 75, 80, 85, 88; religion 89; "shooting irons" remark 90, 169; tavern 81, 85–86, 89–90, 119, 168; tried 77, 158, 162
Surrattsville, MD 65, 81, 89–90, 119
Swain, James B. 28
Swann, Mary 149
Swann, Oswell or Oswald 120, 149
Swegles, Lewis C. 146–47, 163
Swett, Leonard 12, 50, 146

Taft, Alphonso 30
Taft, Charles S. 99, 105, 107–108
Taylor, Zachary 8, 49
Tell, William 121
Tennessee 51, 54
Texas 9, 51
Thatcher, Richard 151
theatrical practices 70–71
Thompson, George 119
Thompson, Jacob: Canada operations 60–63, 160; death 160; finances 62, 160; flight to Europe 160; as secretary of interior 60–61, 160

Thompson's Drug Store 80
Thornton, James 124
Tod, David 37
Todd, Alexander 44
Todd, David H. 44
Todd, Eliza Ann Parker 6
Todd, George B. 105
Todd, Lyman Beecher 105
Todd, Robert Smith 6
Todd, Samuel B. 43
Torpedo Bureau, Confederate 58
Townsend, Edward D. 11
Townsend, George A. 29
The Trappe 124
Trenton, NJ 136
trial of conspirators 39, 77, 136, 151, 153, 155, 162
trial of John Surratt 41, 151, 159, 162
Tudor Hall 85
Tyler, John 50, 52
Tyrrell, Patrick D. 146–47, 163

Ulke, Julius 162, 163
Uniace, Michael 125
Union Party 51
United States (railroad car) 134–36, 164
United States Christian Commission 55
Urquhart, Charles, Jr. 129

Valkenberg, Frank 141
Vallandigham, Clement L. 61, 72
Van Bibles, Chew 107
Van Buren, Martin 40, 52
Van Ness Mansion 64
Verdi, Tulio S. 98
Vermont 62
Vernon, J. R. 29
Virginia 19, 51, 58, 65
Virginia Polytechnic Institute 161
Volk, Leonard W. 144

Wade, Benjamin F. 37, 52, 133
Walker, Leroy Pope 60
Wall, W. L. & Co. 67
Wallace, Lewis 34, 136, 162
Wallace, William S. 7
Walsh, Francis S. 80
Walz, John 125
War Department, Confederate 58
War Department, U.S. 12, 32, 38
War of 1812 11, 19, 133
Warne, Kate 15–16
Washburn, Elmer E. 146, 163
Washburne, Elihu B. 17, 133, 138
Washington, George 12, 20, 50, 132, 134
Washington, DC: assassination rumors in 11, 17; danger to 10–12, 67; defense of 11, 20, 34–37; description 28–30; illumination 40; mourning for Lincoln 132–34; rewards offered by 150; spies in 58, 64–65
Washington Arsenal 131, 153
Washington Theatre 72
weapons of conspirators 82, 86, 90, 93, 119, 152, 167–69
Weaver, John C. 107
Webster, Elizabeth A. 87
Webster, Timothy 15
Weichmann, Louis J.: acquaintance with Booth 76; boarder at Mrs. Surratt's house 75–76; early life 85; friend of John Surratt 84–85; informs on conspirators 76; reaction to assassination 100; testimony against Mrs Surratt 90, 158, 162; testimony against Mudd 84, 155; writes history of assassination 162
Welles, Gideon 37
Wells, Henry H. 149
Wendell, Andrew 125, 128
West, George 140
Westfall, John W. 40
Wharton, John W. 79
Wheeler, Rose 79, 153
Whig Party 6, 8, 51, 59
White, Horace 12
White House 25, 27–29, 34, 38–39, 68, 133
Whitman, Walt 33, 100
Why Was Lincoln Murdered? 163–64
Wickham, William C. 64
Wiget, Bernardine F. 85
Wigfall, Louis T. 10
Willard Hotel 17–18, 21
Williams, Lizzie 116
Wilmer, Lemuel 120
Wilson, John 168
Winder, John Henry 58, 75
Winter, John 125
Winter Garden Theatre 74
Wisconsin 51
Withers, William S., Jr. 94, 168
Wolf, G. S. 42
Woodward, Ashbel 105
Woodward, Joseph J. 107–108, 129
Woolcott, Alexander 35
Woolf, Mr. 41
Worthington, Alexander 35
Wright, Horatio G. 36–37
Wrightson, George W. 140

Yates, Richard, Sr. 133
Yellow Fever Plot 67
Yellowplush, James 25
York, PA 136

Zekiah Swamp 120
Zimmer, Carl 125
Zisgen, Joseph 126
Zouaves, Papal 159

www.ingramcontent.com/pod-product-compliance
Ingram Content Group UK Ltd.
Pitfield, Milton Keynes, MK11 3LW, UK
UKHW050525150426
5217IPUK00026B/1810